MW01201197

NARRATIVES OF WOMEN AND MURDER
IN ENGLAND, 1680–1760

This book is dedicated to my mother, Dr. Ruth O. Saxton

Narratives of Women and Murder in England, 1680–1760

Deadly Plots

KIRSTEN T. SAXTON
Mills College, USA

ASHGATE

Published by
Ashgate Publishing Limited
Wey Court East
Union Road
Farnham
Surrey, GU9 7PT
England

Ashgate Publishing Company
Suite 420
101 Cherry Street
Burlington
VT 05401-4405
USA

www.ashgate.com

British Library Cataloguing in Publication Data
Saxton, Kirsten T., 1965–
   Narratives of women and murder in England, 1680–1760: deadly plots.
   1. Women murderers in literature. 2. Criminals' writings– History and criticism–18th century. 3. Women murderers– England–London–Biography–History and criticism.
   4. Law and literature–England–History–18th century. 5. English literature–18th century–History and criticism.
   I. Title
   823.5'093526927–dc22

Library of Congress Cataloging-in-Publication Data
Saxton, Kirsten T., 1965–
   Narratives of women and murder in England, 1680–1760: deadly plots / Kirsten T. Saxton.
      p. cm.
   Includes bibliographical references and index.
   ISBN 978-0-7546-6364-5 (hardcover : alk. paper) – ISBN 978-0-7546-9452-6
   (ebook) 1. English literature–18th century–History and criticism. 2. English fiction–18th century–History and criticism. 3. Women murderers–Great Britain–Biography–History and criticism. 4. Crime in literature. 5. Women murderers in literature. 6. Murder in literature. 7. Femininity in literature. 8. Law and literature–Great Britain–History–18th century. I. Title.
   PR448.C75S39 2009
   820.9'355–dc22

                                                                                    2009006716

ISBN   978-0-7546-6364-5
EISBN 978-0-7546-9452-6

Mixed Sources
Product group from well-managed forests and other controlled sources
www.fsc.org Cert no. SA-COC-1565
© 1996 Forest Stewardship Council
FSC

Printed and bound in Great Britain by
MPG Books Group, UK

Contents

List of Illustrations   *vii*
Acknowledgments   *ix*

Introduction   1

1   Imagining Murder in Augustan England: Bodies of Evidence;
     Murder and Gender   9

2   Moving Violations: Aphra Behn, Delarivier Manley, and the
     Romance of Violence   31

3   "Interesting Memoirs of the Most Notorious Characters":
     Four Eighteenth-Century Murderesses   55

4   "The Confines of Virtue and the Frontiers of Vice":
     Daniel Defoe's *Roxana* and Henry Fielding's *Amelia*   85

5   "The Prisoner at the Bar": Mary Blandy and Henry Fielding   115

Epilogue   127

Select Bibliography   *133*
Index   *147*

List of Illustrations

3.1   Catherine Hayes Burnt for the Murder of Her Husband. (Hayward, Arthur L. *Lives of the most remarkable criminals, who have been condemned and executed for murder, the highway, housebreaking, street robberies, coining or other offences, collected from original papers and authentic memoirs, and published in 1735.* New York: Dodd, Mead & Company, 1927; 352.)   63

3.2   Catherine Hayes and Her Accomplices Cutting Off Her Husband's Head. (Andrew Knapp, William Baldwin, and Henry Savage, *Newgate Calendar.* London: J. Robins and Co., 1824; 257.) This item is reproduced by permission of *The Huntington Library, San Marino, California.*   64

3.3   Miss Mary Blandy. (James Granger, *A Biographical History of England.* Vol. 28. London, 1769; 81.) This item is reproduced by permission of *The Huntington Library, San Marino, California.*   65

3.4   Miss Molly Blandy. (James Granger, *A Biographical History of England.* Vol. 28. London, 1769; 81.) This item is reproduced by permission of *The Huntington Library, San Marino, California.*   66

3.5   Benjamin Cole. Miss Mary Blandy. (James Granger, *A Biographical History of England.* Vol. 28. London, 1769; 81.) This item is reproduced by permission of *The Huntington Library, San Marino, California.*   67

3.6.   Sarah Malcolm. (William Hogarth and John Trusler. *The Works of William Hogarth Containing One Hundred and Fifty-Eight Engravings, by Mr. Cooke, and Mr. Davenport, with Descriptions in Which Are Pointed Out Many Beauties That Have Hither to Escaped Notice, with a Comment on Their Moral Tendency.* London: Tegg.) This item is reproduced by permission of *The Huntington Library, San Marino, California.*   77

3.7   Elizabeth Brownrigg. (George Daniel. *Merrie England in the Olden Time.* Vol. 2, pt. 2. London: R. Bentley, 1842; 194.) This item is reproduced by permission of *The Huntington Library, San Marino, California.*   79

Acknowledgments

I have written most of this book while teaching at Mills College, and the project was made possible as a result of my being a member of this vibrant community. The material provision of Mills's Faculty Development Grants and Meg Quigley Summer Research Grants allowed me the time and resources to write. My colleagues in the English Department read drafts and contributed essential ideas and suggestions, and I am regularly grateful for their collegiality, generosity, and commitment to intellectual curiosity. Thank you particularly to our Chair, Cynthia Scheinberg, for pushing me to completion. I owe a tremendous debt to my current and past students at Mills who continue to challenge, impress, and inspire me inside and outside of the classroom, and whose questions and observations changed my thinking about this project.

I am also thankful to the many eighteenth-century scholars who have served as audience to the book in a number of its iterations and whose insights and suggestions helped to shape my thinking. The book's faults are of course entirely my own, and what works is due in large part to the generosity of the larger community of eighteenth-century studies. This list of those to whom I owe thanks is too lengthy to enumerate here in its entirety; I would like particularly to thank Toni Bowers, Aleksondra Hultquist, Madeleine Kahn, and Jennifer Thorn as well as the anonymous readers of the manuscript. It has been a pleasure to work with the editorial staff at Ashgate Publishing, and I appreciate Ann Donahue's patience and guidance throughout the process. Much of the book was written in the hallowed halls of the Henry H. Huntington Library and the William Andrews Clark Memorial Library. I am grateful for their extraordinary collections, funding, and knowledgeable and thoughtful staff. Thank you also to Cassie Childs, Elizabeth Matthews, Carrie Pickett, Joni Roylance, Jennifer Sophie Weeks, and Haley Wise for their invaluable research assistance.

My life is richer for all of my friends who provide essential warmth, humor, keen insights, and encouragement. Eve Lynch's work on servants particularly helped me frame my thinking, a service almost as helpful as her consistent and deep friendship. Thank you to my family, without whom this achievement would be neither possible nor meaningful. The unstinting affection, intellectual engagement, and emotional sustenance provided by my parents, siblings, and in-laws account for much of the great joy of my life. My husband, Karl Garcia, has both unfailingly supported and suitably distracted me from my fascination with the eighteenth century. Our son, Nicky, burgeoning lover of books, is both anchor and star. Finally, I dedicate this book to my mother, Ruth O. Saxton, my best reader, whose grace and skill as a mother, teacher, and scholar inspire and humble me.

Introduction

"Murderess, murderess," he whispers to himself.
"It has an allure, a scent almost. Hothouse gardenias. Lurid but also furtive."
—Margaret Atwood, *Alias Grace* (1996)

This book takes as its subject the figure of the murderess in eighteenth-century England.[1] As eighteenth-century writers knew full well, the story of the murderess is one greatly worth the telling. Stories of murderous women abounded in Augustan England: repository tracts, broadsides, ordinaries' accounts, privately published criminal biographies, ballads, journalistic accounts, and the new and disorderly genre of the novel are replete with stories of homicidal women. As Charles Johnson states in *A General History of the Lives and Adventures of the Most Famous Highwaymen*: "[T]is certain, [whether] a Woman always discovers more Art and Cunning than a Man … or whatever else, [that] a female Offender excites our curiosity more than a male" (p. 327).

Narratives of Women and Murder in England, 1680–1760: Deadly Plots reveals the centrality of the female criminal subject in the rise of the British novel and uses the figure of the murderess to explore the constitutive relationship between eighteenth-century legal and fictional texts. Legal narratives informed the budding genre of the novel, and fictional texts shaped emergent changes in legal narratives. The study examines accounts of the murderess in the parallel discourses of letters and law to demonstrate the ways in which these representations established, reflected, and contested eighteenth-century conceptions of femininity, criminality, and genre.

The murderess was and remains a figure of cultural fascination for the ways in which she is seen to contradict and embody tropic notions of female possibility.[2]

---

[1]　I use the term *murderess* rather than the more gender-neutral *murderer* because my project is concerned primarily with the effects of femininity on murder; it is exactly the nonneutral haunting and titillating feminine associations of the term *murderess* in which I am interested.

[2]　This project is particularly indebted to and informed by the following works for their excellent scholarship on criminality and gender: J. M. Beattie's "The Criminality of Women in Eighteenth-Century England"; Ian Bell's *Literature and Crime in Augustan England*; Frances Dolan's *Dangerous Familiars: Representations of Domestic Crime in England, 1550–1700*; Margaret Doody's "The Law, the Page, and the Body of Woman: Murderesses in the Age of Johnson"; Lincoln Faller's *Turned to Account: The Forms and Functions of Criminal Biography in Late Seventeenth- and Early Eighteenth-Century England*; Hugh Gladfelder's *Criminality and Narrative in Eighteenth-Century England*; Lynda Hart's

This study considers the ways in which nonfiction and fiction narratives of the long eighteenth century represent female violence within deadly plots that defy and define notions of textual and sexual license, notions that continue to shape literary and legal mandates more than two centuries hence. The book looks specifically at nonfiction accounts such as trial reports and the biographies of Newgate ordinaries, and at fiction by Aphra Behn, Delarivier Manley, Daniel Defoe, and Henry Fielding.

Narratives of Women and Murder calls attention to marginalized texts and genres, provides fruitful new ways of reading canonical novels, and reveals the ways in which formal and thematic literary critical practices have, however inadvertently, served to replicate received ideologies of gender and genre. Excellent existing studies investigate the roles that either gender or legal and criminal narratives played in the tumultuous history of the early British novel, and this book would not be possible without them. I bring together these two areas of scholarship to demonstrate the ways in which the categories of criminality, gender, and fiction fundamentally intersected in the long eighteenth century. The study serves as a feminist intervention in scholarship on the literature of crime and insists upon the centrality of the literature of crime in feminist histories of the novel.

When I began the project, I was attempting to argue two principal points: first, that the murderess held a particular critical fascination in the long eighteenth century, and that, as such, the murderess provides a useful lens through which to approach the prose narratives of the era in which she figures so largely; second, that female-authored amatory fictions of the murderess provide more "subversive" possibilities than those of legal narratives, criminal biographies, or now-canonized novels.[3] I remain convinced of the first point, but over time I realized that regarding the second I had created a reading that argued that female-authored fictions are not only formally and historically undertheorized but politically "better." Despite my privileging of female-authored amatory texts, I was, in fact, working very hard to try to define them as "real" novels, as meeting Ian Watt's famous conditions, and doing so with extra style and subversive intent. More crucially perhaps, while

Fatal Women: Lesbian Sexuality and the Mark of Aggression; Mary Hartman's *Victorian Murderesses*; Ann Jones's *Women Who Kill*; Jennifer Jones's *Medea's Daughters: Forming and Performing the Woman Who Kills*; Peter Linebaugh's *The London Hanged: Crime and Civil Society in the Eighteenth Century*; Virginia Morris's *Double Jeopardy: Women Who Kill in Victorian Fiction*; Philip Rawlings's *Drunks, Whores, and Idle Apprentices: Criminal Biographies of the Eighteenth Century*; Alexander Welsh's *Strong Representations: Narrative and Circumstantial Evidence in England*; and John P. Zomchick's *Family and the Law in Eighteenth-Century Fiction: The Public Conscience in the Private Sphere*.

[3]   While these writers receive far more attention now than they did ten years ago, their work is still not part of the mainstream canon; in other words, while eighteenth-century academics are now familiar with, for example, Eliza Haywood, most nonspecialists still have not heard of most early eighteenth-century women writers.

the book was superficially attacking canonical categories, it left them intact and created a simplifying counter-narrative.

What fascinates me now is the general fictiveness of broad literary divisions. Just as "amatory" fiction is indeed full of exempla of Watt's realistic novel criteria, so are legal narratives and "realistic" novels permeated with the hyperbolic, the excessive, and the romantic. However, some generic styles are associated with certain authors and these associations carry social privileges. It is not coincidental that the modes in which women tended to write have been devalued, but the modes themselves are not gendered. The authors in this study move freely between what we now define as differing rhetorical styles. They borrow strategies from various narrative forms and from one another. Just as the rational is not the realm of the male or the emotional the realm of the female, so are amatory and realist fiction free of essentially sexed characteristics. This project demonstrates the essential subjectivity, fluidity, and ambiguity of the categories of genre, political intents and effects, and aesthetic formulations.

I am also increasingly careful in my designation of a text or representation as "subversive." Unlike some recent critics, I remain convinced that the term has a useful literal meaning—that texts and representations may, for example, subvert reigning ideological constructs. However, this fact does not imply authorial intent or mean that the text handily anticipates my contemporary feminist politics. That said, I of course cannot read or think without the worldview that my cultural and historical placement provides me, and I do not attempt to re-create an imaginative eighteenth-century critical persona through which to frame my ideas.

Histories of the novel tend to be grounded in the topoi of both fictional and legal narratives; as scholars, we create narratives of circumstance, peopled by protagonists and minor characters, which we arrange according to an overarching plot or argument that reflects our assumptions, as it must. While it is outside the scope of this project (whose murderesses kept languishing in service to the history of the novel in England) to attempt to define exactly what constitutes "real" novelistic narrative, the book does participate in recent feminist interventions in traditional histories of the novel. Genres traditionally coded as feminine and most often written by women were long dismissed and disparaged. It is a critical commonplace now that battles for discursive primacy regulated feminized genres to the margins while centralizing those genres marked as masculine. That the female writers I consider, including convicted murderess Mary Blandy, are often chronologically originary raises the question of literary influence and challenges the passing, but still powerful, perception that Daniel Defoe and Henry Fielding, along with Samuel Richardson, are the sole progenitors of the British novel.[4]

---

[4]   To divide my chapters as I do, with the women writers in one and the men in another, seems to contradict my claims here. I divide them as such, not because of the relative value of either pair, or because of their gender, but because of similarities in their respective formal and thematic approaches to the figure of the murderess. The implications of these similarities remain a fascinating and open question.

In contrast to critical readings that simplify the topical depth and formal expertise of early novels, or those that deny the complex and ideologically challenging potential of later fictions, I investigate the ways in which both lesser-known and canonical novels of the early century engage with and help to shape contemporaneous popular and legal visions of the two contested categories of women and violence.

Situated simultaneously in the fields of historical, literary, feminist, and cultural studies, the project reads fictional and nonfiction narratives of female homicide, individually and against one another. I have chosen to focus on texts that offer a range of perspectives on eighteenth-century notions of female homicide. Yet, despite their diversity, the texts also speak to one another across genres and decades, and the project highlights the connections between them as well as the more obvious differences. The nonfiction narratives of female homicide—whether ordinaries' accounts, journalistic pieces, trial reports, or moral tracts—share the common task of recounting the story of an actual murderess to her contemporary audience. While differing in kind, all of these nonfiction criminal narratives attempt imaginatively to re-create a real murderess as a monstrous anomaly. These narratives offer spaces of identification or sympathetic logic that trouble their overtly regulative ends; however, their project is always to contain violent female potentiality.

Fiction writers, on the other hand, tend to create more obviously complex visions of the murderess. Unlike nonfiction narratives, related after an arrest and usually a sentence, fictional narratives rarely begin by overtly establishing the protagonist as a murderess-to-be; thus she is not as easily disentangled from the social plot in which we encounter her. Moreover, in overt fiction, there is no real human being who has died, so there is more room for narrative complexity than in a text that focuses on an actual, most likely recent, crime. The formal innovations of novelistic narrative also allow complex textual representations, as early prose fiction writers bring elements of, for example, parody and irony to bear on their configurations of characters. I privilege the literary in this project both for its complexity and because I imagine this book as part of an ongoing critical conversation about eighteenth-century fiction. However, the interplay between varying Augustan narrative formulations of female crime remains constant. That this interrelatedness is self-conscious and acknowledged supports an inclusive approach to textual sources.

I take a traditional formal and historical approach to texts, reading each as a structured narrative written within a particular cultural moment. Informed by new historicism, I read each narrative as a piece of crafted literature; as such, I am interested in the ways in which the narrative—whether factual or fictional—functions formally and thematically. I explore the calibrations between the real-life murderesses of the criminal biographies and the overtly fictional murderesses to investigate the complex interactions of genre, gender, and political affiliation in narratives of female homicide. In order to tease out the complicated strands of motivation, stereotype, and desire in Augustan configurations of crime and femininity, the project interrogates the ways in which murderesses were textually imagined and legally codified. Finally, and fundamentally, this project provides me the chance to read and to tell many compelling stories, deadly plots of days past whose voices reach to us and shape our own ways of reading and plotting.

The first chapter, "Imagining Murder in Augustan England: Bodies of Evidence; Murder and Gender," situates popular eighteenth-century narratives of female homicide within the contexts of contemporaneous discourses on criminality, murder, gender, and fiction. It begins with an analysis of the crime panics of the era and then analyzes the ways in which murder, in general, and female homicide, in particular, are defined and represented in both legal and literary discourse. The chapter concludes with a discussion of the prose narratives that the project investigates: nonfiction accounts and early novels. I review the multiple levels of the association of early fiction with crime and the connections between juridical and novelistic narratives. Like recent revisionist critics of the novel, I contest the terms by which Restoration and early eighteenth-century feminocentric fictions were dismissed in their own era as well as the ways in which this "conversion" narrative has been replicated in critical studies. The chapter demonstrates the ways in which gender crucially intersects with discourses of both criminality and early fiction.

Each of the following chapters considers particular textual portrayals of the eighteenth-century murderess, and their order is roughly chronological. Chapter 2, "Moving Violations: Aphra Behn, Delarivier Manley, and the Romance of Violence," examines explicitly literary representations of the murderess, concentrating on early fiction writers Aphra Behn and Delarivier Manley. The chapter examines three short novels: Aphra Behn's *The History of the Nun, or the Fair Vow Breaker* (1689), the ironic tale of a murderous and bigamous ex-nun; Behn's *The Fair Jilt* (1688), a hyperbolic and darkly witty story of a woman who will kill to get what she wants; and Delarivier Manley's macabre *The Wife's Resentment* (1720), a furious prequel to the Lorena Bobbitt case in the USA. I read these novels against the legal fictions outlined in the first chapter and contend that each novel challenges state and socially sanctioned visions of female violence. I am particularly interested in the ways that these early fictions' formal structures of excess and irony themselves create a criminal narrative.

Chapter 3, "'Interesting Memoirs of the Most Notorious Characters': Four Eighteenth-Century Murderesses," turns to nonfiction narratives, focusing on the cases of four convicted murderesses: Catherine Hayes (1726), Mary Blandy (1752), Sarah Malcolm (1733), and Elizabeth Brownrigg (1767). These four cases have, on the surface, little in common save that all four generated an extraordinary amount of textual production and attention in their own eras and beyond. The chapter demonstrates the ways in which these narratives dramatize a reductive and schizophrenic vision of female nature as they simultaneously contain the means by which to critique the delimiting visions of female agency they propose. In addition, read together, the cases tell us something about tensions and contradictions regarding eighteenth-century women's social positions. For example, the cases of Hayes, burned at the stake for the murder of her husband, and Blandy, hung for the murder of her father, demonstrate the complex social and legal attitudes toward family hierarchies, while the cases of Malcolm, a servant hung for the murder of her mistress, and Brownrigg, an employer executed for the torture/murder of her apprentice, emerge from and reflect anxieties regarding domestic service.

The fourth chapter, "'The Confines of Virtue and the Frontiers of Vice': Daniel Defoe's *Roxana* and Henry Fielding's *Amelia*," illustrates the ways in which representations of female homicide in these novels differ in important ways from the fictions of the second chapter. The murderesses are not the eponymous protagonists, but secondary characters; the crimes take place "offstage," and the novels share the overtly didactic and regulatory goal of the criminal biographies. However, the chapter argues that neither *Roxana* nor *Amelia* finally succeeds in containing its murderesses or in convincingly conveying its orthodox moral messages. In addition, the section on *Roxana* continues the previous chapter's exploration of servants and crime by investigating its depiction of the murder of one female servant by another. The section on *Amelia* shows how Fielding's portrayal of the murderess Miss Mathews uses tropic notions of female criminality and libertinism seen in the previous chapter, yet formally and thematically evokes the tropes used by Behn, Manley, and Haywood to critique such limited visions. The chapter ends with a discussion of the ways in which the murderous Miss Mathews's case is a mocking parallel of the story of seduction and abandonment recounted by Mary Blandy.

The fifth chapter, "'The Prisoner at the Bar': Mary Blandy and Henry Fielding," moves from Fielding's fictional foray into Blandy's case in *Amelia* to his theological-jurisprudential account, *Examples of the Interposition of Providence in the Detection and Punishment of Murder* (1752). The chapter reads Fielding's exposition of Blandy's guilt against Blandy's autobiographical plea for clemency, *Miss Mary Blandy's Own Account of the Affair Between Her and Mr. Cranstoun* (1752). I argue that the debate between Blandy's and Fielding's versions of the truth of her case encapsulates a battle for narrative primacy in both the legal and the literary arenas. While Fielding attempts to define Blandy through rhetorical strategies of remove and circumstantial logic now associated with realist fiction, Blandy turns to the rhetorical strategies of amatory fiction to craft her apologia. Despite magistrate-novelist Fielding's attempt to render Blandy outside of human signification, like *Amelia*, the *Interposition* is ultimately a plea rather than a ruling; his authoritative textual mandate is a wishful testimonial that relies on absurdly fantastical evidence to argue that the natural state of daughters precludes filial violence. In contrast, while Blandy's text was deemed too romantic and hyperbolic, in fact, it was—like the fictions of Behn, Manley, and Haywood—too authoritative and too realistic. Blandy structured her tale along the lines of those feminocentric fictions that alarmingly reveal women's crimes and desires to be viable, motivated, and specific.

The epilogue looks at female-authored fictional versions of female crime that arise within and from the politically charged and ideologically volatile climate of the 1790s. I briefly consider four turn-of-the-century novels that take criminal women as their subjects: Elizabeth Inchbald's *Nature and Art* (1796), Mary

Wollstonecraft's *Maria, or the Wrongs of Woman* (1798), Mary Robinson's *The Natural Daughter* (1799), and Charlotte Dacre's *Zofloya* (1806). The chapter suggests that these writers use themes and formal devices from both amatory and criminal narratives to craft novels that resist easy formal categorizations and that dispute regulatory and positivist visions of female nature. While *Maria*, *Nature and Art*, and *The Natural Daughter* all overtly challenge orthodox patriarchal formulations of women and crime, I argue that, looked at together, they represent a literary trend to displace or erase actual female violence. In contrast to the gothic *Zofloya*—the story of the homicidal and sexually rapacious Victoria—the murderess is no longer even a peripheral character in these texts. Instead, the female criminals are nonviolent victims of the criminalization of female agency. From the end of the eighteenth century through the nineteenth, the murderess is writ large only in subgeneric fictions: the gothic novel, the sensation novel, and the penny dreadful become the space of imagined violent female agency. The epilogue shows that their association with the somatic, the feminine, and the fantastic links these texts in a chain of debased popular fiction that began with the female-authored fictions of the Restoration and early eighteenth century with which I began this project.

* * *

I hope that my consideration of popular eighteenth-century textual representations of the murderess offers some useful insights into the literature of centuries past; it is also informed by my awareness of the ways in which our current legal and popular formulations of female violence continue to be framed by regulatory visions of female nature. Delimiting and essentialist visions of female nature currently at play in Western culture are obviously not the same as those of the long eighteenth century, and English juridical and popular narratives of female violence are fundamentally different than those of two centuries past. However, legal and fictional narratives of the murderess continue to imagine female crime within a sexualized context whose tenets are remarkably similar to those analyzed in this project. The murderess is still popularly imagined according to a rubric of sexual deviance, and social location— race, ethnicity, sexual orientation, motherhood, and chastity, for example—continues to frame her representation and her legal sentencing.

In his *Interposition* of 1752, Henry Fielding lamented that "[m]urder is very lately begun ... to be, common among us" (7). His lament is a familiar one in twenty-first-century America, where headlines regularly decry the dangers of contemporary society, the increase in homicide, the loss of an innocence we never actually possessed. Increasingly, concern is directed not only at disenfranchised young men, traditionally the most feared candidates for criminal violence, but also at women. Headlines, law enforcement, and social science monographs decry the perceived increase of violent crimes by that sector of the population traditionally seen as more innately good, more submissive, and less violent than adult males.[5] Images of the murderess provide the plots for countless TV thrillers, films, editorials, and popular nonfiction books; violent girl gangs, murderous housewives, and lethal Lolitas are seemingly running amok.

As in the Augustan era, narratives of our demise are greatly exaggerated: historical perspective makes it clear that the violence we rightly decry has been similarly present and decried for hundreds of years and that the media's broadcasting of increased social ills does not simply reflect such ills but often hyperbolizes them. Now, as in the eighteenth century, statistics do not support the notion of a rise of violent crime by women.[6] Yet the effects of such hyperbolic fears can be deadly to those who are judged the virulent cause of what Fielding termed "the disease in our body politic." In his book *Principles of Sentencing*, D. A. Thomas argues that "if you define a situation as real it's real in its consequences." The literary, legal, and social consequences of the moral panics of the Augustan era were real and disastrous for women. I am concerned about what is currently at stake in our own society's legal and aesthetic demarcations of femininity, and I hope that the body of woman—criminal, fictive, creative—can become a body viewed as a subject in the fullest sense without reliance on or repetition of those deadly plots of feminine possibility whose disastrous effects I trace in this project.

---

[5]   Since the nineteenth century, the argument has been made that female crime rates increase as women gain more independence, more legal and social rights, and more opportunities. This general emancipation–crime thesis correlates women's strivings for independence with an increase in female crime and plays on fears that female independence poses a dangerous attack on the social order.

[6]   What increase in female criminal activity does exist is in the realm of property crimes, not violent crimes against the person.

Chapter 1

Imagining Murder in Augustan England: Bodies of Evidence; Murder and Gender

Murder is where history and crime intersect … .
Murder establishes the ambiguity of the lawful and the unlawful.
—Michel Foucault, *I, Pierre* … (1975)

Women in general are of natures more gentle, of dispositions more harmless than men: yet when the mind of a woman becomes once contaminated she commonly becomes more vicious even than a man of bad character; and the amiable softness of the sex seems to be totally eradicated.
—Andrew Knapp, William Baldwin, and Henry Savage, *The Newgate Calendar, or, Malefactor's Register* (vol. 2, 1791, 109)

Every woman is supposed to have the same set of motives, or else to be a monster.
—George Eliot, *Middlemarch* (1872)

Murder is a crime that requires plot, that story that lurks underneath and apart from the body's remains. To take another's life is violently to act out, against not only an abstract body of legal principle, but also a specific physical body. It is an act that simultaneously requires and refutes social representation. Homicide marks the end of a chain of circumstances and demands the imaginative re-creation of that chain: Who was murdered? By whom? Why? Murder begs the question of motive, of cause and effect, of the mechanics of the crime. It engenders narrations of guilt and expatiating punishment, escape, or disturbing lack of resolution. Whether forensic or fictional, stories of murder shape a dramatic, compulsive, and paradoxical social narrative, one that upholds the notion that divine and civic order will out, as it simultaneously articulates a lurking fear that blood lust will ultimately conquer all structures that attempt to contain it.

Violent crime demarcates what a society will not tolerate, what it wants to excise, avoid, and repress. Belonging to that class of offenses termed *mala in se*, "evil in themselves," murder is defined as a crime of evil intention, prohibited in every Western criminal code and deemed the most damaging of crimes to the body politic. As the crime at the furthest end of a chain of offenses, murder is the gravest of trespasses and the one most often to engender death as punishment. The Mosaic Code of the Old Testament justifies the execution of the murderer as accomplishing his necessary excision from the family of man; in Genesis, God states to Noah:

"Whoso sheddeth man's blood, by man will his blood be shed." Eighteenth-century moralists remained true to this biblical edict; a 1733 writer commented that "the corrupt members of a community must be cut off by the sword of justice, lest by delay and impunity the malignant disease spread further, and the whole be infected." By virtue of his crime, the murderer has moved outside normative social relations. Apart from us, and yet also part of us, the murderer reveals a lethal potentiality, a brutish impulse of the primordial logic of the primacy of self that both repels and fascinates.

Murder at once horrifies and enthralls, engendering a double-edged social stake: the desire to quell and contain the crimes themselves and the concomitant desire to tell the story of murderous crimes. Crimes of violence provide a tantalizing, often glamorized, and always grippingly illicit, subject matter. The eighteenth century was the first era in which narratives about crime were widely available, and the subject of murder—whether for entertainment or social amelioration, through legal, academic, or popular channels—was as ubiquitous then as it remains today. From the Augustan era to our own, popular representations of homicide play upon the fascinating potentiality of violent crime—anyone could do it, anytime—yet they simultaneously assure us that, if we pay attention, we can spot the signs and protect ourselves from the monstrous murderous other. Both popular and legal narratives tend overwhelmingly to read backward from the crime, to frame the murderer as one apart, as an outsider, long before the crime was committed. These murderer-to-be narratives retroactively point to warning signals of incipient violence to shore up the fiction that we will be able to spot the next criminal, banish that which caused the violence, and thus prevent murder.

Most of these narratives of real or imagined homicide leave crucial social stories intact and attempt to lay blame on problems that can be isolated and indicted. While post-twentieth-century pundits argue that it is the media, lenient laws, violent lyrics, computer games, or a bad-seed gene that makes certain individuals break the most sacred of social contracts, in eighteenth-century England, violence was blamed on lack of religion, inadequate respect for social hierarchies, lax laws, Satan, and pernicious reading material, mainly novels. Meaningfully to address complex and difficult prevalent social problems—for example, domestic abuse, poverty, lack of resources for the mentally ill, lack of education or opportunities, political disenfranchisement, and readily available weapons—was, then as now, to unpeel layers of social narratives in which people are deeply invested.

One such primary social narrative, in the eighteenth century and today, is that of the inherently nurturing nature of women, the notion of an innate female capacity for life rather than death and violence. Disqualified in Western societies from active military combat—legally sanctioned homicide—women are deemed incapable of violence, imagined, despite plenty of evidence to the contrary, as intrinsically antithetical to acts of violent aggression. But clearly women do kill. How then do the representations of homicide change when the murderer is a woman? How does her sex affect the ways in which the female murderer is both imagined and sentenced?

Female homicide is never simply a legal or moral issue; rather, in Western cultures across the centuries, a woman's violent criminality is read as a key to her sexual and subjective status as woman.[1] The violence the murderess does—not only to individual bodies but also to legal and cultural mores—combines with the relative rarity of female homicide to render the murderess an extreme figure of fear, anxiety, and fascination. The murderess functions as a crucial site for competing ideologies and mythologies of femininity. She is the mad or bad other against which a delimiting ideal of femininity is constructed, and her configurations, both legal and literary, reveal the teleologies of gender construction at work.

When a murder is committed by a woman, it strikes even more forcefully at social order than when the act is committed by a man. The murderess challenges not only the social contract but deep-seated social conceptions of gender. While murder is a grave offense for both men and women, the woman who kills confounds more than the bounds of law. For a man to kill may be seen as corrupt, but the male murderer is not considered inherently "unmasculine"; whereas a woman who kills is, now as in the eighteenth century, virtually always more shocking, more frightening, because she abdicates her culturally defined position of nurturer. The murderess attacks notions of female nature as nurturing and passive, and her violence recalls the flip side of the fantasy of innate female purity: that of innate female venality, the specter of the monstrous she-devil who endangers rational civic and social order.

Unlike a male murder, a woman who kills is portrayed in terms of the ways in which her violent act either belies or reveals aspects of her gender. The particular ways in which her body, personality, and behaviors deny or affirm cultural stereotypes of appropriate femininity provide ways of framing the murderess's crime. At times, the cause is located in her female body itself. Her crimes are instigated by gendered pathologies such as hysteria, the presence of unnatural "male" physical attributes, a predilection for or against sexual activity imagined as innate, a "savage" racial atavism, or today's premenstrual syndrome defense. To locate a woman's act of crime solely within a discourse of femininity and female sexuality is effectively to erase any social, economic, or cultural specificity that may be at issue in the act of crime. It also annuls the possibility of understanding that crime as a specific act with specific motivations that may or may not be affected *ad hoc* by the criminal's gender.

In eighteenth-century England, female violence was, on the one hand, diagnosed as causally located in the criminal woman's monstrous unwomanliness; her acts rendered her, "scarce deserv[ing] the name of woman" at all (*A Warning Piece* 91). While much literature, particularly conduct books, imagined or tried

---

[1] I only discuss crimes in which a woman has killed another adult. In the eighteenth century, infanticide was an entirely different crime than homicide. Infanticide by women is worthy of, and has engendered, its own analyses as it is a crime with its own sets of legal, sociocultural, material, and causal contexts. For discussions of eighteenth-century infanticide see Hoffer and Hull, McDonagh, and Thorn.

to define natural femininity as passively virtuous, femininity was simultaneously described—in medical texts, satires, and moral treatises—as consisting of natural rapaciousness and venality.[2] Female biology was imagined to result in women being violently passionate, unable to control their desires by reason. A reviewer of Defoe's *History of the Pirates* summarizes the common argument that women must be closely controlled: having "not as large a portion of Reason" women are "more easily seduc'd into Vices."[3] Here, female criminality stems not from the abandonment of femininity, but is its natural result. If women's inherent weakness renders them more susceptible to crime, then women must hold themselves to higher behavioral standards than men, as any misstep by a woman will logically lead to her utter ignominy.

In sum, women might be naturally virtuous or they might be naturally dangerous. While opposed, these two conflicting visions of feminine nature are ideologically inseparable. The notion of woman as split possibility—as virgin or whore, Mary or Eve, nurturer or devourer—is all too familiar. Held responsible for the fall of mankind and the birth of its savior, the category "woman" in the Western world has always carried tremendous and contradictory symbolic baggage. The specter of the violently passionate woman informs the regulatory vision of the chaste, retiring lady of the conduct book; the ideal presents a double-edged production of both desire and fear. On the one hand, woman's obedience and passivity are posited as a "natural" state in contrast to the frightening and aberrant image of the fatal woman. On the other hand, the iconic status of idealized femininity countenances a fear-based hyper-regulation of female behavior to guard against the possibility that such ideal behavior is not in fact natural to woman at all.

Murderous women drag their bloody skirts through literature and history as anti-exemplars. Both fictional and factual murderesses are associated, across centuries and cultures, with excessive or transgressive sexuality or social power, their motives reduced to their inappropriate fulfillment of gendered ideals. An examination of the eighteenth-century depictions of three of the most infamous literary murderesses of Western culture—Judith, Medea, and Clytemnestra— reveals the challenges these murderesses presented to eighteenth-century ideals of gender: dramatists and critics re-imagined the crimes and their causes, attempting to reduce threats to social signification.[4]

While the Bible portrays a highly positive response to Judith's heroic deliverance of her city by the slaying of Nebuchadnezzar, the few existing eighteenth-century readings and visual representations of Judith exhibit tremendous discomfort with the conflation of female sexuality and female violence. Judith self-consciously

---

[2] For a discussion of this split see V. Jones 57.

[3] Quoted in Faller, *Crime* 48.

[4] I am indebted to Edith Hall's informative and persuasive essay "*Medea* on the Eighteenth-Century Stage" for my information on eighteenth-century productions of the Euripides play and for more general information about the adaptations of classical drama in light of eighteenth-century conceptions of gender.

manipulates her sexual attractiveness to achieve this traditionally masculine feat and appeals to God in terms of feminized duplicity, asking Him to "[u]se the deceit upon my lips to strike them, dead … [and] shatter their pride by a woman's hand … . Grant that my deceitful words may wound and bruise them" (*Judith* 9: 10, 13). In the eighteenth century, rather than a savior, she is usually portrayed as a markedly sinister expropriator of masculine authority (Morris 13). It is striking how few representations of Judith appear from the Restoration through the end of the century in contrast to the multiple representations of previous centuries. She seems to present too troubling an image—a sexualized, violent heroine—for eighteenth-century audiences.

Euripides's *Medea* provided a paradoxical subject for eighteenth-century English theater. While *Medea* had the increasingly popular elements of pathos and sentiment—mothers, children, interior monologues, tear-inducing tragedy—its sexual politics remained deeply unsettling and strikingly at odds with eighteenth-century notions of gender. Although Euripides's Medea is eloquent, passionate, devoted, and sympathetic, she is also the epitome of monstrous murderous maternity. Eighteenth-century adapters of the play had to negotiate audiences for whom such a woman defied possibility and who would "perhaps, not have allow'd the Character within the Compass of Nature" (Gildon, *Phaeton*). Gildon's solution in his 1688 adaptation was to refrain from having Medea murder anyone at all; in his adaptation, the children are killed by the local people, causing Medea to go insane. Charles Johnson, in his 1730 production, even further sanitizes Medea to fit the mold of a properly sentimental eighteenth-century "She-Tragedy"; here, Medea sends the children away to Athens before killing herself for the pain she has caused Jason.[5] By 1767, in Richard Glover's adaptation, Medea killed her children, but she is presented as a good woman gone mad for love, and she was played for great sympathy (and to rave reviews) by the extraordinarily popular actress Mary Yates.[6]

While Medea's violence is figured as a violation of maternal feeling, Clytemnestra's violence is viewed as a dangerous abundance of such feeling: she kills Agamemnon to avenge his politically motivated sacrifice of their daughter Iphigenia. Yet her rule of Argos with her lover, as well as her murder of Cassandra—a killing motivated by self-preservation and, perhaps, sexual jealousy—focuses attention away from Clytemnestra's legitimate maternal rage onto her transgressive sexual status. That her son Orestes is ultimately forgiven his avenging murder of Clytemnestra implies that state and divine justice tacitly approves of the annihilation of the assertive, sensual, and violent female, and the myth implicitly warns that mother love can prove dangerous to affairs of state

---

[5] "She-Tragedies" centered on the private experience of traumatized females and were extremely popular in the eighteenth-century theater.

[6] Medea as purposeful, vengeful murderous mother was too much for the eighteenth-century stage; however, "Medea" was still a term used, as it is today, as shorthand for maternal monstrosity when applied to actual cases of female child murder.

because it is ruled, not by husband, king, father, or law, but by female blood. While Aeschylus's play casts Clytemnestra as a strong and motivated murderess, the eighteenth-century stage followed Homer and imagined her as a weak pawn of powerful men. In James Thomson's 1738 production of *Agamemnon*, Clytemnestra was played, by the famous Mrs. Porter, as a tragically manipulated woman; not only does she lack agency, but this Clytemnestra also actually refuses Aegisthus's suggestion to murder Agamemnon and thus is no murderess at all.[7]

These depictions of Judith, Medea, and Clytemnestra reveal conflicting, conflicted, and persistent themes that circulate throughout the eighteenth century in representations of female violence. The legal and fictional narratives of eighteenth-century murderesses examined in this project inherit the overdetermined legacies of the homicidal women of mythopoetic history as they simultaneously are shaped by and reflect the specific sociocultural concerns of their historical moment.

In the eighteenth century, female transgression of even the most minor ilk was thought to implicate a woman's natural role. Talking at dinner, making double entendres, chastising one's father or husband all came under the rubric of immodest female behavior. The popular conduct book *The Lady's Calling* cautions that:

> Modesty [is a] … a thing so essential and natural to the sex that every the least declination from it, is a proportional receding from Womanhood … abandonment of it ranks them among the brutes. … An Impudent woman is … a kind of Monster, a thing diverted and distorted from its proper form. (Allestree 114–15)[8]

Imagine, then, the dangers and implications of a woman's commitment of an actual *crime*, particularly a crime of violence. If mere "impudence" metaphorically rendered a woman an unsexed monster, what then was one to make of the woman who transgressed not only the bounds of prudence, but those of jurisprudence as well?

Augustan legal writings and codes about the status of women exhibit a schizophrenic view of female criminality similar to that in the popular imagination. English common law wavered between the notion that women were inherently modest and weak creatures and the notion that they presented an exceptionally virulent threat to social order. Historian Bridget Hill comments that the legal status of eighteenth-century English women, "in so far as they had one at all, was that of under-age children" (108): women could not vote, could rarely sign contracts, could not frame or implement law, and, if married, were collapsed into part of their husbands' legal bodies.[9] One odd benefit of a married woman's legal nonstatus as

---

[7]   The production was a piece of political commentary in which Clytemnestra represented Queen Caroline, Agamemnon George II, and Aegisthus Robert Walpole.

[8]   While first published in the late seventeenth century, this conduct book was widely reprinted into the eighteenth and is typical of its sort.

[9]   Blackstone's *Commentaries* states: "By marriage, the husband and wife are one person in law; that is, the very being or legal existence of the woman is suspended

femme covert was that her husband could be held legally responsible for crimes that she committed in his presence, as it was assumed she was obedient to him in all things.[10]

Women also had the opportunity, if convicted of a crime, to "plead the belly," appealing to pregnancy to receive lenience in sentencing. "Pleading the belly" granted the woman a stay of execution until three months after delivery; in that time she might get pregnant again or gain a pardon. To qualify, it had to be proven that the fetus was "quickening," that it had begun to move in the uterus; this was determined by a jury of matrons, women who thus had power to save or condemn other women to death. In 1719, an eighteenth-century Frenchman wrote of the English custom that "if they are not with child already, they must go to work immediately to be so ... they may get time, and so perhaps save their lives. Who would not hearken to such wholesome advice?" (Misson 330). In addition to buying time, delivery and lying in offered at least one capitally convicted woman a means of escape; in 1766, Katherine Nairn, sentenced to death with her brother-in-law for incest and the murder of her husband, escaped from the Tollbooth Prison two weeks after delivering her daughter there.

Beattie states: "Taking all property crimes together, the treatment of women was substantially different from that of men, for women were more likely to be acquitted, and if convicted, to be found guilty of a lesser charge than that stated on the indictment" (*Crime* 438). Historian G. R. Elton attributes the relative bias in favor of women as an "often instinctive chivalry or embarrassment" about the punishment of women (13). However, "instinctive chivalry" did not prevent women from being publicly whipped naked, nor burned alive. I agree with Beattie that this tendency toward less severe sentencing probably reflects the fact that women simply posed less of a threat to lives, property, and civic order than did men (*Crime* 439).

A 1750 proposal that all women should be transported for a first offense, no matter how small, reflects the belief that *all* female crime was fundamentally unnatural, suggesting that even the smallest instance of it revealed a woman's inherent monstrosity and thus required her literal expulsion from English society.[11] While accounts of male murderers constructed the killer as deviant "other," often defining his crimes according to logic of unlawful tendencies, these tendencies were not imagined as having anything to do with his sex *per se*. Augustan England was a violent place: men often beat their wives and children, and participated in boxing matches, duels, drunken brawls, or fights over gambling tables. Often someone died as a result of a fight gone out of control or a "legitimate" beating (of spouse, child, or servant) taken too far. While these events were punished and condemned, they were also understood to be part of the risks and commonalities of

---

during the marriage, or at least is incorporated and consolidated into that of her husband" (2: 430).

[10] *Femme covert* did not apply to burglary, treason, or murder.

[11] See *Gentleman's Magazine* 532–33.

male social life. And, of course, state-sanctioned murder was common as English soldiers engaged in various wars and uprisings. For women, however, violence was figured as a sign of stepping entirely outside of their constituted space, not, as was often the case with male murderers, a sign of simply overstepping it.[12]

Eighteenth-century common law collapsed women's domestic crime and crime against the state, viewing them as equally dangerous to the social order. For a woman to kill her husband was not a crime of homicide, but one of petty treason, as she had rebelled against her God and state-sanctioned master. The 1722 *An Institute of the Laws of England* defines petty treason as "[a] Crime where One out of Malice Taketh away the Life of a Subject, To whom He oweth a Special Obedience" (Wood 346). Men who committed petty treason—for example, servants killing their masters—were hung, the standard punishment for a capital offence. Men who committed high treason, or crimes against the crown, were drawn and quartered or drawn and hung, the more painful and unusual punishment marking the crime as extra-depraved. In contrast, women received extraordinary punishment for crimes of *both* petty and high treason. If a woman killed her husband she was thus not hung, but burned alive at the stake.[13] Her taking of inappropriate power was such a threat it necessitated exceptional punishment; to be burned alive overtly evokes witchcraft and is a particularly slow and gruesome way to die. Tellingly, women continued to be burned at the stake for petty treason or spousal homicide a *century* after the punishment was last invoked in a case of high treason. In all eighteenth-century cases in which women were convicted of high treason, judges simply stopped ordering death by burning and chose more humane options of execution. In contrast, women's death by burning for petty treason remained constant until Parliament abolished the burning of women in May 1790.[14]

---

[12]   Even contemporary historians often describe the eighteenth-century murderess in strongly emotive terms. For example, Frank McLynn notes that "when aroused, the homicidal instincts of women could be tigerish in their ferocity" and refers to murderess Sarah Malcolm as "another demon in female form" (118). His discussion of male murderers never falls into such reductive, hyperbolic terms. Historians Tom Hitchcock and Robert Shoemaker posit a causal link between the relative rarity of female violence and brutality: "[w]hereas male violence was circumscribed by unwritten rules, female violence was unexpected and therefore unregulated. As a result, while such violence was relatively rare, it occasionally led to brutal injuries and death" (42).

[13]   Blackstone argued that for a woman to be burned alive was actually merciful as "the natural modesty of the sex forbids the exposing and publicly mangling their bodies" (4: 95). Such "natural modesty" did not preclude women from being whipped topless in public, but it did result in their being hung in their shifts.

[14]   The last woman to be burned for petty treason was Margaret Sullivan, who was burned in 1788 after first being hanged. As the century drew to a close, the punishment began to rouse much public outcry, as evidenced in the following newspaper commentary: "There is something inhuman in burning a woman, for what only subjects a man to hanging. Human nature should shudder at the idea. Must not mankind laugh at our lay speeches against African slavery, and our fine sentiments on Indian cruelties, when in the very eye

This discrepancy of sentencing suggests that the perceived danger and horror of women's violence against the family resonated far more than the risk she was seen to pose to the crown. Throughout the century, murders within the family—that institution newly invested as affective, feminine, domestic, and thus presumably safe from such bloody mis-adventures—were always "the most attention-grabbing crimes to report" (Bell, *Literature* 70) and, I argue, the locus of this attention and fear was women. A 1752 treatise decries:

> [t]hat the horrid and unnatural crime of murder, has within a very few years ... become much more frequent in this kingdom, than it was ever before known to be, is too sad a truth to be disputed ... alas! of late it has not only been as common as almost every week, to produce a fresh instance; but dreadful to tell! ... not the nearest tie of kindred has been any security against it. (*Warning Piece* 1)

This exposition marks the social arena as mortally endangered by murderers and points specifically to the fear that the familial sphere, supposedly secure from the violent potentiality of the public, provides no security against the uncontainable bloody passions of the killer. According to this treatise, murder has become a sort of banal commonality, a once a week occurrence reminiscent of a demonic domestic routine.

The link between the shadowy domains of crime and womanhood hinted at in this passage is made explicit in the story that immediately follows it, a dire tale of a "female monster," who poisons her lover and her husband.[15] The link between crime and femininity and the correlative anxiety regarding the safety of the domestic realm is also directly ventured in the following excerpt of a letter from a "learned counselor," to Mary Edmondson, convicted of murdering her aunt in 1759. He writes, "What a shudder must human nature receive, when it recollects that there is now no place where security may be depended on; for at the same time persons are barring their doors without, they are enclosing worse enemies within" (*A Refutation* 9).

Fear of contemporary eighteenth-century English female criminals led to accusations that present-day murderesses were worse than their historical and mythic predecessors. For example, the writer of a 1726 letter to *Mist's Weekly Journal* claims that Clytemnestra at least had "a colourable excuse" for her crimes and decries that:

> Our women now, whenever they lift the knife against their husbands ... are content to say, either *that the Devil was busy with them*; or to have found a

---

of the Sovereign we roast a female creature alive ...? Shame on it, thus to attack the female sex, who by being the weaker body, are more liable to error and less entitled to severity" (qtd. in Gatrell 388).

[15] The treatise narrates the stories of Victorina and of the Marchioness de Brinvillier, both women who killed members of their families.

provocation from some trivial *misusage*, or being *stinted* in the *necessaries* of
life ... the objected *misusage* is too often ... by their own *provoking conduct*;
and ... what they call *necessaries* may more properly be stil'd *unreasonable
superfluities*.

In this account, Englishwomen murder because they are bad wives—ill behaved,
unwilling to take responsibility for their actions, and extravagant rather than thrifty
consumers who murder on a whim when their superfluous and illogical desires
are denied.

The Augustan murderess not only rent blood and bone, but also challenged
a newly forming conception of modest and private femininity. Female domestic
homicide resonated with contemporaneous anxieties about the changing
configuration of the family home and woman's role within it. As the century
unfolded in England, boundaries around the home began to tighten as bonds of
kinship began to loosen, and this narrowing domestic space produced a newly
pressurized focus on domestic felicity. Structural changes in the economy, social
hierarchies, and family resulted in the gradual and erratic, but ideologically and
materially powerful, reformulation of the concept of the home and family as
women (of a certain class) were becoming identified as a moral, affective, and
nurturing force in the home. Much has been written about the consequences and the
material truth of this ideological shift, and critics now largely agree that the divide
between public and private was predominantly conceptual, a line women crossed
frequently in actual eighteenth-century life.[16] Certainly criminal women crossed it.
So, for that matter, did almost all women, if we recognize that boundaries between
"public" and "private" are far more porous than we might tend to assume.

No clear public/private divide was in place in Augustan England, nor were
women who ventured into the loosely defined "public" sphere *ipso facto* viewed
as transgressive. However, the conception of women's proper role as affective and
private carried much social and psychic weight in eighteenth-century England, as
did the notion that the home was a feminized space. I am particularly interested in
eighteenth-century writers' notion that the household, while ostensibly a safe and
wholesome retreat from the competitive civic arena, might be a dangerous feminine
realm, free from the clarity, reason, and laws that regulate the public sphere.

Eighteenth-century writings on female domestic crime both hark back to the
specter of Medea and anticipate a fear Sigmund Freud addresses centuries later: that
women may have different ethics from men, possess an inferior sense of justice,
and thus potentially endanger civic peace and reason-based lawfulness. The fear of

---

[16]   Barbara M. Benedict, in her essay "Recent Studies in the Restoration and Eighteenth
Century," states this claim most concisely: "The separation between the public and private
spheres in the long eighteenth century is dead. This is a truth universally acknowledged in
Restoration and eighteenth-century studies this year." See also Klein for a critique of the
ways in which contemporary scholars assume a material division between gendered public
and private space.

what the woman might do within the bounds of the house was accentuated by the fact that women who killed tended, then as now, to commit murder primarily within the domestic arena.[17] The murderess not only abdicates her role as moral guardian of the private sphere, but she is also simultaneously thrust from that realm into the masculine space of the public. In a society that associated female fame with infamy, the accused woman was rendered public property. When she was accused of a crime, a woman entered the public sphere of law, a sphere that defined her most appropriate status as that of private property. As mentioned earlier, common law recognized women as full subjects *only* when they transgressed a judicial system that held them subject to its regulations, denying them agency of any type other than criminal.

The criminal woman also entered into a publicly circulating body of text, becoming the unwitting protagonist in the printed narratives of her misdeeds. In her excellent essay on eighteenth-century female criminals, Margaret Doody points out that "the women who took part in crime were enshrined in the narrative of crime. These characters were 'Heroines' in the sense that they had figured in printed stories" ("The Law" 129). As Doody explains, few women made the news in Augustan England; other than royals, the most prominent female figures in the popular press were those who had committed a crime. For a woman, to be written about was virtually unthinkable, and the female criminal became the protagonist in the voluminous pages recording her crimes.

The specter of the murderess haunted the eighteenth-century imagination as a threat to masculine authority and patriarchal familial order. This threat was, however, largely imagined: actual female homicide rates were low; then as now, women were far more likely to be victims than perpetrators of violent crime.[18] Captain Charles Johnson's 1801 comment in *Lives of the Most Remarkable Female Robbers* bears repeating in this context: "[A] female Offender excites our curiosity more than a male" (327). Despite, or because of, her relative rarity, the murderess became the topic of nonfiction accounts, broadside ballads, derisive cartoons, and published legal opinions in eighteenth-century England, and her appearances in this public world of letters presented powerful images of dystopic femininity.[19]

---

[17]   Beattie notes, in his categories of homicides in the Surrey Assize Proceedings (the most definitive records available), that 81.8 percent of female homicides were committed within the family while 18.2 percent were committed in the course of another crime (105).

[18]   In his research on the Surrey Assize Proceedings, Beattie notes that, between the years 1660–1800, 334 individuals were charged with homicides, of which 91 percent were men and 9 percent women (106).

[19]   From the 1670s through the early decades of the eighteenth century, sessions papers, trial accounts, and ordinaries' accounts—reports by the Newgate prison chaplain—were regularly printed in short broadside form. These accounts were extremely popular and began to run into pages; book-length collections of criminals' lives began to appear in 1710 (Faller, *Crime* 4–5).

In large part, all of these texts work in a regulatory fashion, marking the female criminal as an anti-exemplar in order to shore up, by contrast, the figure of the exemplar she is so decidedly not. Popular visions of female criminality, including the criminal biography and the fictions that grew out of and coincided with it, helped to constitute a vision of domestic femininity. This passive and moral vision of femininity, in turn, bolstered a newly forming contrasting vision of secular, civic-minded, economically useful, internalized law-bound masculinity. Conduct literature defined the private, domestic arena as the natural space for women and articulated this arena as the rejuvenating and purifying tonic for the "public" men of the Enlightenment. At the same time, the criminal biography, or as I term it, the "mis-conduct book," shored up this formulation by defining the public arena as an unnatural and fatal space for women, figuring the criminal woman as one whose excessive desire proves toxic to the body public.

Nonfiction narratives of female homicide construct female juridical transgression according to didactic tropes that resemble those outlined in the conduct literature of the era. Both genres are invested in a vision of passive, chaste, pure, and domestic femininity. Yet the female criminal biographies panegyrize this vision by telling the tales of those women who explicitly assail it. These "mis-conduct" books are some of the few early eighteenth-century works that represent women as active, powerful agents, women whose actions move them outside of a prescriptive realm of feminine passivity.

"The Characteristic of the Age": Crime and Public Panic in Eighteenth-Century England

> Gentlemen, our News-Papers, from the Top of the Page to the Bottom, the Corners of our Streets up to the very Eves of our Houses, present us with nothing but … Fury … grown to so enormous a Height, that it may be called the Characteristic of the present Age … the Rod of the Law, Gentlemen, must restrain those within them Bounds of Decency and Sobriety, who are deaf to the Voice of Reason, and superior to the Fear of Shame.
>   —Henry Fielding, *A Charge Delivered to the Grand Jury*, 1749

The fascination with criminal biographies—of both men and women—was linked to a trend of public anxiety regarding crime. In Augustan England, like today, crime was seen as a sign of the times, evidence of the increasing degradation of society, and crime and its dangers were the focus of extreme cultural attention and anxiety. Increasing urbanization, changing family roles, class anxieties, issues of legitimacy, the Jacobites, foreign and civil wars, new ways of making money, and challenges to established religious doctrine all contributed to the fearful sense that cultural foundations were shifting and dislocated, a fear which lent itself to the notion that disorder was at hand and criminal lawlessness was running amok.[20] Throughout the eighteenth century, there were repeated outbursts of public panic regarding crime rates; these panics were articulated in terms that collapse specific fears of criminal behavior into more general fears regarding a sense of cultural violation and disturbance. The association of criminality with perceived threats of gender, class, or racial others continually informs the somewhat hysterical tones of eighteenth-century writings on crime. In fact, there is no solid corroboration for any perceived crime waves during the century; what *had* changed was the monumental increase in the circulation of printed reports of crime, an increase that created a new hyperawareness of criminal activity.[21]

Eighteenth-century calls to arms about crime demonstrate a particular fear of criminal behavior that slides into a generalized fear of the moral and physical decline of English society. This was an era concerned with empirical definitions and marked by an increasingly secular mode of comprehension and conception. The topic of crime resonated with the anxiety that these newly organized modes of authority might not be strong enough to contain those elements that challenged stable social order; that the body of law might not, in fact, be capable of containing the bodies of those who challenge its precepts. For example, in *An Enquiry into the Causes of the Late Increase of Robbers &c.*, Henry Fielding posits that criminals, the poor, "loose" women, and the politically suspect are epidemic parasites endangering the health and life of English people (of a certain class, gender, and political bent) and thus the nation itself. Fielding analogizes English society to a sick body, doomed to die unless properly attended to and cured of those self-destructive "Faults in the Constitution" that nourish and encourage its mortal illness.[22]

---

[20]   For further discussions of this perception of rising crime, see: Beattie, particularly 213–29; Bell, *Literature and Crime* 12–18; McLynn, chapter 1; and Rawlings.

[21]   Beattie convincingly argues that rising rates of prosecution usually dovetail with periods of peace that follow relatively low crime rates during periods of war (218ff.). However, this argument was not one made in the eighteenth century and Beattie posits that the perception of crime waves was not, in fact, based in fact. Rawlings comments that parliament rapidly increased the number of capital offenses between the 1680s and the middle of the next century "as the new political order sought to establish the roots of its power" and argues that this fact may affect the increasing focus on criminality (17). Faller notes that "though it seems now that crime was actually declining in early eighteenth-century England, contemporary observers were sure it was catastrophically on the rise" (*Crime* 7). Each of these scholars argues that the new proliferation of crime literature added to the sense of rising crime.

[22]   Daniel Defoe and Henry Fielding, whose fictional accounts of crime I turn to in Chapter 4, each published multiple nonfiction texts in which they decry a loss of traditional order, bemoan a society "ripened up to crime," and locate the perceived rise of crime and concomitant threat to England in the "lower orders" (Defoe, qtd. in Beattie 217). See Defoe's *Conjugal Lewdness*, *Street Robberies Consider'd*, and *An Effectual Scheme*. Fielding's writings on crime include: *A True State*, *An Enquiry*, *Examples*, and *A Proposal*. Fielding's threats about rising crime were at least in part a rationale for his and his step-brother

Throughout the century, eighteenth-century writings on crime express, in equal and linked parts, nostalgia for an idealized agrarian past and anxiety about the "lower orders." These writings generally share a sense that there was once a time when England was peaceful and safe, an always already past era aligned with a pastoral, hierarchical fantasy of cultural containment that stands in contrast to the increasingly urban, class-shifting reality of eighteenth-century England. For example, in a 1701 treatise exhorting more severe capital penalties for homicide, the writer of *Hanging Not Punishment Enough* inveighs against what he sees as the overwhelming threat of rising crime in England:

> Were it not so, our Roads would not be so pester'd with that wicked Generation of Men, nor our Sessions-Papers Monthly, and the Publick News daily so full of so many relations of Robberies and Murthers. If some Remedy not be found to stop this growing Evil, we will shortly not dare to travel in England unless, as in the Deserts of Arabia, it be in large Companies, and Arm'd. (2)

The treatise expresses the fear of rising criminality and its effects on the nation in terms of a curtailing of mobility: a future of a barbaric Arabic aura, in which "the satisfaction of traveling" the green hills of England will be "destroyed" and replaced by a dystopic desert of armed companies. This vision resonates with an anxiety that is more far-reaching than that of discrete criminal behavior; it evokes a fear of England losing its national character to become indistinguishable from the "uncivilized" East. The rise of urban London, and the concomitant increase of mobility this rise engendered as people moved from town to city, created a sense that England was being "uprooted," that stability and accountability were in danger as people began to relocate. Relocation to London also allowed the possibility of anonymity, a possibility that was far more difficult when labor was linked to an agrarian model dependant upon stability of place. The new possibility of "losing oneself" in the city carried with it the fear that people might not be what they seemed, that the city offered a potential for deviant misrepresentation and guile.[23] Samuel Johnson's satiric poem *London* calls for the past golden age of Alfred when "a single jail ... Could half the Nation's Criminals Contain ... Best Age! but ah! How diff'rent from our own!"[24]

(and fellow Bow Street magistrate) John's attempts to establish England's first detective/ police force and to improve the system of the magistrates.

[23]   Ironically, in this passage, mobility is seen as endangered while in fact it was increasing. The most actively mobile class was the poor, who traveled to London to make their fortunes and were those associated with the criminal class. The increased freedom of movement of the lower classes is seen as a murderous curtailing of the movement of the wealthy.

[24]   This poem is typical of a host of similarly elegiac writings on the state of England at the time. London's population grew from roughly 60,000 in 1500 to around 400,000 in the mid-seventeenth century, and over a million by the early nineteenth (Sharpe, *Crime and*

In eighteenth-century England, the criminal functioned as a catchall category, as it remains today, for troubling aggregates perceived to pose a potential threat to entrenched authority. As Newgate Ordinary Paul Lorrain preached, "All Thieves and Murderers were Rebels" (*Remarks*). The most impassioned and sepulchral fear of unruly criminal bodies was directed at murderers, those criminals whose crimes violated not only an abstract body of legal principle, but also a discernible individual body. The detection and punishment of the murderer were of paramount concern, and the fear that murderers were running free, undetected and unpunished, terrified and outraged the populace throughout the century as it simultaneously seized their imaginations.

Criminal Imaginations and Illicit Interests: Early Prose Fictions

His History will astonish! And is not compos'd of Fiction, Fable, or Stories plac'd at York, Rome, or Jamaica, but Facts done at your Doors, Facts unheard of, altogether new, Incredible, and yet Uncontestable.

—Daniel Defoe and Jack Sheppard, *The History of the Remarkable Life of John Sheppard* (1724)[25]

A person used to this kind of reading [fiction] will be disgusted with every thing serious or solid, as a weakened and depraved stomache rejects plain and wholesome food.

—Clara Reeve, *The Progress of Romance and the History of Charoba, Queen of Aegypt* (1785)

Stories of criminals—real and imagined—proliferated in eighteenth-century England. In the first third of the century, no clear epistemological, generic, or legal means of division existed between prose narratives—such as news, travel writing, criminal or spiritual biographies, conduct books, the romance, and the new genre of the novel—and the boundaries between them were legally and critically fluid.[26] For example, criminal biographies, while themselves not novels but novel

---

the Law 32). Historians and sociologists have written extensively on similar reactionary responses in our own era; for example, Kappeler, Blumberg, and Potter argue that "[m]yths of crime and justice, when blended with threats to religious beliefs, economic systems, sexual attitudes or orientation, the traditional family, or political preference become a volatile mix" and "the argument is simple: a growing menace is plaguing society ... and endangering tradition" (18–23).

[25]   Quoted in Bell, *Literature and Crime* 67.

[26]   Extensive scholarship charts the reasons the English novel as a genre became possible at this historical moment; technological improvements, most crucially the printing press, coincided with complicated shifts in the historical web of economic, religious, political, and philosophical thought and practice that made realistic prose narratives of

commentaries on legal cases, follow what we recognize as fictional conventions rather than attempt what we would consider historical objectivity. They present "novel" experiences in what we consider "novelistic" terms: the authors created dialogue, invented scenarios, and ascribed motivation in order to "plot" criminals' lives.[27] And, the reverse is also true. As historians of the novel have demonstrated, "legal-criminal categories in general have an enormous organizational significance in the history of the novel" (Bakhtin 124).[28] Fiction was both formally and thematically influenced by legal narratives, and the term *novella* itself implies not only newness, but in Late Latin refers to an addition to the legal code.[29]

Subject matter is the most obvious connection between early English fiction and crime: early novels are full of rogues, highwaymen, bastards, and whores. Like the criminal biography, the early novel is organized around the ideal of telling the truth of the life of an individual, often, in the early part of the century, the life of a criminal. Novels, news stories, and treatises are replete with apologies for the unsavoriness of their criminal subjects and declarations of the virtue of the authors' intentions. Writers of nonfiction accounts were, however, protected in

---

individual consciousness imaginable and desirable. See, for example, Armstrong; Davis; Doody, *True Story*; Hammond; McKeon, *Origins*; Richetti, *Popular Fiction*; Warner, *Licensing Entertainment*; and Watt.

[27]   The veracity and objectivity of criminal biographies was an issue even at the time of their writing; eighteenth-century readers (the most famous being Defoe) argued that many biographers showed little regard for the facts of the criminal's life and were motivated by mercenary or didactic principles. Whatever their motivation, the writers of criminal biographies wrote the stories of unarguably real people who had unarguably been convicted of crimes. In this crucial sense, they are different from imaginative fiction. Yet these representations are odd amalgamations of factual history and fictional story. As Faller and Richetti demonstrate, the biographies present real people as semifictional characters, assigning them those characteristics that rendered them "representational" to readers.

[28]   See Welsh for an essential and in-depth analysis of the effects of circumstantiality on law and literature. The nature and import of "truthful" representation was actively debated in Augustan England on both the legal and the literary fronts. In law, notions of how the truth should be told—issues of testimony and evidence—changed radically during the Restoration as the courts shifted from favoring immediate, unmitigated testimony (from the witness) toward an ideal of natural necessity and neutral remove (with evidence and testimony narrated by the attorneys). Legal discourse began to privilege ideals of clarity and authority; for example, after the Settlement of 1688, it was "accepted that offenses should be fixed, not indeterminate; rules of evidence should be carefully observed; and the judges administering the law should be learned and impartial" (Sharpe, *Crime* 15). For discussions of the links between the early novel and legal discourse also see Lennard Davis's chapter "The Law and the Press"; Michael McKeon's chapters "Histories of the Individual" and "The Destabilization of Social Categories"; John Richetti's *Popular Fiction* chapters "Rogues and Whores: Heroes and Anti-Heroes" and "Travelers, Pirates, and Pilgrims"; and Ian Watt's chapters "Realism and the Novel Form" and "Defoe as Novelist."

[29]   See Bender's clarification of the etymology of the term *novella* in his discussion of eighteenth-century fiction (*Imagining the Penitentiary* 11).

part by the umbrella of truth under which they labored. Recognizable fictions, in contrast, risked being attacked as inherently untrustworthy and immoral. As Lennard Davis explains:

> While actual criminals might recount the steps by which God led them through crime to repentance, the novelist must impersonate God in sending his character through a series of "divinely" inspired—but really "writerly" inspired—revelations. Authors thus put themselves in the blasphemous position of equating plot with providence. (133–34)[30]

In the face of such accusations and generic confusion, writers of fiction regularly exhorted readers that their tales were, in fact, true; the prefaces of early novels abound with lengthy authorial commentary regarding the authenticity of the representation, the sources from whence it came, and the author's claim to be recounting the story for moral purposes.[31]

As Davis comments, however, "[T]he formula for creating a criminal in the eighteenth century was to take a youth, have him read novels, which action leads him to crime, prison, and the gallows" (125).[32] Like Fielding's criminals, novels were seen as a threat to the health of the public body:

> The press groaned under the weight of Novels, which sprang up like mushrooms every year .... [They] did but now begin to increase upon us, but ten years more multiplied them tenfold. Every work of merit produced a swarm of imitators, till they became a public evil.[33]

The purveying of fictional stories was seen as a lowly and a shady business rather than a noble or artistic vocation. Novels, like criminals, were imagined as a

---

[30]   Hence the virulence of the attack by Charles Gildon on his contemporary Defoe: Gildon claimed Defoe was a blasphemous retrograde, as "the Christian religion and the doctrines of providence are too sacred to be delivered in fictions and lies" (*Epistle* 28). Defoe, however, did not define himself as a beleaguered fiction writer; he also attacked novels as a genre and defined his own fictional texts as "histories."

[31]   Swift's satire of such practices, in *Tale of a Tub*, bespeaks the omnipresence (and likely failure) of such claims: "If I should go about to tell the reader, by what Accident, I became master of these papers, it would, in this unbelieving Age, pass for little more than the Cant, or Jargon of the Trade. I, therefore, gladly spare both him and my self so unnecessary a Trouble" (Swift, *Tale* 2). Criminal biographies also regularly assured readers that the stories they told were "no Fiction, as is commonly used in Pamphlets of this Nature" (qtd. in Faller, *Crime* 24), a caveat that speaks to doubts regarding the authenticity of these texts as well.

[32]   See Davis's chapter, "Criminality and the Double Discourse," for extensive examples of the Augustan belief in the criminal force of novelistic fiction.

[33]   John Dunlop's *History of Fiction*, cited in Warner, *Licensing Entertainment* 4–5.

persistent and pernicious fungus, a swarming, mutating virus that was infecting the nation's moral health.

These "criminal fictions"—both fictional and factual—were the subject of moral and critical anxiety in part because of their tremendous popularity. Moralists and critics evinced the greatest concern regarding the ill effects such criminal narratives would have on those who might most easily learn scandalous, rather than scrupulous, lessons from the texts: the lower classes (of both genders) and women. In 1725, James Arbuckle complained:

> Your Robinson Crusoes, Moll Flanders, Sally Salisburys and John Shepards have afforded notable instances how easy it is to gratify our curiosity, and how indulgent we are to the biographers of Newgate, who have been as greedily read by the people of the better sort as the compilers of last speeches and dying words by the rabble.[34]

Here, Arbuckle tellingly imagines novelistic characters and the real-life subjects of criminal biographies as fundamentally interchangeable, and his quote exemplifies the Augustan tendency to situate fictional and actual criminality within the same framework. Reading any of these unsuitable texts was seen as a sign of moral retrogression. Arbuckle's comment suggests the class concern associated with both fiction and crime: he equates the reading of criminals' lives with the habits of the "rabble." That the upper classes were eagerly reading such fictions evoked the fear that lower class tastes were infecting "the better sort," that class that should rightly be inured from commercial and criminal crudeness.[35]

Narratives of criminal activities were assumed to possess the power to unsettle stable social hierarchies and to reflect and encourage, by their criminal content and their presumed transgression at the level of form itself, a trend of immorality and public corruption. A rhyme from the 1729 *Flying Post* overtly associates fictional criminal narratives with the lower classes: "Down in the Kitchen, honest Dick and Doll / Are Studying Col. Jack and Moll."[36] The comment reflects the persistent fear that "honest" servants might "study" the tales of dishonest criminals to ill effect. That such a fear would concentrate on the symbolically fraught bodies of the disenfranchised is logical, as these bodies pose the greatest danger to hierarchical authority.

---

[34] Quoted in Davis 123.

[35] While the meta-association of fiction with criminality and impropriety resulted in its regular alignment with the "lesser" populace, the association of fiction with the lower classes did not reflect the actual reading audience for novels or lengthier criminal biographies as these texts lay largely outside of the purchasing power of laborers (Watt 42).

[36] Quoted in Backscheider, *Moll Flanders* 11.

Similarly, the association of women and the novel was suspect (a phenomenon well documented in contemporary studies of the novel).[37] As Paula Backscheider points out, "Women novelists outnumbered men, and prefaces openly appealed to female readers" (*Daniel Defoe* 182). Women writers such as Aphra Behn, Delarivier Manley, and Eliza Haywood—referred to in 1722 as the "Fair Triumvirate" for their fame and success—wrote and sold their works commercially, needed or wanted the money (versus wealthier women writers such as the Countess of Winchilsea or Katherine Philips), and tended to come from the middle and lower social ranks or to have suffered a financial set back that left them in need of an income (Todd, *Sign* 37). The extraordinary popularity of these writers must have irked their male contemporaries. The politics of early fiction writers also tended to be out of line with majority interests; Behn's, Manley's, and Haywood's politics leaned toward unpopular and ornate Stuart royalism, while Defoe was a committed Dissenter. The association of women and paid labor was also suspect, linked by critics, moralists, and popular opinion to servitude and to sexual laxity.

Given the social constructions of femininity combined with market and political pressures, it is unsurprising that early English women who wrote fiction engendered some of the most vitriolic critical responses of the era.[38] Women writers were damned on multiple fronts, and critics consistently used regulatory conceptions of proper gender roles as ammunition in their attacks.[39] For example, John Duncombe's poem, *The Feminiad*, imagines early English women writers as antithetical to true and moral literary production as well as to natural and nationalized femininity:

> The modest Muse a veil with pity throws
> O'er Vice's Friends and Virtue's Female foes;
> Abash'd she views the bold unblushing mien
> Of Manley, Centlivre, and Behn;

---

[37] The feminocentric association of early fiction is well charted; I will simply comment briefly. See, for example, in order of date of publication: Gilbert and Gubar; Perry, *Women*; Spencer; Armstrong; Todd; Langbauer; Ballaster, *Seductive Forms*; Gallagher; and Bowers, *Politics*.

[38] Restoration and early eighteenth-century attacks on women writers were influenced by particular material, as well as aesthetic and moral, conditions. Most crucially, the Restoration was the first period when women as a group began clearly and openly writing for money. The association between theater and fiction is also at play; women writers often wrote and worked for the theater, and the association of spectacle and sin that accompanied the actress or the public woman affected women fiction writers in parallel and often materially overlapping contexts.

[39] It is unclear to what extent these attacks were motivated solely by the authors' gender and to what extent they were motivated by their participation in and association with Grub-Street, the popular Hack literature positioned as at odds with the neoclassical formalism of the Scriblerians, as well as by particular political affiliations. For an excellent discussion of these issues, see Brewer.

And grieves to see one nobly born disgrace
Her modest sex, and her illustrious race.

Like the female criminal, the woman writer affronts the muse, herself truly modest, and boldly disgraces her gender and her country through her corrupt "unveiled" material.

To write fiction in Restoration and early eighteenth-century England was to participate in a profligate practice aligned with criminality, danger and pleasure, and inappropriate sexual and political license. The widely circulating prose narrative was generically novel, not regulated by strict rules of form or content, but unruly and imaginatively unlawful. By later in the century, the novel's reputation was to some extent reformed as it began to be seen as a didactic tool. With the publication of *Pamela*, *Clarissa*, *Joseph Andrews*, and *Tom Jones* over the course of the 1740s, the novel became less associated with the criminal, the lower class, and the feminine and began to receive critical praise for its moral potential. Over the centuries, critics have defined this shift as one from romance to realism and heralded it either as a moral or an aesthetic improvement. The shift is often imagined in gendered terms, and critics who have embraced it (from the eighteenth century to the present) tend—to greater or lesser degrees—to dismiss early female-authored fictions as plot-driven diversions in contrast to the more rich and substantive realism of Defoe, Richardson, and Fielding.

As contemporary historians of the novel have shown, Restoration and eighteenth-century novels do not follow a linear trajectory toward moral seriousness or aesthetic realism. The critical reformation of the mid-century did not reflect any substantive change in the moral content of fiction, and the newly rehabilitated and realistic nature of the novel was largely imagined, rooted in party and sexual politics.[40] Such a trajectory, rather, tends to delineate genre divisions according to gender stereotypes, reading early women's fiction as a guilty, frothy sexual secret replaced by the principled, complex realism of later male writers.[41] This reading erases many writers all together. It defines Defoe, stuck in the wrong era with the flashy/trashy women, as a sort of protonovelist, a harbinger of good men

---

[40]   Like others before me, I argue that fiction did not in fact break off in the 1740s to begin, in Fielding's words, "a new species of writing"; however, that such a claim has been argued and accepted from the mid-eighteenth century until the recent present means it has a cultural effect, if not veracity. In other words, whatever the nature of later fiction, it was more often praised as morally redemptive than any fiction written in the Restoration or early decades of the eighteenth century, and it was often contrasted explicitly and positively with earlier fiction.

[41]   In his fascinating history of the novel, William Warner argues that, while the novel remained a porous term, "the targets of the antinovel campaign [of the early eighteenth century] were quite precise: seventeenth-century romances, novellas of Continental origin, and those 'novels' and 'secret histories' written by Behn, Manley, and Haywood" ("Licensing Pleasure" 1).

to come. And it relegates to the footnotes those early didactic women writers—such as Aubin, Barker, and Rowe—who preceded Fielding and Richardson in gaining moral approbation for their fiction. Such readings simplify the fiction on either side of a false divide; *Clarissa* can take on *Love in Excess* for erotics anytime, and Behn's discourses on vows and moral obligation could make Pamela feel guilty.[42] All of the fictions discussed in this project are formally complex texts that engage with serious topical, ethical, and epistemological questions. The question with which this book is fundamentally concerned is: how did early eighteenth-century narratives imagine female homicide? In the remaining chapters, I look closely at the murderess as she is imagined both in the news and novels and examine the ways in which these eighteenth-century narratives of female homicide reflect and refract the contemporaneous legal, social, aesthetic, and literary contexts in which they were produced.

---

[42] My readings of Behn and Manley (and elsewhere of Haywood) do not support the characterization of their novels as plot-driven texts that provide, at best, a simplistic engagement in the moral significance of that plot. Here, I differ from some recent critics, who, while often thoughtfully attentive to early women's fiction, still argue, when comparing it to the fiction of contemporaneous male authors, that it asks of its readers only a superficial interest in plot. See, for example, Hammond's comparison of Defoe's *Roxana* with Haywood's *Idalia* (227) and Richetti, "An Emerging New Canon."

Chapter 2

Moving Violations:
Aphra Behn, Delarivier Manley,
and the Romance of Violence

Woman! By heav'ns the very name's a Crime ...
Averse to all the Laws of Man, and heav'n ...
Be cautious then, and guard your Empire well;
For shou'd they once get power to rebel,
They'd surely wage a Civil War in Hell.
> —Robert Gould and Thomas Brown, *Love Given O're: or, a Satyr against the*
> *Pride, Lust, and Inconstancy, &c. of Woman* (1682)

What are your laws, of which you make your boast, but the fool's wisdom and
the coward's valour, the instrument screen of all your villainies, by which you
punish others what you act yourselves, or would have acted, had you been in
their circumstances? ... Thus you go on deceiving and being deceived, harassing,
plaguing, and destroying one another, but women are your universal prey.
> —George Lillo, *The London Merchant* (1731)

This chapter closely examines three early novels with female protagonists who
commit, or attempt to commit, murder: Aphra Behn's *The History of the Nun, or
the Fair Vow-Breaker* (1689) and *The Fair Jilt, or The History of Prince Tarquin
and Miranda* (1688); and Delarivier Manley's *The Wife's Resentment* (1720).
These fictional versions of murderous women are stories of love with a vengeance
in which good girls go bad, bad girls make good, and female subjectivity is enacted
and redacted in a shifting web of intrigue. These novels were long dismissed as
hyperbolic, unrealistic amatory fictions that fail to meet the criteria for "real"
novelistic fiction; in a less overly critical but similarly delimiting fashion, they
have also been read as cultural artifacts, interesting or valuable primarily because
they are female-authored. In fact, as recent critics have recognized, they are
complex and highly sophisticated short novels that are typical of early fiction in
their commentaries on Restoration party and monarchical politics and their focus
on the gendered themes of seduction, abandonment, women in distress, and female
power. In my readings, I focus on the ways in which Behn's and Manley's fictional
representations of murderesses engage with contemporaneous sociopolitical
notions of female morality and criminality. These texts engage explicitly with

women's roles in the civic realm, their exclusion from legal subjectivity and protections, and the implications of these exclusions on notions of feminine virtue and vice.

The History of the Nun and *The Fair Jilt* are thematically and formally similar: each tells the story of a beautiful votary who becomes brutally violent. Because the novels intermingle subjects and styles, they resist easy thematic or formal categorization. In both texts, Behn interrogates the subjects of vows, chastity, honor, familial duty, sexual desire, civic rights, violence, and subjectivity. Each novel baits its readers by moving between moments of what appear to be straightforward moralization and countermoments that directly defy easy moralistic conclusions. Most critically, for my purposes, each novel presents femininity as a cultural construct rather than a natural condition. While other Augustan narratives of female homicide, such as criminal biographies and juridical texts, imagine female violence through prescriptive fantasies of female nature, these novels represent female violence as motivated and specific. Behn's texts challenge comfortable classifications of gender, morality, and legality and reveal the flaws in the categories themselves.

The History of the Nun

The History of the Nun traces the fall of Isabella de Vallery, paragon of virtue, into bigamy and double homicide.[1] Behn portrays her murderess as neither entirely good nor entirely bad. She is neither wholly angel nor wholly whore, but both. In Isabella, Behn creates a complicated character who continually subverts the conspicuously overdetermined readings the text seems to provide. As the novel may be unfamiliar, I will begin with a brief plot summary. As a child, Isabella is sent by her father to a convent until she comes of age, when she must decide whether to remain a nun or to marry. There, she is raised by an Abbess who is intent on keeping Isabella's considerable fortune for the nunnery. Isabella remains a model nun until she meets and falls in love with the brother of a sister nun, the young and handsome Henault. Undone by passion, she breaks her religious vows and elopes with Henault, who ultimately proves both greedy and inept. After squandering Isabella's fortune, he joins the military and leaves her in order to win the graces and gold of his estranged father. He is reported dead in battle, and after a proper mourning period, Isabella is destitute. She marries Villenoys—a rebuffed suitor of her youth and the leader of Henault's military battle unit. They live happily for years until Henault miraculously returns. Isabella then murders him to save her current marriage and subsequently murders Villenoys as she fears he will disavow her as a bigamist. She lives on for some time as a wealthy widow until she is caught and beheaded.

---

[1]   For a useful discussion of the history of the novel's many adaptations, see Pearson.

From the novel's outset, Behn destabilizes the rigid demarcation between moral narrator and murderous subject. Rather than shoring up her already tenuous moral position as female writer by clearly delineating a separation between the narrator and the criminal protagonist, Behn aligns them. The narrator's connection to Isabella crystallizes in her declaration that the she, like Isabella, was once a

> humble votary in the house of devotion, not endued with an obstinacy of mind, great enough to secure me from the efforts and vanities of the world, I rather chose to deny myself that content I could not certainly promise myself, than to languish (as I have seen some do) in a certain affliction. (5)

The alignment of the narrator, the novel's sole source of moral commentary, with the protagonist—the murderess Isabella—reverberates on at least two levels. First, it disturbs the traditional boundary between the moral recounter and the immoral criminal subject, a boundary set firm within criminal biographies. The narrator's identification with the immoral character whose deeds she recounts calls into question her position as reputable moralizer as well as calling into question Isabella's position as entirely disreputable sinner.

Second, as fiction writers were seen to be tainted by the immoral tales that they told, as well as by the very act of writing fiction, the author, the narrator, and the fictional subject (as well as the reader) are all implicated here in an enterprise with an aura of disrepute. Narrator, protagonist, author, and female reader are linked in their fascination with the "efforts and vanities of the world." The narrator refuses religious life for worldly pleasure; Isabella elopes for romantic fulfillment and kills for personal gain; the author writes for profit and fame; and the female reader chooses to spend her time on lascivious entertainment. Each thus repudiates the social dictates of appropriate femininity, refusing to remain cloistered, "languish[ing] in a certain affliction," and instead seeking personal dominion.

Through its tropic use of vows, the novel critiques not only England's contemporaneous monarchal politics, but also contemporary gender politics.[2]

---

[2] Bowers's and Messenger's readings point to the ways in which Behn's fiction negotiates complex sociopolitical issues. In her excellent reading of the novel, Bowers notes that vows and their breaking not only resonate within the popular plot of seduction and betrayal, but also go "to the heart of Augustan questions about the status of personal honor and the authority of words in a world where sacred vows to God and king recently had been rendered negotiable and contingent" ("Sex, Lies" 63). In late seventeenth-century England, "oaths were regarded as political weapons," and "the dissonance between old and new notions concerning the efficacy of oaths could be exploited by those most ready to deploy the new nominalism against the old idealism" (63–64). Bowers asserts that "the story represents sympathetically the moral and religious uncertainty many were experiencing in the context of the Glorious Revolution, the sense of being without a choice but nevertheless at fault" (67). Messenger observes that "although the sexual passion of a French nun may seem far removed from the turmoil of England's government in 1688, the issue of broken loyalty unites them" (46).

The novel opens with a discourse on the particular dreadfulness of the sin of vow-breaking: "Of all the sins, incident to Human nature, there is none, of which heaven took so particular, visible, and frequent Notice, and Revenge, as on that of violated Vows" (3). The narrator does not actually define breaking a vow as the worst sin, but contends that it has the worst consequences in terms of divine punishment. The narrator moves to discuss the breaking of romantic vows and disputes the claim that romantic perjury is unworthy of divine retribution:

> Cupids may boast ... that heaven never takes cognizance of Lovers' broken vows and oaths and that 'tis the only perjury that escapes the anger of the gods. But I verily believe, if it were searched into, we should find these frequent perjuries, that pass in the world for so many gallantries only, to be the occasion of so many unhappy marriages and the cause of all those misfortunes, which are so frequent to the nuptialed pair. (3)

Behn defines nonromantic perjury as a sin that will suffer divine retribution, thus locating the current political "sins" of broken oaths within a framework of clear guilt that eventually will be punished by heaven. That she sees the broken vows of romance as purportedly free from such divine retribution opens them up to questions of necessary social retribution or critique, as well as implicitly questioning a divine authority who would ignore what the text defines as such harmful perjuries.

The beginning paragraphs of the novel proceed directly to the issue of gender and vows, commenting that both sexes are guilty of breaking vows of love. However, the narrator implies that women are instructed in the art of romantic deceit by male examples, arguing that female vow-breaking stems from a desire to avenge the suffering women have sustained at the hands of untrue men:

> [T]aught, perhaps, at first, by some dear false one, who had fatally instructed her youth in an art she ever after practiced in revenge on all those she could be too hard for, and conquer at their own weapons ... women are by nature more constant and just than men, and did not their first lovers teach them the trick of change, they would be doves. ... But customs of countries change even Nature herself. ... The women are taught by the lives of the men, to live up to all their vices. (4)

Behn acknowledges that men and women are both inconstant, but figures male inconstancy as innate and female as learned, freeing women from the charge of natural fickleness and positioning female transgression within a framework of originary male abandonment. In the novel, it is men who suffer violence at the hands of a female vow-breaker; however, the language of the description of male deceivers points to the historically far more likely outcome of romantic vow-breaking, women's lost virginity and resultant ruin: "What man that does not boast of the numbers he has thus ruined, and, who does not glory in the shameful triumph?" (4).

In the seventeenth century, a promise of marriage was binding and failure to follow through on such a promise was grounds for legal action; marital vows were affected by shifting notions of the binding nature of oaths.[3] Behn's fiction, along with that of her successors Manley and Haywood, explores a world in which such regulations are shaky, in which if a woman is seduced with false promises and abandoned she is likely to reap contempt as well as condolence.[4] Behn's interrogation of the ascendancy of gendered vows is made explicit by her text's dedication to Hortense Mancini, Duchess of Mazarin. Forced into an arranged marriage with an autocratic husband who frittered away the money she brought to the marriage, the Duchess tried to gain a legal separation. Upon failing, she left her husband and fled to England, where she became a mistress of Charles II.[5] Behn's dedication is flattering to Mancini and thus calls into question the relative virtue of vows made to church and husband in the case of cruel treatment. The dedication is doubly charged when we consider that Mancini's sister Olympe, Comtesse de Soissons, was famously banished in 1680 over the La Voisin affair and was accused of murdering her husband (Pearson 244).

By framing her text with a dedication with such notorious connotations, Behn overlays the novel's pious statements regarding the sacred nature of religious vows, described as those that, if broken, "receive the most severe and notorious revenges of God" (4). She raises a notion of relativity that conflicts with the text's apparent claims for moral absolutism. Behn again clarifies the *punishment*, not the nature, of the sin of religious vow-breaking itself as the most severe. The narrator is outraged at the sin of romantic perfidy, whose ruins she traces. Behn diffuses the power of the critique of sacred vow-breaking by immediately following it with a comment on the impossibility of holding to a holy vow, that of chastity, when it is made in youth: "[T]his resolution we promise and believe we shall maintain is not in our power" (4). The comment clarifies the seriousness of the offense, but the narrator proposes that it is an offense impossible to avoid. Thus, the narrator sets up Isabella's crime of vow-breaking not as a sign of her innate criminality, but as the logical consequence of forcing any woman—protagonist, narrator, author, or reader—to make such a decision when she is uninformed.

Behn examines women's lack of options and power within a patriarchal society that punishes them for straying from the dictates of modest and chaste femininity.

---

[3]   The first parliamentary divorce was granted less than a decade later, in 1698.

[4]   Historically, it is assumed that women suffered far more than men from this change in marital oaths, as a promise of marriage would often be used by men to gain sex, and if that promise was not binding, women had no legal recourse to insist upon the marriage to repair their lost reputations, or to gain legal paternity for the children they may have conceived from the union. See Bowers, "Sex, Lies" 64.

[5]   Manley also praises Mancini in her the introduction to *The Adventures of Rivella* (1714), and Mary Astell was inspired by Mancini's dilemma in her writing of the famous polemic *Some Reflections upon Marriage* (1700). For a discussion of Mancini's effect on Astell's work see Perry, *The Celebrated Mary Astell* 150–56.

The novel critiques England's refusal to grant women full status as subjects and reveals the ways in which women are harmed by their exclusion from active participation in family and state affairs. The narrator's final introductory comment decries the results of this denial of female agency:

> I could wish, for the prevention of an abundance of mischiefs and miseries that nunneries and marriages were not to be entered into 'till the maid, so destin'd, were of a mature age to make her own choice; and that parents would not make use of their justly assumed authority to compel their children neither to the one or the other; but since I cannot alter custom, nor shall ever be allowed to make new laws, or rectify the old ones, I must leave the young nuns inclosed to their best endeavors of making virtue a necessity; and the young wives to make the best of a bad market. (5)

The narrator locates female error in abused patriarchal fiat, arguing that if women were allowed to make their own choices, as adults, many "mischiefs and miseries" would be avoided. Behn portrays female crime as a result of the criminalization of female agency, implying that the dictates of feminine passivity and male prerogative provoke "bad" behavior. She places the blame for female crime on a society that refuses to allow women active roles in their own lives. The novel overtly links women's lack of power in the domestic/familial arena to their exclusion from the civic. Women's lack of substantive power in the civic arena—their status as second-class citizens without the capacity to make or change laws—results in their inability to effect the broad social change the text implies is necessary.

Behn disputes such ideologies throughout *The History of the Nun*. Her descriptions of Isabella play with reigning iconographies of femininity: Isabella embodies both the purely holy and the wholly sensual. Early in the story, elaborate descriptions of Isabella's purity wittily echo conduct book discourse: "[H]er life was a proverb, and a precedent, and when they would express a very holy woman indeed, they would say, 'She was a very Isabella'" (11). Behn also describes Isabella according to the popular vernacular of over-sexed femininity. After meeting Henault, Isabella "grows pale and languid" with desire that made her "rage within, like one possessed, and all her virtue could not calm her" (12, 15). Through use of such feminine stereotypes, Behn calls attention to the extremity and the folly of familiar and oppositional demarcations of femininity.

The novel situates female sexuality within a human framework that opposes both the contention that women are the modest sex and the conflicting claim, famously stated by Alexander Pope, that "every woman is at heart a rake." Isabella is not a creature of naturally insatiable appetite; she is unable to contain her love, not because of a lack of reason, but because she is uneducated about, and unfamiliar with, sexual desire. *The History of the Nun* critiques the ways in which nuns, and by extension all women "cloistered" in the role of idealized virtue, are forced to consider their passion unnatural. Behn implies that what is unnatural is the notion that women should feel no passion, stating that Isabella has been living "more like a saint than a woman; rather an angel than a mortal creature" (16). Behn suggests that Isabella, and by extension all women, cannot repress natural desire, and that their attempts to deny its existence simply increase its power. In a comment that anticipates a modern psychological grasp of repression, the narrator states that:

> the more she concealed her flame, the more violently it raged ... life could no longer support itself, but would either reduce her to madness, and so render her an hated object of scorn to the censuring world, or force her hand to commit a murder upon her self. (15, 16)

The language of crime and censure here anticipate the story's violent ending, but Behn's heroine directs the violence outward through murder, rather than inward through suicide.

Behn paradoxically renders Isabella's romantic love, unlike Henault's, as honorable in that, once it is acknowledged, her commitment to her love is unqualified. In contrast, Henault is unsure "though he adored the maid, whether he should not abhor the nun in his embraces" (19). While piety may stand as the surface explanation of Henault's trepidation, ultimately he is revealed as a fickle hypocrite who questions his commitment to her, not for her sake or that of religious principle, but because he will lose his fortune to his younger brother upon marrying her. Henault's lack of industry and his frivolous expenditure of Isabella's savings leave them economically imperiled. He ignores Isabella's pleas and, rather than working or saving, he joins the army to regain his father's approval and fortune. Isabella's consequent grief-stricken miscarriage of their child symbolizes the selfishness of Henault's abandonment of his pregnant wife and critiques his kowtowing for prestige, money, and paternal approval. The narrator dismisses any discussion of the war itself with the dry comment that "it is not my business to relate the history of the war, being wholly unacquainted with the terms of battles" (30). The passage ironically nods to the story's dramatization of the war between the sexes, a war, in this text, in which the woman ultimately takes up the sword.[6] The negative characterization of Henault highlights the dangers of a system in which women are forced to rely on male protection no matter how ineffectual that protection might be.

The narrator continues to frame Isabella's crisis with consistently critical comments on the lack of viable plots for woman. After Henault reportedly falls in battle, Isabella is devastated and grieves for some time until, left with no feasible economic options, she is "forced to submit herself to be a second time a wife ... and fancied the hand of Heaven had pointed out her destiny, which she could not avoid without a crime" (32). This passage suggests that Isabella's destiny requires a crime and syntactically positions that crime as an unavoidable result of an external situation. Unexpectedly, Isabella's blissful and wealthy

---

[6] The comment also resonates ironically with Behn's own experience as a spy for Charles.

five-year marriage to Villenoys constitutes a crime, bigamy, punishable by death. When Henault returns, Isabella is horrified and accurately recognizes that, as a bigamist: "I am ruined" (34). She will be:

> not only exposed to all the shame imaginable; to all the upbraiding [of Henault]; but all the fury and rage of Villenoys and the scorn of the town, who will look at her as an adulteress. She sees Henault poor and knew she must fall from all the glory and tranquility she had. (35)

Isabella recognizes that female honor and worth are not measured in terms of production or deeds but by reputation, or bodily borne chastity. No longer a virgin, unable to be a nun, and now a bigamist—Isabella not only *has* nothing, she is reduced *to* nothing. Isabella embodies the dangers of a system that defines the roles available to women as either virgin, chaste wife or widow, or virago. An unwitting bigamist, Isabella is disenfranchised by the loss of the "fair" exchange of her only capital—"her charming face and mien" (32); she thus assures her economic capital through a capital offense. She smothers Henault, pretends he has died of shock, and convinces Villenoys to dump the body. However, she then becomes immediately afraid that Villenoys will "be eternal[ly] reproaching her" (39) when the fact that their marriage is illegal sinks in. So she murders Villenoys as well.

In a deliciously ironic perversion of domestic art, Isabella uses needlework to murder Villenoys. *The History of the Nun* turns stitchery and witchery on their heads, making the female art of needlework—a symbol of female self-expression as well as repression—the means of murder. Behn astutely manipulates the irony inherent in Isabella's homicidal method. Shortly before the murders, the narrator portrays Isabella as occupying herself by "innocent diversions of fine work" (34), an act which ironically precedes that "black" (needle)work which will soon prove far from innocent. Her decision to commit her second murder of the night is described in language of feminine fate: "[W]hen Fate begins to afflict, she goes through stitch with her black work" (39). Isabella is explicitly aligned with those female Fates who weave men's destinies when she engages in her murderous act: She sews, "with several strong stitches," her second husband's coat to her first husband's body bag, imploring Villenoys to "give him a good swing" when throwing Henault's body into the river (39). The trope of witchcraft here suggests both female depravity and empowerment. The imagery also aligns Isabella with the female author, the woman who through her "black work," the ink of writing, seizes the prerogative of authority by taking control of the plot. Isabella gains forbidden and tantalizing authority by sewing up her own fate as she sews up her husbands', as Behn gains authority by shaping fate through her fictional designs.[7]

The second murder scene, while shocking, is irresistibly comic as well; its reliance on a sophisticated use of irony as well as physical farce is an unlikely

---

[7] See Gilbert and Gubar for their groundbreaking exploration of the association of women writers with transgressive authority, including witchcraft.

combination in a description of petty treason. Criminal biographies describe the female criminal in terms of her failure to exemplify appropriate feminine behavior. They finish with a lengthy account of the accused's utter self-hatred, or, if she defends her innocence or offers a defense, with a diatribe on the depth of her evil. In contrast, *The History of the Nun* locates female criminality within a complicated web of social circumstance in which "appropriate" feminine behavior is revealed to be potentially lethal. The text does not present Isabella as simple virago. Behn's heroine suffers extreme remorse and proclaims her wish for death, but Behn troubles the surface morality of Isabella's prostrations by skewing the plot.

Unlike Richardson's Clarissa, Isabella does not in fact pine away with remorse, nor does she turn herself in to the magistrate and confess her crime. Instead, she lives on happily, wealthy and beloved by her community, until she is caught. It is only *after* being charged that Isabella confesses her guilt, and then, rather than being burned, or even hung as "the murderess of two husbands in one night" (42), Isabella is rather aristocratically beheaded, "generally lamented and honorably buried" (42). Behn shifts the issue from Isabella's nature to the nature of the community's reaction to her; the text implies that the social system determines the ways in which we read crime and suggests that Isabella's crime does not rest in female nature but in the ways in which that nature is transformed by and within a community. Behn creates a criminal whose character leads us to question the assumptions that the criminal biography leaves intact, assumptions about femininity, about criminal action and motivation, about the efficacy of divine providence and judicial practice, and about the nature of subjectivity. *The History of the Nun* exposes the pat plots of criminal biographies and the moral and juridical apothegms that inform them.

The History of the Nun negotiates party, sexual, and textual politics in a skillful and subtle investigation of personal and political agency in which the boundaries between subject and object and the complicated negotiations of power are continually shifting. The novel resists traditional formal genre definitions: its exotic setting, foreign locale, aristocratic characters, elaborate linguistic flights of fancy, and sexual lushness are seen as characteristic of the romance. Yet *The History of the Nun* is also notable for its "realistic" characteristics: the aristocratic characters have interiority and complex psychological motivations, and they negotiate with contemporaneous issues, and the text focuses on illegal doings and forbidden passions as defined by law rather than classical conceptions of honor.[8] Rather than occupying a liminal space between genres, the novel reveals the instability of the critical demarcation between romance and novel.

The thematic qualities of the work, as well as its critical reception, expose the inseparability of the personal and the political arenas. Behn creates a story of sexual passion that critiques the political climate of its day, commingling closely rendered erotic palpitations with incisive sociopolitical critique. *The History of*

---

[8]   These divisions are based on Lennard Davis's schema of the differences between the novel and the romance discussed in the first chapter.

the Nun explores the ways in which the lack of political power affects the fabric of personal lives. Her novel suggests that those who are denied the power of self-government and political participation may prove dangerous, as, without lawful recourse, personal violence may offer a more expedient or inviting option than passive acceptance. In this light, Behn's text may be read as a defense, or explanation, of both female aggression and the aggression of subjects displaced from party and monarchical politics in late seventeenth-century England.

The History of the Nun's formal and thematic attenuations dislocate gendered stereotypes. In her figuration of women as essentially or innately good and honest before male instruction in the arts of dissemblance, Behn inverts the notion of Eve's daughters leading men into sin, reversing the binary by positioning male sin as the origin of female sin. However, her portrayal of Isabella steps outside of the terms of the binary rather than simply reversing it to favor women. In Isabella, Behn imagines a woman neither innately good nor innately bad. She illustrates the possibility of a woman who is neither wholly angel nor wholly whore, and her portrayal reveals such categories themselves to be flawed. Isabella is both victim and violator. She is sensual, pious, charming, innocent, dissembling, amusing, tragic, greedy, repellent, and appealing, the faithful adulteress and the innocent murderess, and she presents a paradox that challenges comfortable classifications of gender, morality, and legality.

The Fair Jilt

While *The Fair Jilt* closely resembles *The History of the Nun*, this text presents a more troubling vision of criminal female violence. *The Fair Jilt* initially appears more superficial than *The History of the Nun*; however, it ultimately provides a more profound attack on governing conceptions of both femininity and female criminality. Miranda, the protagonist of *The Fair Jilt*, lacks the implied, if morally questionable, motivation of Isabella. Miranda is simply selfish; her violence is instigated by greed and egocentricity. *The Fair Jilt* is a violent female fantasy of unleashed female desire that refuses to be contained by sexual or textual boundaries. The energy and black humor that appear sporadically throughout *The History of the Nun* inform virtually all of *The Fair Jilt*. Behn luxuriates in the vivacity and authority of her wicked heroine and revels in the imaginative potentiality of unrestrained female will that Miranda embodies. Miranda is a powerful, ferocious, and voracious character that controls her own plot and wreaks havoc on others in the pursuit of her desire.

The novel does not provide the castigation, punishment, or moral instruction we anticipate, even today, in a story of ungoverned female appetite and violence. While Isabella's death garners pity from the townspeople and is less brutal than the burning she legally deserves, she still dies repentant for her murderous sins. In contrast, despite her violent transgressions and their blatantly selfish motivation,

Miranda utterly escapes traditional legal and narrative punishment: she "lives on in as perfect a state of happiness as this troublesome world can afford" (72).

The novel, as critics have noted, reschematizes the traditional gendered power dynamics of sexual desire through the medium of textual fantasy.[9] The novel also explores the gendered power dynamics of female textual authority. In a text that is itself a narrative of excess desire, Behn investigates fictional prerogative—the crafting of illicit plots—through her protagonist's textual inscription of her illicit desire. Like Isabella, Miranda is an intelligent and dazzling young votary, but unlike the more modest Isabella, she has not taken vows of chastity and she revels in male admiration, relishing the striking power her beauty affords her over men: "[T]housands of people were dying by her eyes, while she was vain enough to glory in her conquests, and make it her business to wound" (33). This language of war, orgasm, and power positions Miranda as a violating vamp whose pleasure is largely masturbatory in scope if not kind. Miranda seems to enjoy actual sexual pleasure as well as narcissistically winning hearts; she was "infamous[ly] possessed by a great many men and strangers" (52). Behn seems to delight in her portrayal of Miranda as a traditional Restoration rake, obdurate and inconstant in her affections. The descriptions of Miranda's beauty, its effect, and her single-minded pursuit of pleasure add up to an exaggerated version of the infamous and venal *femme fatale* who wounds "thousands with her charms." The narrator goes on at length to delineate, not only the breadth of Miranda's charm, wit, education, and beauty, but also her lack of romantic commitment; Miranda "knew the strength of her own heart, and that could not suffer itself to be confined to one man and wisely avoided those inquietudes, and that uneasiness of life she was sure to find in that married life which would … oblige her to the embraces of one" (33). Miranda is

---

[9]   Aercke reads the novel in light of her argument that early fiction should be read through the lens of cross-genre experimentation with theater. Behn's life also offers interesting motivations for her creation of a victorious woman who ruins men's lives and does not end up ruined or dead. Salvaggio reads *The Fair Jilt* through the biographical lens of Behn's failed romance with bisexual lawyer and wit John Hoyle. Salvaggio argues that *The Fair Jilt* operates as a fantasy in which Behn enjoys being in the position of Hoyle, and she reads the novel as emblematic of the attempts of the woman writer to retrieve, by figuring an imaginative space for female desire through the medium of fiction, what love has "undone" in her own "Amorous World" (268–69). Hammond argues that in this text, and others, Behn loses control of the point of her narrative. I disagree with Hammond's reading for number of reasons, the most crucial being the assertion upon which it rests: that the novel's argument is one about Tarquin rather than Miranda herself. Hammond states that "the standard didactic purpose of fiction is being overwhelmed altogether by a loving attention to grisly realistic detail. *The Fair Jilt* is trying to tell the story of Prince Tarquin, whose infatuation with Miranda is so total that he is prepared to go to any lengths of criminality to appease her. As the story ends, its attempt to articulate this moral is entirely drowned out by a description of a botched execution so mordantly exact that it becomes a source of interest entirely in and of itself" (110). I posit that this critique misses Behn's precise interest in the "grisly details" and their implications.

the self-aware and determined seducer who employs devious machinations and seductive poses in her attempts to win the complaisance, or the destruction, of virtuous men whom she desires.

Miranda desires a friar, a former prince who abdicated his position and took holy orders after the loss of his true love. Miranda has won the hearts of the populace, but, like early fiction writers, she cannot gain the approval of the critical moral authority. The friar remains silent, making "no return" to her missives and thus nullifying her literary outpouring:

> All her reasonings … he despised. … Yet … she ceased not to pursue him with her letters, varying her style, sometimes all wanton, loose and raving; sometimes feigning a virgin-modesty all over, accusing herself, blaming her conduct, and sighing her destiny … . But still she writes in vain, in vain she varies her style, by a cunning, peculiar to a maid possessed with such a sort of passion. (43)

Miranda writes because she is "possessed" by the passion of love, a possession that mirrors the female author's "peculiar" passion for writing. Her love letters mirror the fiction writer's texts as they attempt to win their reader through a series of disguises, the "cunning" capacity to produce controlled representations of uncontrollable feelings. Miranda's letters fluctuate between vice and virtue and mirror the novelist's narrative shifts between wanton description and moral prescription in her attempt successfully to tell a story of iniquitous desire while representing herself as conscientiously virtuous. Both character and author feign veracity for their texts: Miranda falsely claims sexual innocence and modesty; Behn falsely claims to be innocently recounting fact rather than knowledgeably producing fiction. Behn shapes Miranda's textual false front as initially unsuccessful, suggesting the impossibility of success through narrative authority, yet she ultimately imagines Miranda's writing as far more powerful as an instrument of potent revenge and destruction than her seductive physical body.

When Miranda's chameleonlike masquerade of letters fails, rather than folding in despairing acceptance of his "cold neglect," Miranda replaces the body of text she has sent to the friar with her own body. She declares her love and attempts to seduce him, "snatch[ing] him in her arms" and giving him "a thousand kisses" from which "he could not defend himself" (46). Despite his vows and protestations, Henrick finds himself diverted by Miranda's amazing beauty, and the irony of the fact that this full-grown man could not escape from a full thousand kisses was, I am sure, not lost on Behn or her contemporary readers. When the friar castigates her for her "wanton blood which has so shamefully betrayed [her]," Miranda becomes enraged, informs him she will ruin him if he denies her and, in the face of his rejection, cries out, "Help, help! A rape!" (47). The friar is imprisoned and condemned to death by burning. He receives a reprieve from his death sentence, but for the rest of the novel he languishes "in prison, in a dark and dismal dungeon," while "Miranda, cured of her love, was triumphing in revenge, expecting and daily giving new conquests" (50).

While Miranda's letters are produced in court as evidence of the friar's innocence, they are superseded by the counterfeit text she composes of her own beleaguered innocence. Miranda successfully changes the plot, casting herself as virtuous victim and ensuring her own victory. Her heydays of seduction continue as she falls in love with the handsome and wealthy Prince Tarquin, "a Prince of a mighty name, and famed for all the excellencies of his sex" (50). He marries Miranda in spite of her loose reputation, and they live in splendor until the arrival of Miranda's younger sister, Alcidiana, whom Miranda torments, keeping Alcidiana from marrying the man she loves in order to retain control of her share of the sisters' fortune. Alcidiana refutes "the tyranny of her sister" (54), runs away, regains her lost love, and Miranda must come up with her sister's portion of the estate, a portion she has squandered. Realizing she will be unable to continue to live in the manner to which she has been accustomed if she loses her sister's money, Miranda decides to have Alcidiana murdered before the wedding.

Miranda's power struggles continue in her battle with her sister, and in this case her desire for the ruin of another is based entirely on money-hungry greed, rather than the sexual desire or revenge for hypocrisy that fueled her deceptions with the friar. As in *The History of the Nun*, readers are placed in the uncomfortable position of identifying with, or at least focusing on, a protagonist whose actions are simultaneously morally reprehensible and strangely exultant. The novel does not frame Miranda through comments of moral censure, but, like *Roxana* some three decades hence, paints a picture of a selfish antiheroine whose energy is that which fuels the text. Alcidiana offers a competing site of identification; however, as the passive ingénue and murder target, her character offers the female reader only the all too familiar option of identifying with the pathetic female victim.

Ruth Salvaggio argues that Behn fractures the female subject into villainess or victim, and that this binary splitting reveals Behn's inability to conceive of a successful female subject position. In fact, the disturbingly nonexemplary status of her murderous protagonists enriches her texts' inquiries into the politics of gender, as the texts refuse to allow readers simply to celebrate feminine goodness and denigrate masculine baseness. It is tempting and often satisfying to read female-authored texts in terms of the ways in which they present positive alternatives to the numerous delimiting portrayals of female characters. Yet, rather than read simply to find anachronistic exemplary female models, we should read Behn's fictions for the ways in which they probe the possibilities of textualized female subjectivity, and we should attend not just to the plot she creates but to the ways in which she relates that plot. Salvaggio's distress at the malicious protagonist Behn creates neglects the playful and ironic means by which she constructs her. Miranda's actions are despicable; Behn's hyperbolic description of these actions calls attention to their fictionality and to the ways in which the text is not a meditation on appropriate or inappropriate female behavior per se but may be read as a sly celebration of authorial control.

Miranda's attempts to murder her sister result in comical failure, and, as in *The History of the Nun*, the narrator never engages with the moral or physical consequences of Miranda's reprehensible acts. As the plot becomes more and more ludicrously improbable, we remain distanced from what could be a deeply disturbing narrative. Miranda's first murder attempt involves her use of sexual promises to convince her handsome page to administer poison; when Alcidiana lives, he is discovered and hung for his bungled attempt. The dying page is described as a sight that "moved all the beholders with … pity," but his death is very quickly passed over, and his death-bed pleas for Miranda's forgiveness (for his confession's implication of her) ironically point to the foolishness of male lust and undercut the moment's pathos.

Miranda is charged as an accomplice and forced to stand on public display under the gibbet with the nature of her crimes inscribed on paper displayed on her back and breast. Miranda loses control of her plot, and her body becomes the public bearer and readable text of her misdeeds. Yet rather than retreat, Miranda wrests authorial control. She spins a lengthy and ludicrous tale to her husband of how Alcidiana is "the author of her shame," as Miranda never would have been publicly humiliated, nor would her husband face debtor's prison, if Alcidiana had simply not existed. Miranda brazenly refigures her sister as the "author" of her wicked narrative and inscribes herself as concerned wife and ignorant sufferer. The stupendous illogic of her dissembling rationale renders her husband's acceptance of it shockingly stupid. Just as the page desires the beautiful lady Miranda's favor even as he is to be killed on her behalf, so is the prince a likable buffoon who assumes her lovely face and piteous demeanor are transparent signs of feminine goodness and agrees to do her murdering for her, consenting to arrange the death of her sister.

Miranda may easily be read as a stereotypical embodiment of the female rake, the wanton hussy who deludes good-natured men with her sexual wiles, and thus the novel may be read as thematically reifying binary conceptions of femininity: evil criminal she-devil or passive angel. Yet, Miranda's self-assurance and her glib and outrageous behavior are so unrealistic that she exists as a cartoon version of outlaw femininity, a character that invites grudging admiration for her very extremity, as the text continually allows her to succeed when she should fail and refuses to explore the serious repercussions of her behavior.

The hysterically excessive quality of the narrative is at a high pitch from Prince Tarquin's murder attempt on Alcidiana to the end of the novel. When his attempt fails, Tarquin is arrested and sentenced to death. The account of his failed murder attempt and resultant escape efforts is followed by the highly unlikely information that everyone "had but a real sorrow and compassion for him" after his arrest, since he exhibited such "valour and bravery" in his attempts to fight off his arrestors (64). That the prince's new status of public hero has been achieved through his violent efforts to escape being arrested for his attempted murder of a defenseless young girl is patently improbable. The populace adores him and begs him to renounce Miranda, whom they hold responsible. Here, Behn interestingly reverses traditional notions of legal responsibility by rendering the husband the witless tool of the dominating wife. Tarquin is seen as unable to bear responsibility for his own actions while Miranda is assumed to be fully in control and thus culpable. Behn's plot mocks the legal configuration that woman has no identity or capacity for action without her husband's overseeing dictate and also calls into question the idea that any person, male or female, should not be accountable for his or her actions.

Behn's sarcastic portrayal of illogical mob reaction and the exculpation of actions that imply the abdication of individual responsibility resonate with issues of political accountability raised after the Whig ascendancy and Restoration. The final pages of the text narrate an improbable restoration of order: experiencing real grief at the forthcoming death of her husband, Miranda "at last confessed all her life," including the truth about the friar, who just happens to be held in the same prison and is joyfully released. The prince amazingly survives a botched execution attempt and is carried away to freedom by a rejoicing crowd. He pretends to abandon Miranda to avoid public censure, but secretly still loves her. In spite of being doubly targeted for homicide, Alcidiana is mortified at having been the "prosecutor of the great man," and works to gain the couple royal pardons, after which Miranda secretly joins her husband and his wealthy father in Holland, where she is received by Tarquin with "a joy unspeakable" and they live happily ever after in good fortune (71–72).

The feverish propulsion of the narrative toward marital bliss and familial accord is unconvincing, amusing in its brazen improbability, and noteworthy in its refusal of a conventional moral ending. The second-to-last sentence of the text claims Miranda's repentance and her happiness:

> They say Miranda has been very penitent for her life past, and gives Heaven the glory for having given her these afflictions, that have reclaimed her, and brought her to as perfect a state of happiness as this troublesome world can afford. (72)

Miranda's penitence is a story "they say," one that may or may not be true and that resembles in structure the dying repentances of the criminal at the gallows, a protestation of guilt represented to readers and circulated like a rumor. Ironically, instead of dutifully repenting before lawful execution for her crimes, fearfully praying to heaven for a dying reprieve, and thereby shoring up both law and punishment, Miranda repents for being reprieved from expiating punishment. "Thanks to Heaven" may indeed be due and heartfelt, coming from the criminal who thanks God for not being caught. In this passage, Miranda resembles the novelist who cites history as author and obscures her own role as plotter: she neatly rescripts to providence the blame for her afflictions, afflictions decidedly of her own design.

Miranda's being "reclaimed," or given a new chance, has nothing at all to do with either afflictions or remorse: Tarquin's love for her is never in question, and her happiness is achieved by the bad aim of the executioner and her husband's inheritance upon the death of his father. The novel unequivocally calls Miranda's presumed spiritual makeover into question in the final line of the novel, in which the narrator dryly states: "Since I began this relation, I heard that Prince Tarquin died about three quarters of a year ago" (72). With this brief line, Behn explodes any narrative closure the text might have offered. The sentence further subverts the already subversive narrative closure of happy marriage by reinserting the threat of violent female appetite into *The Fair Jilt*. We are left not knowing whether Miranda killed Tarquin, making herself a widow and thus gaining full control of her husband's huge estate. Did Miranda's early and "wise" inability to conceive of monogamy bear true? Was her foolish husband taken in and taken to his death? Or did Miranda truly experience happiness with him and mourn his natural passing? Behn refuses to relinquish Miranda to us for total judgment; we are left in the dark as to her character. Behn moves Miranda outside of the plot, ultimately refusing to deliver her to the reading audience for sentencing. In *The Fair Jilt* Behn pushes her narrative beyond the plot limits of marriage or death. She undermines the surface morality of her text by infusing the narrative with irony and black humor and mocks the extremities of dichotomous female possibility. Behn's murderous protagonist finishes neither repentant nor dead; instead, Miranda is left victorious, alive, and wealthy, perhaps a saddened widow, perhaps a murderous one.

The History of the Nun demonstrates the negative effects of women's economic and social exclusion from successful recourse in the face of adversity. In rendering Isabella's actions understandable and motivated, *The History of the Nun* may attack the strictures of sexist formulations of female violence more effectually than *The Fair Jilt*. Yet the latter's denial of narrative closure, its refutation of any established understanding of its main character's motive, or even any clear grasp of her actions, destabilizes more than notions of femininity. By refusing to provide an authorial verdict on how we should read the criminal subject of its narrative, *The Fair Jilt* complicates the idea of definable, categorical subjectivity and calls attention to the active roles of writers and readers in the creation of narratival meaning. This early novel refuses a didactic closed-loop moral, refutes notions of authoritative textual truth, and revels in the unstable "cunning" and "passion" of "letters" themselves (*Fair Jilt* 41).

The Wife's Resentment

Like *The History of the Nun*, Delarivier Manley's novel *The Wife's Resentment* (1720) opens by describing its heroine, the aptly named Violenta, as a feminine exemplar, traces the ruinous consequences of her embodiment of this role, and ends with her violent attack on the position of feminine passivity. Violenta's forays into crime, like Isabella's, are contextualized within a deleterious social system, not an overdeveloped nervous system, and the novel portrays female violence as motivated and specific.[10] Like Behn's fictions, Manley's novel counters dominant

---

[10]   The novella is a retelling of the story of Didaco and Violenta in William Painter's *The Palace of Pleasure* (1566). Its origin is a tale by Matteo Bandello (c 1480–1562).

narratives that locate female violence in relation to the female body. However, while Behn's novels destabilize the very category of femininity itself, *The Wife's Resentment* remains vested in the notion of feminine virtue that is defined by virginity and chastity.

Some thirty years after Behn published *The Fair Jilt*, Delarivier Manley explicitly established her literary identification with her predecessor when she reincarnated Behn's fictional and poetic persona, Astrea, in her first major scandal novel, *The New Atlantis* (1709). Manley, like Behn, was a professional woman writer whose work was extremely popular and critically condemned. She followed Behn's tradition of using fiction to critique sexual and party politics and wrote in numerous genres, including pro-Tory political journalism.[11] In *The Wife's Resentment*, Manley subtly reworks contemporary ideological debates and politically charged meanings, investigating the terms of honor as Behn investigated the terms of vows.[12]

In a textual fantasy that attacks the figure of the beleaguered and passive heroine with a vengeance, Manley refigures violent female action as heroic rather than horrific. *The Wife's Resentment* demonstrates that female honor (or reputation) defines female subjectivity and argues that, as such, female honor may require violent defense by the dishonored subject. Manley contends that just as a man is deemed heroic in his expected physical defense and reclamation of his honor through physical conflict (dual or battle), so should a woman be lauded for justified defense of hers. In fact, for a woman the stakes are higher than for a man since, as Manley points out in *The New Atlantis*: "Men may regain their Reputations, tho' after a Complication of Vices ... but a Woman once departed from the Road of Virtue is made incapable of a return ... the World suffers her to perish loath'd and unlamented" (83–84).

The story's premise anticipates—down to the closet scene—that of Richardson's *Pamela*. Violenta is a poor, chaste beauty pursued by the rakish Count Rodrigo, who is finally worn down by her virtuous resistance and marries her. The count of Valencia is a classic seducer, a man whose "business was pure gallantry," who "knew not how to love," simply enjoying the conquest and ruin of beautiful women and being "wholly unacquainted with [the virtue of] remorse." Violenta recalls the idyllic early Isabella: while very poor, she is uncommonly beautiful, "had more wit than all the women of Valencia," and "no virgin in Valencia had so fair and honest a report" (144, 146). The count espies Violenta from the street and becomes enamored of her; she too is engaged with interest, although she remains vehement in the protection of her virtue.

---

[11] For discussions of Manley's scandal fictions, political pamphleteering, and other fiction, see Todd's, Ballaster's (*Seductive*), and Spencer's chapters on Manley.

[12] Manley's decision to rework this tale with its fascination with the concepts of honor and justice may reflect her political involvement with the Tory party, including her being sued by Whigs for libel, and her distaste for what she perceived as the Whig's focus on money and commercialism at the expense of rational aristocratic virtues.

Manley's descriptions of the perfidious nature of men and the consequent dangers for ill-informed and unprepared women recall Behn's prefatory remarks in *The History of the Nun*. But while Behn complicates the traditional trajectory of the seduction tale by firmly locating desire and the acquiescence to it in her female protagonists, Manley does not. Violenta—at this stage in the novel—abides perfectly by conduct book strictures; she represses her desire for Rodrigo and insists upon marriage, responding to his yearlong campaign of letters and gifts with letters attesting to her passionate regard for her honor and virtue.

Manley inserts Violenta's letters into the narrative in a move that interrupts the omnisciently narrated plot with the utterances of the female protagonist. As plot devices, Violenta's letters are relatively superfluous; their content could be presented in standard narrative recitations of Violenta's virtue. As insertions into the text, however, the letters allow Violenta to articulate the terms of her own honor. Unlike Miranda's letters of illicit desire and their evocation of the dangers and joys of female-authored fiction, Violenta's letters stand as didactic moral treatises, evidence of female modesty and strength of character. These female-authored texts narrate the value of traditional embodied female virtue and put the reader in the place of Rodrigo, the seducer, who must, like Samuel Richardson's Mr. B—, be reformed by moral nonaristocratic female textual power.

In a move that becomes both famous and standard with Richardson's *Pamela*, Manley locates honor in the impoverished virgin maid. Her claim of "plain" speaking in response to his "eloquence" points to the class difference between them and defines her motivation as unvarnished and pure in contrast to his embellished prostrations. Her letters balance appreciation of his attentions with defenses of her chastity; she reiterates the conventional equation of female chastity with honor and figures female sexual virtue as a life or death phenomenon. She designates herself as "a maid … who knows the true estimation of virtue, and who would die in defense of it" and responds to his seductive pleas by stating: "You very eloquently tell me you shall die if I continue unkind; but I very plainly tell your Lordship, that I must perish if I prove otherwise; since I know it will be impossible for me to live after the loss of my honor" (146). While she is "not insensible" to the effects of love, she "would see the whole world in a conflagration, and myself in the middle of it, before I could be brought to do anything contrary to the rules of modesty" (147). Violenta's articulations of female modesty and its value as sum total of female worth do not stray from time-honored gendered formulations.

Where Manley skews the plot is in the novel's imagining of the consequences of such ideological conceptions. Like *Pamela*, *The Wife's Resentment* critiques masculine aristocratic excess and locates reform in the virtuous lower-class woman. After a year and a half of failed seduction attempts, the frustrated Rodrigo realizes that "though she was neither of such birth or fortune as his quality deserved, yet her virtue and accomplishments, her beauty and discretion, deserved greater advancement. … He owned that … 'twas hard, a life so faultless should be attended upon with infamy and ruin" and was pleased therefore to be the one who could "reward her chastity, raise her abject fortune, and draw forth of obscurity a bright example, which virgins of the age might imitate" (150). And so he marries her, unlike the reader dismissing as meaningless his dream of her stabbing him to death for his inconstancy.

The dream is, of course, telling; like the battle imagery that fills their earlier courtship discourse, it foreshadows the violence to come. It is after the marriage that Manley's and Richardson's texts diverge, and Manley's bleak vision of eighteenth-century hypergamy is by far the more realistic. Rodrigo has asked Violenta to keep their marriage a secret because of the difference in their stations, until he can "take care to inform his friends and relations gradually" (153). After a year of secret wedded bliss, disrupted only by the fact that her neighbors believe Violenta to be a whore, Rodrigo tires of her. He blames his fickleness on her low station, bemoans that he has married down—"matching himself with the lees of the people,"—and grows to despise his wife, whom he visits only "to gratify the call of nature" (155, 156). Rodrigo convinces himself that, by virtue of her social class, Violenta is fit only for a mistress, and he marries again—this time an heiress. He believes that since Violenta has no social standing or money she poses him no threat.

The Wife's Resentment demonstrates the dangers of a social system in which women's survival relies on men's virtuous caretaking, a caretaking that is presumed but not legislated (this argument continues Behn's similar complaints and predates Defoe's famous portrayal of these dangers in *Roxana*, published four years later). Violenta has not impugned her virtue and is guilty only of proper feminine acquiescence when she accepts his desire for a secret marriage. The novel reveals such acceptance as naive when he is revealed as base bigamist. Manley takes a jab at the traffic in women when Violenta is let down by not only her lawful husband and master but also, like Roxana, her brothers as well. After his second, bigamous marriage becomes public, Rodrigo successfully pays off Violenta's brothers so that they will not avenge her ruin. The narrator explains dryly that the brothers lacked that "honorable resentment which is always found in the well-born" (156).[13] The irony of the quote is, of course, thick given the count's immoral and illegal behavior, and, in the last section of the text, Manley castigates hierarchical and sex-based machinations of law and conceptions of honor in tumultuous detail.

The novel suggests that female violence may arise out of a social system that refuses women recourse when presumed male protection fails them. When she hears of her ruin, Violenta does not die of shame or retreat to a convent, but emerges a spectacular avenger on her own behalf:

---

[13] Manley's description of Violenta as utterly innocent in her bigamous marriage may have been an attempt to imply her own innocence in her bigamous marriage to her cousin, Whig lawyer and politician, John Manley, an affair in which it seems Manley was complicit. She became pregnant, without friends or money and with her husband still married to his previous wife. Todd comments that "[t]he usual narrative ending is withdrawal and death for distressed innocence, and suicide for betrayed passion, but of course Delarivier Manley does not kill her self or pine and die. Instead she becomes a writer and uses her infamy to her advantage" (96).

> Her Sense of Honor lost, of her virtue demolished, her chastity overthrown, her ruined reputation swelled her to an extremity of Resentment ... she travers'd her apartment like a raging Bacchanal; like Medea, furious in her revenge; like the fiends with fatal torches in their hands, to set the world on fire: she was more than all of these, she was herself, that is to say, most miserable and most outrageous. (159)

Violenta's lost reputation transfigures her into an embodiment of resentment. As in *The History of the Nun*, the heroine becomes aligned with mythic figures of female power in response to the implications of her loss of female dominion and as a precursor to her acts of murderous violence. Violenta's body seems to grow larger in this passage; she becomes pregnant and powerful with rage and righteous fury as she is linked to a chain of female avengers. Yet Violenta is *not* a fiend or reincarnation of Medea but is "herself"—like them only in her explicitly female outrage and fury—and *more* than them because of her "reality" as a violated subject. The sharp contrast between the modest and the murderous Violenta echoes Behn's construction of Isabella. Like Behn, Manley attacks the hyperbolic qualities of stereotypical figurations of femininity and calls attention to the futility of a system in which female identity is defined solely by mythologized bodily status.

Violenta's very identity, like Isabella's, is symbolically erased by her unwitting loss of both virginal innocence and wifely dominion. While she has not lost her actual honor (she remains chaste in marriage), her reputation in her community has been shattered. Even this perceived loss of sexual honor destroys her ability to function as a speaking subject. Her loss of reputation results in a temporary loss of voice: she could not speak, "even the relief of words were denied her; she could only beat her breast [and] groan" (157). She who was once in command of her voice and her narrative becomes all body with no capacity to narrate her plight. Manley reveals the ways in which Violenta, and by extension any woman, is defined and erased by her attenuated relationship to her sexual status within a civic and social arena in which she has no power *except* as pure body.

Unlike Behn's sly and comic demonstration of women's violent responses to their limited options, Manley approaches this dilemma with an initial high seriousness informed by Enlightenment notions of logic and individual sovereignty. After portraying Violenta's descent into embodied and nonverbal female rage, the novel repositions this rage as familiar rather than fabulous and as reasonable rather than hysterical. When she regains the power of thought and speech, Violenta's desire for violent revenge does not lift, as might be expected, but deepens as it is now supported not only by archetypal female power but by the twin pillars of Christianity and reason traditionally evoked in opposition to any female act of violence.

Violenta's potent anger is furthered, rather than tempered, by her employment of secular and religious logic. She argues eloquently that both reason and God support her desire for violent vengeance, declaring:

Those are light and small offences that we can be reasoned out of the sense of;
what Rodrigo has committed against me, reason itself supports me in my desire
of vengeance! ... God caused me to be born his instrument of wrath to punish
the injury done to my honor .... That base seducer who used to say ... maids of
my base birth had no pretensions to honor, what had we to do with such fantastic
notions? As if courage were only appropriated to men of quality, or modesty to
noble women! (161)

Violenta's violent revenge is sanctioned and directed by empirical logic and God.
She denounces a system of justice and morality in which high feelings are only
ascribed to those of high birth and in which *droit de seigneur* conceptions of
the worth of chastity preclude individual claims to moral authority. As well as
critiquing class-based notions of honor, Manley collapses the gendered equations
of masculinity/courage and femininity/modesty in the character of Violenta, who
embodies both courage and modesty in the avenging of her lost reputation. The
novella condemns the flawed standard that defines female honor as chastity but
denies women active recompense for its loss and insists that it is as heroic for
a woman violently to avenge her lost honor as it is for a man, from whom such
violent reprisals are not only accepted but expected and celebrated.

The text implies that men actually have less reason than women to turn to
violence to defend attacks to their honor as they have at least the possibility
of avoiding bloodshed through legal recompense. Violenta, in contrast, has no
powers of legal redress, for as she astutely comments, "[J]ustice waits upon the
great, Interest holds the scale, and Riches turn the balance" (161). Justice does
not, implies Manley, stoop to cover poor, chaste women. Appropriate behavior for
a female character who has lost virginity, love, and reputation, is, of course, self-
immolation; she should suffer and slowly die from shame (as Richardon's Clarissa
will soon do so poignantly), thus becoming a tragic victim whose death can ruin
Rodrigo's life when he realizes the extent of his sins. Or she should enter religious
orders where she would live a pious life, never remarrying, dedicating her no longer
virginal self to God, and serving as a moral exemplar of self-sacrifice. Manley,
however, like Behn before her, writes her heroine out of these proscriptive plots
and instead inscribes Violenta according to a plot of heroic action.

While Violenta is still innocent and chaste, Rodrigo's unfair actions have
resulted in her community's fatal misreading of the text of her body. But Violenta
takes none of the traditional or appropriate options open to a publicly ruined
moral woman. Instead, she separates the social and emotional consequences of
her loss of virtue and directs her rage where it is appropriate, at Rodrigo. Rather
than sliding into depression, she hurtles into aggression. In a letter that recalls
those of Miranda to the friar, she professes her love, understanding, and desire to
Rodrigo as a trap to lure him to his death. This letter, which does not appear in
the text, contrasts the earlier didactic epistolary articulations of her virtue; instead,
her letter is a declaration of battle that only the writer and reader can accurately

decode. Violenta abandons the publicly sanctioned female-authored didactic text and replaces it with a scandalous fiction that better serves her.[14]

Deeming her "a creature of no consequence whom he might use as he pleased," Rodrigo falls for Violenta's claim that she still desires him and accepts her invitation to bed, whereupon she avenges her honor according to classical heroic codes: she kills him. Manley's lush textual erotics and verbal pyrotechnics come into play not in the actual seduction scene, which is referred to only in a metaphoric clause, but in the scenes of Violenta's rage and the long passage devoted to the homicide. Violenta stabs Rodrigo with "undaunted resolution and heroic spirit," "gouges out his eyes," "tears his heart from its seat," cuts off *all* of his limbs, and throws his body out of the window, declaring that his "carcass be exposed as publicly as was my reputation" (165). Rather than punishing her own body for her loss of virtue, Violenta revenges her publicly destroyed reputation with his publicly destroyed flesh in an extravagant supplantation of power in which Rodrigo's phallic violation is avenged by Violenta's protophallic stabbing of him with his own dagger. She violently replicates her loss of virginity in her breaking open and into his flesh. Her "infinite gashes" symbolically reenact his hymeneal rendering, with the blood of maidenhood being replaced with that of violent death (167).

Her body seems to have extended its limits and overtaken his. Violenta is once more beyond language, but in this case she is enlivened by the violent actions of revenge, actions the text explicitly portrays as heroic rather than demonic. Manley employs familiar tropes of female monstrosity in this hyperviolent moment, but she does not reduce her protagonist merely to grotesque body. Violenta's comparison to Medea reminds us that the source of Medea's violence lies in Jason's betrayal. And Manley emphasizes Violenta's rational and honorable motives by stressing her resolution and "heroic spirit." In Violenta, Manley figures the origins of female violence as twofold: situated in idealized heroic values traditionally associated with masculinity and in archetypal feminine rage, understood through the lenses of reason and honor rather than through hysteria and pathos.

Violenta, like Isabella, faces the consequences of her unlawful action with dignity. After killing him, "as if conscious of well doing," Violenta immediately and "nobly" requests to be executed to expatiate her sin (169). She tells her story to the justices, "without either rage or passion," and, moved by her modesty and its betrayal, they publicly denounce Rodrigo. The story ends not with the required instructional self-loathing of the criminal biography, but with a clear condemnation of the system that allowed Violenta to be abused. The narrator makes the brief and biting statement that, "[N]otwithstanding the pity of the people, the intercession of the ladies, and the applause her chastity and magnanimity deserved, Violenta was condemned to be beheaded" (170). Again, the murderess is executed by beheading when not simply hanging but burning at the stake would have been the appropriate

---

[14]   That the letter itself does not appear in the novel seems tantalizingly important, and while I am unsure what it finally suggests, its absence hints at the parallel between Violenta's final fictional output and the text of *The Wife's Resentment* itself.

legal punishment. The author's refusal to levy the punishment of petty treason critiques the law that unequivocally defines women as subjects to their husbands, and the failed "intercession of ladies" points to a female recognition and support of Violenta's status as violated wife. Manley represents Violenta, not as the vicious she-devil or weak strumpet of criminal biography, but as a heroine who dies in defense of a cause, that of her own sovereignty. Violenta died "with the same spirit and resolution with which she had defended her chastity" (170). She does not kill because of greed, sexual perversion, or insanity, but in defense of her integrity, a fact the community recognizes and lauds.

The Wife's Resentment denounces a system of male privilege that venerates female passivity and self-abasement. On the one hand, Violenta is a less complicated protagonist than either Isabella or Miranda; she is clearly wronged, and her violence is motivated by socially sanctioned feminine ideals. The novel positions Violenta's act of criminal violence within a schema of socially understandable behavior and refutes the idea of female violence as intrinsically monstrous. However, Manley's text ultimately remains within the dichotomy of gender binaries themselves. Violenta presents a vision of female subjectivity that remains bound by conventional ideology of sexualized virtue and sacrifice. If we read the novel as reversing the site of the privilege of honor and agency from male to female, it inverts tradition, but like the carnivalesque, does not fundamentally dismantle it. The text does not posit that sexual virtue is an inadequate and inaccurate definer of female selfhood.[15] Rather, it critiques classist assumptions that deny some women their rights to such virtue and it condemns sexist laws and customs that limit a woman's capacity to defend her virtue and avenge attacks upon it.

This reading, however, does not adequately account for the text's forays into outrageous excess—most notably the extraordinarily bloodthirsty quality of Violenta's revenge—and the contrast between this excess and the text's rational arguments. This tension exists at the level of form as well as plot. The novel is largely narrated in a didactic and informative, if ornate voice, one that informs us of Violenta's virtue and Rodrigo's deceit, or recounts passionate but logical social diatribes. However, the prose becomes almost hysterical in the scenes of Violenta's initial rage and the homicide itself; like Violenta, the language can barely be contained. These passages consist of volcanic outpourings more commonly associated with the articulation of impassioned seduction than homicide.

At the level of plot, Violenta's logical defense of her crime, her "heroic resolution" while committing it, and her peaceful sense of "well-doing" afterward do not correspond with the violence of the murder itself. In a simple gendered reversal of the defense of honor, Violenta would kill Rodrigo, but her method of killing does not recall a knight's honorable dual or the acts of a noble soldier during war. Gouging out a victim's eyes, dismembering him, and proudly displaying his mutilated corpse is not behavior associated with aristocratic heroes. But the text

---

[15]   And, like Behn's eponymous Oroonoko, Violenta is an exception to her class and gender rather than the rule.

positions Violenta not as a monster, but as a martyred heroine. The text's capacity to position Violenta as heroine relies on her status both as a victim and as a fictional character. The psychological satisfaction the reader gains from the novel is tied to the very real social and legal conditions that the novel condemns. Nevertheless, the reader would presumably not condone in a criminal biography the violence that she is able to relish in the novel, no matter how justified this violence might be. *The Wife's Resentment* is the stuff of fantastic revenge; its violence spills outside of any social codes. As such, Violenta's appeal relies on the reader's continual awareness that the novel is fiction, that it is preposterous, like a nightmare from which she can awake.

It is this combination of contemporary social critique and absurd excess that makes Manley's novel so fascinating. Through its absurdity, *The Wife's Resentment* demonstrates the preposterous effects of the paradoxical sexist ideologies it critiques. It reveals the inevitability and fetishizing of violent revenge when there is no legal recourse available for the ill used. Justice may eventually denounce the wrongs of the abused; however, only after the disenfranchised victim has spectacularly taken justice into her own hands. Manley's text moves between approbation of its wronged heroine, gleefully unmitigated fantasies of her ferocious revenge, and acknowledgment of the hollowness of her victory in a society in which the verdict of the law remains too little, too late.

Chapter 3
"Interesting Memoirs of the Most Notorious Characters": Four Eighteenth-Century Murderesses

Wife and Servant are the same,
But only differ in the Name:
For When that fatal knot is ty'd,
Which nothing, nothing can divide:
When she the word obey has said,
And Man by Law supreme has made,
Then all that's kind is laid aside,
And nothing left but State and Pride.
—Lady Mary Chudleigh,
"To the Ladies." *Poems on Several Occasions* (1703)

This chapter moves from fictional representations of the murderess to nonfiction accounts of four women convicted of homicide: Catherine Hayes, Mary Blandy, Sarah Malcolm, and Elizabeth Brownrigg. In 1726, Catherine Hayes, wife of a tradesman, was burned at the stake for decapitating her husband. In 1752, Mary Blandy, a genteel spinster, was hung for poisoning her father. In 1733, Sarah Malcolm, an impoverished Catholic charwoman, was convicted for killing three women during a robbery. In 1767, Elizabeth Brownrigg, a respected midwife and mother, was convicted of torturing and executing her female apprentice. The circumstances of each of these cases differ dramatically. I chose them for three reasons: (1) each case generated an exceptional level of public attention and press; (2) read together, they offer a useful overview of the complex and often contradictory characterizations of eighteenth-century murderesses and of the broader ideas about femininity that underlie these characterizations; (3) these cases demonstrate the tensions and complexities of eighteenth-century ideas of the domestic: the domestic family, the domestic servant, and the domestic space. Specifically, read in conjunction, the cases of Hayes and Blandy reveal the ways in which notions of female guilt and agency are enmeshed in ideas of women's position related to men in the domestic family; those of Malcolm and Brownrigg shed light on the tensions and intersections between women's roles in the family and in domestic service. This chapter looks at the intersections and gaps between the roles of "wife" and "servant" that Lady Mary Chudleigh describes in the epigraph that frames the chapter, and it explores what happened in four cases when the laws of state and the customs of servitude were broken, when the "fatal knot" tropes not only kinship, but also the hanging tree.

Nonfiction accounts of the crimes, personal histories, and executions of criminals proliferated in England from the Restoration through the eighteenth century. From the late seventeenth century on, the various ordinaries produced:

> an *Account* following each hanging day and there might be as many as eight of those in a year. It has been claimed that the *Accounts* "enjoyed one of the widest markets that printed prose narratives could obtain in the eighteenth century." In them were reported the behavior, biographies and confessions of all those from Newgate who had been hanged. (Rawlings 114)

As Lincoln Faller notes, criminal biographies "tracked the careers of individual criminals from birth to death" and tended to fall into two categories: those designed more to entertain and titillate and those structured as morally serious and instructional (*Turned* x). Because of the seriousness of the crime, accounts of murderers virtually always fell into the first category. On the one hand, the accounts reveal the means by which the ordinary struggled for the criminal's soul, hopefully bringing the criminal to a state of repentance.[1] However, as Rawlings points out:

> It is important to recognize that the *Accounts* were formed by the intersection between the religious and the secular. The biography was shaped by the fact of the capital conviction, by the views, including the religious views, of the Ordinary and any other writers or editors who may have been involved, by the cultural tradition within which such crime literature fitted, and, because this was first and foremost a commercial venture, by an estimation of what would make the Accounts sell. (116)

And sell they did. In 1750, Horace Walpole complained to a friend of "the ridiculous rage" of buying biographies of criminals (Lewis 199).[2] Not including newspaper articles, between two and three thousand biographies have survived from the eighteenth century, figures that hint at the wide proliferation of such texts (Rawlings 2).

The biographies did not attempt what we would consider historical objectivity, but followed what we now recognize as fictional conventions. They present

---

[1]   Eventually, biographies were written by persons other than the ordinary. For example, a relative of the victim or of the convicted criminal might write one. In some cases, most notably that of Mary Blandy, the criminal herself may write her own story. The "requirement" seems only to have been the ability of the writer to claim some close relation to the criminal. That the ordinary was the last person to whom the criminal spoke, and that he took his confession, or "dying words," tended to give him a perceived access to the truth of the crime.

[2]   For discussion on prices and readership, see Faller, *Turned* 47ff.

"novel" experiences in what we consider "novelistic" terms: the writers created dialogue, invented scenarios, and ascribed motivation in order to "plot" criminals' lives. The veracity and objectivity of criminal biographies was an issue even at the time of their writing; eighteenth-century readers (the most famous being Defoe, who wrote criminal biographies himself) argued that many biographers showed little regard for the facts of the criminal's life and were motivated by mercenary or didactic principles.[3] As Faller demonstrates, the eighteenth-century literature of crime served complex social functions "showing the full range of attitudes their society encouraged—or found it expedient to allow—toward criminals, crimes, and their fates on the gallows" (*Turned* 4).

Whether biographies, ballads, or trial reports, narratives of female homicide demonstrate the ways in which what was on trial in eighteenth-century cases of female homicide was not simply the individual woman, but her symbolic relation to, among other things, attitudes about women's roles and natures. These narratives dramatize a reductive and schizophrenic vision of female nature and yet simultaneously they contain the means by which to critique this vision by offering narrative sites in which women are presented as active and effective, if atrocious, subjects. To explore this tension is not to celebrate the violent woman as a sort of antiheroine who was self-determined or a rebel—none of the women I discuss serves as a remotely positive icon; rather, these cases provide a way to see and to think about the ways in which eighteenth-century representations of the murderess emerge from paradoxical notions of gender and deep anxieties regarding the roles of women in a shifting social, political, and national landscape. Each case provides us a window, not into the actual woman who killed and was consequently killed by the state, but into the ways in which her representations attempt to appease certain fears and to feed others in service of complex social needs.

Catherine Hayes and Mary Blandy

Popular narratives of the cases of Catherine Hayes and Mary Blandy offer strikingly different visions of the murderess: Hayes is presented as a monstrous and sexually voracious harridan; Blandy, with some variations, is presented as a flighty, romantic, and dangerous fool. Reading these two cases together reveals the competitive narratives of feminine possibility at play in eighteenth-century England and points to the ways in which female crime was presented according to a master plot of feminine deficiency. The cases also shed light on heavily defended notions of female submission within the family romance.

In March of 1726, an unidentified head was found floating in the Thames. It was displayed on a pole until its smell caused it to be put in a bottle of spirits. After a few days, the resemblance of the head to that of missing tradesman

---

[3]   See, for example, Defoe's critiques of and attacks on the ordinary Paul Lorrain: *A Hymn*; *A Trip Through London*; and *A Trip through the Town*. For Lorrain's reply see *Remarks*.

John Hayes caused suspicion to fall on his wife, Catherine. She was arrested along with Thomas Billings and Thomas Wood (who was the first to confess to the crime). At trial, Wood and Billings pleaded guilty while Catherine was tried for the offense of "being traitorously present, comforting and maintaining the said Thomas Billings in the murder of the said John Hayes, her husband" a charge that held the same punishment as that of active petty treason or murder (*Old-Bailey Sessions Papers*).

I focus on two of the biographies of Catherine Hayes: *A Narrative of the Barbarous and Unheard of Murder of Mr. John Hayes* and "Catherine Hayes, a Murderess." The biographies are typical in that they read her life, from childhood on, as that of a "murderess-to-be." The texts reconstitute her life backward from her crime, plotting her life story to delineate her as aberrant. The biographers are less concerned with providing factual evidence regarding the crime itself than with providing evidence of her inherent wickedness; what is, quite literally, at stake is Hayes's status as woman.

A Narrative opens with a discourse on the "great privileges and immunities of the English wife" (7), ruefully noting that "when we consider how particularly benevolent [the laws of England] have been to the women of this island, the horrible murder we are going to speak of, will appear the more black and shocking" (6). The writer sets up Hayes as a shocking ingrate, a woman who does not appreciate, and thus by implication does not deserve, the "benevolence" of English laws as they apply to her sex. The narrator rhetorically evokes a lurking "barbaric" country with less "civilized" laws than England in which, he implies, Hayes would deservedly have met far worse conditions, both before and after her crime. Each narrative describes Hayes as a restless girl, who, in direct contradiction of proper daughterly obedience, fought with her mother, ran away to London at sixteen, and "rambled about" with military gentlemen.[4] "Catherine Hayes, a Murderess" remarks that "as a girl she discovered marks of so violent and turbulent a temper, that she totally threw off all Respect and Obedience to her Parents, giving loose to her passions, and gratifying herself in all her vicious Inclinations" (2:2). Hayes is marked by a violent selfishness described in language more commonly associated with sexual debauchery than with childhood disobedience. The writer imagines a she-devil whose "loosed passions" present an unleashing of desire, a desire that seems to encompass both an illicit and voracious sexual appetite

---

[4]   As Faller and others have noted, opening or closing with an excoriation of the criminal's history of disobedience is common in criminal biographies. For example, the following quote from the 1752 biography of Ann Whale and Sarah Pledge, convicted for the murder of Whale's husband, says of Whale: "[E]arly in life she gave evidence of an uncontrollable disposition; and, having a dispute with her mother, she wandered into the country and associated with people of bad character" (Knapp, Baldwin, and Savage, vol. 3, 226). In a 1721 case of coining, the convicted woman's guilt is laid at the feet of the "violence of her temper, and her want of duty to her mother ... no crime is more likely to lead to destruction than that of disobedience to parents" (Knapp, Baldwin, and Savage, vol. 1, 128).

and an uncontrollable criminal malevolence. Her excessive will and her implied promiscuity coalesce in her public "rambling" outside of her household. She is at once literally and figuratively defined as improperly contained within the domestic plot. The biographies tell us that Hayes became a servant on a farm, whereupon she "used her wiles to bewitch" the farmer's son into falling "violently in love with and marrying her," against his family's will. The narratives establish her as breaking apart the family home, associate that transgression with witchcraft, and position her husband as a hapless victim-to-be—his falling into love already associated with her violence and sexual power.

The writers comment that "her husband was indulgent," while Hayes was a "nag" who was "not careful with household management" and who "neglected to provide her husband with children." Hayes belies the newly forming conception of dutiful housewife: she is disobedient, not frugal, and, by virtue of "neglect," unmaternal. "Catherine Hayes, a Murderess" adds more details of Hayes's household extravagance, stating that "in her artful and insinuating way, [she] once spirited him to break almost all the goods in their house, she always being violently prejudiced against them" (24). Hayes's irrational dislike of her household goods implicates her in a plot of excessive, hysterical, and dangerous feminine greed at odds with sober, rational mercantile consumption. Her hunger for money is figured as an even more direct threat to stable social and kinship relations in the subsequent observation that Hayes attempted to convince her husband to murder her parents for monetary gain (24).

Hayes is shown to have abdicated any accepted filial position as daughter, and her conviction for petty treason removes any wifely status to which she might have appealed; the biographies end by marking her maternal status as corrupt. In a bizarre plot twist, the biographies state that Hayes had an illegitimate son, Thomas Billings, who, as an adult, visited her and whom she then "unnaturally seduced" and then convinced to commit the murder. After her execution, *The British Journal* reported:

> [S]he affirmed in Newgate that Billings was her own son, got by Mr. Hayes, tis supposed before her marriage with him. If so, Billings murdered his own father, assisted in quartering him, and then lay with his own mother, while his father's mangled limbs were under the bed. A most horrible scene of wickedness!

No proof exists that Billings was Hayes's son, or even her lover. However, even twentieth-century historians seem to find the accusation irresistible; in his 1989 discussion of the case, McLynn blithely improves on the biographies' claims, doubling her lovers and contextualizing Hayes within a mythic framework of feminine evil: "With her two lovers Hayes played Clytemnestra to her husband's Agamemnon" (122). Rather than castigating Billings for having sex with his supposed mother, McLynn portrays Billings as a man of good character who is ruined by Hayes's monstrous influence.

The introduction of the incest theme, a theme unsupported in the trial by any facts, shockingly crowns the case that Hayes is guilty, not just of murder, but of acting out against the founding fictions of the social order. Although she does not wield the axe, Hayes is uniformly positioned as the architect of the murder who uses her guile to ensnare Billings and Wood to be her henchmen. Hayes is portrayed as an archetype of female evil: a creature of extraordinary power that is half siren and half harpy and can force men to do her bidding, seducing and destroying them. The writers of the biographies configure murder as the natural outcome of *any* female transgression, narratively linking teenage flirtation and household mismanagement with incest and homicide. The ungrateful and disobedient girl grows up to be the monstrous, murderous wife and mother. Her maternity breaks out of patrilineal boundaries as she creates a bastard child whom she then perverts, leading him into an abyss of sexual and capital criminal sin.

The following verses from a popular ballad provide a glimpse of the ways in which popular coverage of Hayes's case elevated her husband while figuring her as a murderous over-sexed virago. The ballad's wit aligns her with the traditional figure of the female shrew, horrifying in one sense, ludicrous in another:

A Song, on the Murder of Mr. Hays [sic], *by his Wife*
To the Tune of Chevy-Chase

In Tyburn Road, a Man there liv'd,
A just and honest Life,
And there he might have lived still
If so had pleased his wife.
But she, to vicious Ways inclin'd,
A Life most wicked led,
With Taylors and with Tinkers too
She oft defil'd his bed.
Full twice a Day to Church he went,
And so devout was he,
Sure never was a Saint on Earth,
If that no Saint was he!
This vex'd his Wife unto the Heart,
She was of Wrath so Full,
That, full no Hole in his Coat,
She pick'd one in his Skull.
But then her heart b'gan to relent,
And griev'd she was so sore,
That Quarter to him for to give,
She cut him into Four.
All in the dark and dead of Night,
These Quarters she convey'd,
And in a Ditch at Marybone,
His Marrow Bones she laid.
His Head at Westminster she threw,

All in the Thames so wide;
Says she, my Dear, the Wind sets fair,
And you may have the Tide.

The ballad links wifely promiscuity and vicious spousal murder in a bawdy and macabre chain of causality. It removes Wood and Billings entirely and repositions John Hayes as a super-virtuous victim. Since Catherine Hayes was dead by the time the ballad was printed, her power is mockingly diffused and the uncomfortable threat of her violence is reduced to a comic trope.

Criminal biographies of murderers usually reach narrative closure in the criminal's dying declarations of his or her guilt and sincere repentance; these declarations, often delivered in the first person, function as didactic textual apotheoses. Hayes, however, never confessed, and so the biographers must create narrative closure without the repentant sinner's confession, a confession that testifies to the reliability of the narrator. Without this confession, Hayes's biographers portray her insistence on her innocence (even while burning at the stake) as final evidence of Hayes's unrepentant guilt and monstrous character. Her insistence on her innocence may, on the other hand, also be read as evidence of the unreliability of the narrators' conclusions. The biographies state that she enlisted Billings's and Wood's sympathy and support by claiming that her husband was a drunken profligate who violently abused her regularly, spent all their money on alcohol and gaming, and murdered two of their newborn children. In his *Ordinary's Account*, James Guthrie includes Hayes's claim that

> Mr. Hayes was a very unkind husband, beating and mortifying her upon every trivial occasion in a cruel manner; and when she was with child, he would never suffer a midwife to be called but once which with his other ill usages proved the cause of an abortion, and commonly put her in hazard of her life.

While it does not support her claim of innocence, the information does provide the reader with an understandable, if not defensible, motive for the murder. The narratives, however, resist this reading and ascribe Hayes's motivation to her inherently deviant status, defining her as separate from, and dangerous to, the community. *A Narrative* and "Catherine Hayes" offer these claims as evidence of the scheming lengths to which Hayes went to gain support for her wicked plan.

While attention to the possible material motivations for her crime would not have provided Hayes with an effective legal defense, it is probable that serious attention to the allegations of her husband's abuse in the narratives of her crime might have gained her at least some popular sympathy.[5] For example, Lydia Adler

---

[5]   See Dolan (32–38) for her persuasive reading of the cases of Alice Clarke and Mary Aubrey (or Hobry), who were executed for petty treason for spousal homicide in 1635 and 1688, respectively. Dolan argues that while the articulation of the abuse Aubrey suffered calls attention to, and implicitly critiques, a husband's abuse of his wife, the text ultimately

received a sentence for manslaughter (punishable by being burned on the hand) for killing her husband in 1744 (Knapp, Baldwin, and Savage, vol. 3, 131–32). While it seems she did indeed murder him, that she had recently discovered he had four wives, thus dislocating familial unity and damaging patrilineal laws of inheritance, seems to have affected the mildness of the verdict. Hayes received no legal or popular quarter for her claims of spousal violence. Of course, eighteenth-century readers of the biography might have read her claims and sympathized with Hayes. However, no instances of sympathy appear in the extensive literature surrounding the case. One letter writer comments that "the best excuse" she offered for "her execrable action" was that "her husband beat her," but the writer dismisses her claims as unrealistic as "to believe them true, we must suppose her a woman of more *patience* than can be easily allow'd" since she remained with him for nearly twenty years before killing him (*Mist's Weekly Journal* 1726). From the eighteenth century to the present, Hayes's crime is regularly referred to as an archetypal example of female blood lust and fury. The crowd at her execution, for example, insisted that the executioner follow the letter of the law by burning her alive while it was generally common for a woman to be strangled first (Illustration 3.1).

The writer of "Catherine Hayes, a Murderess" recounts the remarks an unnamed visitor made to Hayes in prison; these remarks refer to a tendency of the populace to pity "those afflicted" and stress the fact that Hayes is seen as so wicked as to be beyond such pity:

> The Clamour of the World is very strong against you, and though common fame be very indifferent Evidence in some Cases, yet in your Case it is a Sign of more than Ordinary Guilt, because the common Sort, being unable to distinguish nicely, generally pity everybody whom they see under Affliction, unless there be a particular Degree of Wickedness in what they have been guilty of, and such as seems to transcend the Malignancy of human nature, and hath consequently rendered the Criminal unworthy of human Regard. (2:31)

The quote implies that the "common sort" might sympathize with the criminal if they are provided with some level of possible identification with him or her. But Hayes's crime has moved her beyond any space of identification even by those who might tend to sympathize with a prisoner "under Affliction." Here, popular disgust at Hayes is read as evidence of her monstrosity, of her demarcation as one outside not only normative social relations but also humanity itself.

The next case I examine, that of Mary Blandy, convicted of murdering her father, stands out as a rare example of a familial murder, and one by a woman no less, whose narratives allow space for sympathetic identification between the reader and the criminal.[6] In 1752, Mary Blandy was hung for deliberately

---

condemns her violence and, by extension, the hierarchical threat inherent in her privileging of her own life over his.

[6]   See Faller's discussion of the "familiar" murder (*Turned* 4, 21–42).

Illustration 3.1   Catherine Hayes Burnt for the Murder of Her Husband.
(Hayward, Arthur L. *Lives of the most remarkable criminals,*
who have been condemned and executed for murder, the
highway, housebreaking, street robberies, coining or other
offences, collected from original papers and authentic memoirs,
and published in 1735. New York: Dodd, Mead & Company,
1927; 352.)

murdering her father by poison, a charge that she, like Hayes, denied to the end. The frontispieces of Hayes's and Blandy's biographies immediately reveal a difference in the texts' treatments of the two murderesses.[7] Hayes's crime and its location outside of sympathetic identification are established by the title: "*A Narrative of the Barbarous and Unheard of Murder*" (1). In contrast, Blandy is rhetorically imagined as victim, and her crime remains unnamed: her biography is entitled "A General and Impartial Account" of "the crime for which she *suffered*" (1; emphasis added).

Pictorial representations of each murderer also read very differently: One of Hayes's biographies includes a large drawing of Hayes with Billings and Wood, who are cutting off John Hayes's head while Catherine Hayes holds a bucket to catch the blood streaming from his neck (Illustration 3.2).

Illustration 3.2   Catherine Hayes and Her Accomplices Cutting Off Her Husband's Head. (Andrew Knapp, William Baldwin, and Henry Savage, *Newgate Calendar*. London: J. Robins and Co., 1824; 257.) This item is reproduced by permission of *The Huntington Library, San Marino, California.*

---

[7]   I refer to the *Account* of Hayes's case, as the "Catherine Hayes, a Murderess" piece does not reproduce the original pamphlet and thus there is no frontispiece. The Blandy frontispiece reads: "*A General and Impartial Account of the Life of Mary Blandy, Particularly From the Time of her Commitment to Oxford-Castle, to her Execution at Oxford, Monday, April 6, 1752, for poisoning her Father. With Her own Account of the Affair between her and Mr. Cranstoun, from their first Acquaintance, in 1746: In a Narrative of the Crime for which she suffered.*"

This image stresses the violence of the crime and its grotesque details, such as the axe on the floor and the use of the bucket to catch the blood from the severed head. The scene is a tableau with the feel of a stage set: the opened curtains frame the action, and the marital bed behind the three figures emphasizes violated matrimony—both through the literal death of the husband and through the scene's suggestion of cuckoldry.

Blandy, on the other hand, is regularly depicted in terms familiar from genteel portraiture. On one frontispiece she appears in a locket-like frame in a position that recalls traditional portraits of young ladies: she is properly attired in a modest mourning dress and wears a demure bonnet laced under her chin. She is seated and has her hands primly in her lap, holding what appears to be a teacup, and she appears chaste and unremarkable (Illustration 3.3).

Illustration 3.3   Miss Mary Blandy. (James Granger, *A Biographical History of England*. Vol. 28. London, 1769; 81.) This item is reproduced by permission of *The Huntington Library, San Marino, California*.

Eighteenth-century images of Hayes leave no doubt as to her status as a murderess—she is either depicted in the process of the crime or at the stake. Eighteenth-century images of Blandy, however, displace her venality; her criminality is a detail at odds with her socially acceptable status. We see this disjunction in the image of her in a lovely dress, befitting a well-bred woman, standing in a lovely meadow; only upon closer inspection are her leg irons visible above her stylish shoes (Illustration 3.4).

Illustration 3.4   Miss Molly Blandy. (James Granger, *A Biographical History of England.* Vol. 28. London, 1769; 81.) This item is reproduced by permission of *The Huntington Library, San Marino, California.*

The bifurcation is perhaps most clearly writ in a painting that is divided into two parts: the top two-thirds depicts a framed image of Blandy in a fashionable hat and gown, holding a flower and looking demurely to the left, a perfectly common image of young womanhood until one moves to look at the painting's bottom third, which shows her hanging (Illustration 3.5).

Illustration 3.5   Benjamin Cole. Miss Mary Blandy. (James Granger, *A Biographical History of England*. Vol. 28. London, 1769; 81.) This item is reproduced by permission of *The Huntington Library, San Marino, California.*

The tension in these images is supported by the narratives of Blandy's life and crime that present her, not as an aberrant monster whose sins are of her own volition, but as a good woman who has been led astray. As per usual, *A General and Impartial Account* begins with a discussion of Blandy's girlhood, which defines Blandy in terms of her femininity. However, unlike Hayes, Blandy is described as successfully feminine, possessing all of the proper and positive attributes of her sex:

> She was sprightly, affable and polite, and though not beautiful, yet her Person was agreeable, and her Conversation remarkably engaging. She was dutiful to her Parents. ... To her Superiors behav'd with becoming Reverence; was open and unreserved to her Equals, and to her Inferiors courteous. (3)

This portrait of proper feminine conduct is clouded, however, by the author's comment that, despite her promise, Blandy "shew'd an early Propensity to Coquetry ... by which her Character was soon sully'd, either thro' Envy or of real Misconduct" (3). The writer continues by stating that he has no wish to "blacken" her name (one presumably blackened enough by virtue of her capital conviction), but that he "is not at Liberty to think her Conduct blameless, and the more so, as she was endowed with so extraordinary a share of Understanding" (3; the writer has earlier commented on her being well-read and articulate). We see an oddly chivalric and paternalistic treatment of Blandy that at no time appeared in regard to Hayes. Her position as unmarried daughter seems to render her a perpetual child, rather than an adult woman (she was thirty-three the year of her arrest), and the writer is loath to criticize such a traditionally "good" girl, but feels he must. What damns Blandy here is, interestingly, her intelligence; it suggests to the biographer that she must have been aware of the effects of her behavior, and so, he concludes, her intelligence adds credence to what is acknowledged to be hearsay evidence of flirtation. The text refers to her "remarkable" love of reading, a taste that also points to her intelligence, a trait the biographer implies is somehow connected to her lack of beauty (she had suffered from smallpox).[8]

The biography continues by telling us that Blandy's father committed a "pious fraud" by erroneously implying that his daughter was to be the recipient of a large fortune upon marrying. We are told that Mr. Cranstoun, having heard of Miss Blandy's supposed fortune and gaining Mr. Blandy's ear, became one of the family, "enjoy[ing] the young lady's Company without Controul" (4). This last statement, coupled with the previous suggestion of her flirtatious misconduct, implies that Blandy and Cranstoun were improperly sexually involved. The narrator tells us that Cranstoun is ugly, short, and disfigured by smallpox, stating wryly that we must suppose he won Blandy by his "——Eloquence" (4), the long dash implying his unlikely seductive/sexual prowess and her undiscriminating response to male flattery and sexual attention. His unattractive physical description prepares us for his malfeasance, signs of which we soon encounter as the writer tells us that Cranstoun had a wife and children in Scotland. Upon his discovery that Cranstoun was married, Mr. Blandy forbade his relationship with his daughter. Cranstoun responded by falsely insisting that his marriage was not a legal one and returning to Scotland. He sent Blandy a packet of white powder (later discovered to be arsenic) that she claimed he told her was a love potion that would induce her father to love him. The writer includes a dry comment here regarding the fact that Blandy cautioned the maid not to eat the gruel she prepared (evidence presented at trial as indicative of her knowledge of its ill effects); he writes that either she knew the powder was poison or else she must have feared the maid falling in love with Cranstoun, thus providing him with too many admirers. After her father ingested the powder prepared in the gruel, he fell ill, and she was arrested for murder (her father died from the poison while she was in prison).[9]

---

[8] Dryden's "To the Pious Memory of the Accomplisht Young Lady Mrs. Anne Killigrew," which addresses both Killegrew and Katherine Phillips, links female intellect and agency with smallpox; I am unaware if such a link was common or at play in Blandy's case, but it is evocative nonetheless.

[9] Poisoning cases carried a *de facto* mandatory death sentence. After her arrest, Cranstoun ran off to France, from where he published accounts that blame Blandy for the murder.

From this point on, the narrative becomes alternately critical of Blandy's behavior and sympathetic to her distress. The writer praises her composure and seriousness while he decries her calm ability to eat a big meal after being sentenced and denounces her inappropriate remarks in prison (one worth noting is her reported statement that "[a] Bill was going to be carried into Parliament, for a Law to hang all the sensible Women, and let none but Fools live" [11]). The account is unable firmly to fix Blandy either as a truly "good" woman, misused by a man to poison her beloved father inadvertently (her version of the events) or as a wicked coquette, shamelessly murdering her father for romantic and economic gain (the prosecution's version of events). Instead, the account wavers between these two possibilities.

Before its concluding pages, the account includes Blandy's autobiographical version of the events, *Miss Mary Blandy's Own Account of the Affair Between Her and Mr. Cranstoun*, an account that is formally and thematically indebted to the amatory fictions of writers such as Aphra Behn, Eliza Haywood, and Delarivier Manley.[10] In her own account, as well as on the witness stand, Blandy constructs herself as a damsel in distress, an innocent ruined by love, or, as she puts it, one destroyed by "loving and relying too much on the Human part" (10). At his deathbed even her father reportedly remarked: "Poor love-sick girl! What will not a woman do for a man she loves?" Her appeal to a conception of sentimental, affective femininity presents Blandy and her crime within acceptable codes of gendered behavior; she elides the hard evidence that indicts her for murder by positioning herself as a girl unwittingly undone by a villainous rake. That she should not, by all accounts, have been allowed into such close proximity to such a dangerous character is implicit and is an indictment of her father's lack of appropriate paternal authority; Blandy neatly relocates blame away from herself and onto two men who have failed to fulfill their socially prescribed masculine roles.

Blandy entreats her reading audience to pity her and "hopes her hard case will win her clemency," for, she pleads, "Sure it is hard to die for Ignorance, and too good an Opinion of a Villain?" (12).[11] Blandy's intelligence and her skill at presenting herself sympathetically in text make it a bit hard to swallow her claims regarding her lack of knowledge of the powder's ill effects, as do the letters she sent to Cranstoun, which refer to her fear of discovery and the fact that she continued to administer it even after her father fell ill. However, she is extremely adept at manipulating popular conceptions of femininity, both in her writings and in her public behavior. To be a good girl who has been led astray from her family by a fiendish rake is to fit into an understandable gendered plot; this characterization does not, as Blandy wishes it to, spare her life, but it does allow her, unlike Hayes, to remain recognizably worthy of

---

[10]   I discuss Blandy's account and its narrative link to amatory fiction at length in Chapter 5.

[11]   Her direct address of the reader to consider her misfortunes echoes similar narrative moves in popular amatory fictions. She had at least some success; for example, Lady Ailesbury of Park Place used all of her influence to attempt to obtain Blandy a pardon.

human regard, to, as Margaret Doody points out in her discussion of the case, "save and re-create her femininity" ("The Law" 154).[12]

The biography's conclusion begins with the author's refutation of each of Blandy's claims. He then compounds her guilt by listing, in language that, as in the Hayes accounts, conflates sexual and economic overindulgence. He notes that Blandy gave Cranstoun money that her father had given her for "mourning for the Prince of Wales" and that she borrowed her maid's savings to provide Cranstoun support. In these actions, she transgressed filial duty, precluded her duty to royalty, and abused class privilege. The expenditures are deemed proofs of the "Extravagance of her passion" (14) and indict Blandy within a rhetoric of feminine unsuitability. However, the narrative next praises her gallows demeanor as "well suited to her deplorable Circumstances" (15) and approvingly notes the proper feminine modesty and piety she demonstrates at her death. In a wonderfully extraneous nod to dainty sensibility, Blandy requested of the executioners: "Gentlemen, do not hang me high, for the Sake of Decency" (16) and, the rope having been put round her neck, "she pulled the handkerchief over her face and gave the signal to hang her by holding out a book of devotions from which she had been reading" (16). At this point, the biographer comments, the crowd, estimated in the *State Trials* at 5,000 strong, fell to weeping.

Blandy knew how to enact the role of pious and modest femininity even as her actions belied it. Her success in rendering herself an object of pity rather than one of revulsion is evidenced by the account's final exposition:

> When we reflect on the Excellence of her natural Qualities and Endowments, improv'd by the best education; when we consider her firm and intrepid Behavior at her Trial; her steady and uniform Seriousness (except in some few Instances) during her Confinement; and her persisting in Vindication of her Innocence even to her latest Breath at the fatal Tree; all plead strongly in her Favour; and whether really guilty or not, must be left only to the Supreme Judge. To conclude, she was either the most *wicked*, or the most *unfortunate* of Women, but Pity and Christian Charity would incline one to believe the latter. (17)

---

[12]   The prosecutorial narrative in the trial, needless-to-say, presents Blandy in entirely negative terms. The barrister describes the case as: "no less a crime than that of Murder. And not only for Murder, but for the Murder of her own Father; a Father passionately fond of her. And not only so, but for the Murder of a Father passionately fond of her, undertaken with the utmost Deliberation; carried on with an unvaried Continuation of Intention; and at last accomplished by a frequent Repetition of the Baneful Dose, administered with her own Hands. A Crime so shocking in its own Nature, and so aggravated in Circumstances as will (if she is proved to be guilty of it) justly render her infamous to the latest Posterity; and make our Children's Children, when they read the horrid tale of this Day, blush to think that such an inhuman Creature ever had an Existence" (*The Tryal of Mary Blandy* 3–4).

See Chapter 5 of this book for a discussion of the judicial treatment of her case, including Fielding's jurisprudential-theological narrative of her guilt.

Blandy's case has continued to attract sympathy across the centuries. While some commentators remained unconvinced of her pathos (an 1882 article in *The New York Times* comments that her declaration of innocence "must have been a lie"), most discussions of the case, from the eighteenth century to the present, posit Blandy as a victim. She is memorialized as a tragic heroine in the 1827 poem *Henley*:

> Alas! the record of her page will tell
> That one thus madden'd, lov'd, and guilty fell.
> Who hath not heard of Blandy's fatal fame,
> Deplor'd her fate, and sorrow'd o'er her shame?

In a 1926 book on famous trials, *The Mayfair Calendar: Some Society Causes Célèbres*, Horace Wyndham pithily positions her as a victim: "Mary Blandy died for love. The tragedy of it was, she died on the gallows" (19). In 1950, Joan Morgan published a novel vindicating Blandy entitled *The Hanging Wood*, and, most recently, Henley publisher Victor Bingham published a book, *The Noose Around the Wrong Neck*, in which he blames Cranstoun for the murder; in 2005, Bingham applied to the Criminal Cases Review Commission to overturn Blandy's conviction.

We have seen the ways in which Blandy's self-presentation helped enable biographers from the eighteenth century on to deem her "unfortunate" rather than wicked. However, in large part, there are similarities between Hayes's and Blandy's cases and demeanors that would seem to preclude this judgment. Neither confessed, both are defined as sexually improper, and both murdered the men who were, according to social law and custom, their rightful masters. Blandy's apt self-representation clearly affected the tone of her account and the outpouring of popular sympathy she engendered, yet it does not seem quite enough to account for the ways in which she is able to be at least partially recuperated while Hayes, whose case seems to offer a more valid, if still legally inexcusable, rationale for murder, cannot be.[13]

Alexander Welsh argues that "we cannot take murder for granted the way we can death. Thus murder always raises the evidentiary question—strikingly in a forensic scene, hauntingly perhaps most of the time" (iv). The evidentiary question most hauntingly crucial in the cases of Hayes and Blandy is that of their positions as women in relation to patriarchal social hierarchies. That Blandy was a daughter led astray by her seducer allows her story to stand as a cautionary tale of filial obedience and female chastity, a story that shores up conventional social and

---

[13]   Further evidence of the disparity in the tone of the accounts is revealed by the ways in which the writers discuss rumors linking the criminals to other deaths. Blandy's biography mentions that she has been thought guilty of her mother's death, but the claim is defined as rumor, whereas in Hayes's account the claim that she wanted to kill her parents is included without comment as to its veracity.

moral gendered conventions. Rakes will be rakes, and it is a woman's job to be well defended with virtuous piety against them; see what can happen, even to a "good" girl, if she missteps? If Blandy's version of the facts were true, that indeed she was misled by Cranstoun to believe the vial contained love potions, then she is guilty of disobedience and inappropriate romantic inclinations, faults that put her outside of the realm of "proper" femininity, but that are understandable within a palatable discourse of feminine possibility. She can then be an object of pity and education—a "there but for the grace of God" case of womanly crime—and the true blame for homicide falls on Cranstoun, the man who presents a danger to the familial unit, not only the Blandys but also his abandoned family in Scotland. If she was lying, and she knowingly poisoned her father, a decision the biographer cannot finally bear to make, her guilt, while far more serious than filial disobedience, may still be traced back outside of the familial (and national) unit to Cranstoun (who sent her the poison) and her motivation—that of a love too strong—coincides with passive, sentimental notions of femininity and obedience, however misplaced.

Hayes, on the other hand, is either innocent, which is unlikely, or her guilt arises out of her own desire for her husband's death. Even assuming that her allegations were true, that her husband's behavior was despicable, her response to that behavior was self-generated. No one, including Hayes, ever proposed that Billings or Wood originated the plan, although they committed the actual act. If indeed she plotted his murder, she acted of her own accord. Moreover, if Hayes's allegations about her husband were true, many of them, while offering motivation, consisted of behaviors that were covertly ignored within Augustan society. Excessive gambling, wife-beating, and immoderate drinking were socially frowned on, even legislated against, but they were rarely actions for which men were formally punished. Gambling and drunkenness were publicly derided but manifestly common male activities for which a man was legally at fault only if he incurred a bad debt to another man or was guilty of public drunken disorderliness that created a social problem, such as brawling or physical attack. While wife-beating became a legal offense by 1650, it continued to be "widely practiced and regarded as a husband's right, underpinned by the Holy Writ" (Burford and Shulman 135), and Hayes's accusations of paternal infanticide would have been nearly unthinkable to a society in which the crime was legally, as well as culturally, figured as feminine.[14] In addition, the fault of husbandly misbehavior was commonly understood as resting with the wife, whose spousal behavior was usually presumed to be unsatisfactory, thus causing her husband's errant ways.

If the biographers had seriously considered Hayes's contended motives for murder, the entire patriarchal power system that excluded women from lawful recourse in the face of marital mistreatment would, by default, have been under attack. While there are moments when biographies nod to extremities of wives'

---

[14]   There is only one recorded case in the century of a man accused and convicted of infanticide. See McLynn 114.

abuse at the hands of their husbands, such moments are rare and are almost always subsumed into a rhetoric of marriage that finally will not support a woman putting her own life above that of her husband. The following long quote, from George Savile, Marquis of Halifax's *The Lady's New Year's Gift: or, Advice to a Daughter* (1688), is notable for its use of legal terms as well as its content—a defense of the inequities of women's position within marriage. While the quote dates from thirty years prior to Hayes's trial, the text from which it comes had been reprinted over twelve times by 1726 (the date of Hayes's crime), and the sentiments and the legal situations to which it refers are those of the era as well.

> It is true that the laws of marriage, run in harsher stile toward your sex. It might be alleged by the counsel retained by your sex, that as there is in all other laws, an appeal from the letter to the equity, in cases that require it, it is as reasonable, that some Court of a larger jurisdiction might be erected, where some wives might resort and plead specially ... they might have relief, and obtain mitigation in their own particular of a sentence which was given generally against woman kind. The causes of separation are now so very coarse, that few are confident enough to buy their own liberty at the price of having their modesty so exposed. But ... the institution of Marriage is too sacred to admit a liberty of objecting to it. [That you are the] weaker sex ... maketh it reasonable to subject it to the masculine domination. It is safer that some injustice should be conniv'd at than to break into an establishment upon which the Order of Humane society doth so much depend. (Qtd. in V. Jones 17–23)

Savile's quote highlights the illogical nature of the gender inequity of marriage it strives to defend. He contends that even justified complaints by married women constitute unsafe attacks that must be ignored in order to shore up marriage as a social institution. His rhetorical move paradoxically reveals the institution to be far less secure than he intends; marriage is unable to support equitable jurisdiction, and so it must be shored up forcefully. The Marquis's legal language oddly defers and excludes the possibility of legal action, dividing the realm of marriage from that of the realm of rights and equity in terms that work at cross purposes to his intentions, calling attention to the harshness of marital laws for women, the ways in which female modesty logically precludes female liberty, and the fact that, within the current marital economy, a woman's only option is that of submission. Or, one might argue in light of Hayes's case, the only alternative to submission is violent defiance of a system of law that does not provide her recourse.

Hayes's crime struck too hard at social structures of marriage and gendered behavior to sustain the possibility of her narrative construction as an understandable, if deplorable, part of her community. In addition, in contrast to Blandy, Hayes was guilty on other counts: she crossed class lines and married up and was still not content. The nonhomicidal accusations leveled at her—including scolding, sexual perversion, and the destruction of property—were faults not recoupable into a discourse of feminine passivity. And she was, finally, unwilling or unable convincingly to present herself as a victim. All of these things combined to doom Hayes to be immortalized as the eighteenth-century villainess *par excellence*. An 1884 discussion of the case describes it as "[p]erhaps the most revolting murder ever perpetrated, not excepting those of later date" (Griffiths 350). Her story became one of female depravity that was widely circulated for the next 150 years, including William Thackeray's version of her case in his first novel, *Catherine*, a lengthy fictionalization of the case that posits her as devil incarnate.[15]

A 2003 book, *Written in Blood: A History of Forensic Detection*, describes Hayes as "a rather attractive woman" (175) who was "dominant and quarrelsome" and states that Wood and Billings "were both Catherine's lovers." (Wilson and Wilson 176).

The disparity between Hayes's and Blandy's accounts and in the reception of their accounts demonstrates the ways in which what was "on trial" in Augustan female homicide cases was not only the female criminal herself. At stake were the status of her perceived femininity and the status of her crime's perceived effect on heavily defended social institutions or traditions. Often those involved gender norms, but they also included issues of class, nationhood, economics, and religious authority.

Sarah Malcolm and Elizabeth Brownrigg

Sarah Malcolm was convicted in 1733 for multiple murders in the course of a robbery; Elizabeth Brownrigg was convicted in 1767 for the torture and murder of a female apprentice. Narratives of Malcolm's and Brownrigg's crimes, while dissimilar at the level of plot, exemplify the ways in which female violence generically threatened eighteenth-century social signification. While the cases of Hayes and Blandy reveal the ways in which the accused murderess was textualized in terms of her more or less satisfactory submission to male guardianship, Malcolm's and Brownrigg's cases demonstrate the ways in which the physical body of the accused woman could be positioned as both proof and cause of her guilt. The cases also draw attention to topical anxieties regarding the roles of domestic women and domestic servants. Malcolm was a servant convicted of killing a mistress, Brownigg a mistress convicted of killing her servant, and the legal and popular treatments of these cases reflect and illuminate mid-century concerns about gender and class.[16]

Sarah Malcolm was indicted in 1733 for a triple murder committed in the process of a robbery. On Sunday, February 4, 1733, two elderly women, Mrs. Lydia Duncomb and Elizabeth Harrison, her companion, were found strangled

---

[15]   The novel uses Hayes as the focus of Thackeray's stated "attempt to make vice appear entirely vicious" in contrast to "the prevailing style of literary practice" that is, he claims, too sympathetic to crime (160).

[16]   Seleski provides a persuasive reading of the role of class in the Brownrigg case. Also see Magrath for a lucid discussion of gender and the body in the case.

in Duncomb's rooms with Ann Price, her young maid, whose throat was cut. Malcolm was arrested that night on the information of her master, Mr. Kerrol, who had chambers in the same staircase as Duncomb, and who found some bloody linen under his bed and a silver tankard in his close stool (Malcolm had been staying in his chamber while he was away).[17] According to *The Old-Bailey Session Papers*, Malcolm, Mary Tracy, and the brothers Thomas and James Alexander were arrested for the murders of Duncomb (for whom Malcolm had worked), Harrison, and Price. While all were arrested and indicted, only Malcolm was charged with and hung for the murders (she was not guilty of petty treason as she was not in the direct employ of Duncomb); the others were eventually released, as it was thought that Malcolm "accused them only to save her own life" (*London Magazine* 7). While she confessed to the robbery, itself a capital offense, Malcolm consistently insisted on her innocence of the murder charge. When she stepped into the courtroom, Sarah Malcolm was already guilty twice over: first for being charged with any crime at all; second, for confessing to the one but refusing to confess to the other.

Malcolm's testimony—that she was guilty of one crime and not the other— explicitly countered eighteenth-century conceptions of female criminality that claimed a woman could not make one wrong step without inevitably progressing to the worst step, a narrative plotted according to the logic of progressive female sin. By the time she stood trial for the murders, she was already guilty of endangering property and authority, a charge that played on deep-seated class anxieties. Malcolm was a Catholic raised in Dublin, a laundress and charwoman, and was convicted of murdering a gentlewoman and two servants while in the process of a robbery. Her religion, perceived nationality (she was actually born in England), class, and sex combined to mark Malcolm as exceptionally untrustworthy and her crimes exceptionally dangerous, as she represented the threats of lower-class, Irish, Catholic female agency in a society preoccupied with the perceived dangers of each.

Malcolm's case also reveals the ways in which the quotidian matter of the female body could not be expressed in an eighteenth-century court of law that viewed women's bodies through a predominant socioreligious narrative that positioned the female body according to a virgin/whore dyad: either chaste, passive, and obedient or virulent, violent, and rebellious. The defense's case rested on Malcolm's claim that the blood used as evidence against her was not the blood of the victims but menstrual blood. Malcolm's defense is remarkable in that it rests on the issue of menstruation. Malcolm relies on the product of her female body—her menstrual blood—as evidence of her innocence, while the prosecution turns to her lack of proper femininity as the source and proof of her guilt.

At her trial, the clerk of the arraigns stated that Malcolm was indicted for "being moved and seduced by a devilish Instigation" (*Old-Bailey Session Papers* 2), an instigation he defines as her desire to gain money and independence to convince one of the accomplices in the robbery, a Mr. Alexander, to marry her.

---

[17]   Some sources refer to him as Mr. Kerrel.

The prosecution implied Malcolm was unlikely to win a husband without money because she was not adequately feminine—in behavior or body. Malcolm disputed the clerk's version and maintained that she and Mary Tracy planned the robbery because they were in dire need of money for food and explained that they convinced a known criminal pair, the Alexander brothers, to help them. She swore that the brothers committed the murders in the course of the robbery without the women's knowledge or consent. Malcolm's insistent response in her own defense offered a logical counterpoint to the court's claims of the chains of events and concurrently shored its claims of her failed femininity.

The physical evidence levied against Malcolm was the blood found on her shift, apron, and bed sheets. Malcolm's response was that this blood was menstrual and not the blood of one of the victims. Her logic is compelling; she states:

> Modesty might compel a woman to conceal her own Secrets if Necessity did not oblige her to the contrary; and 'tis Necessity that obliges me to say, that what as been taken for the Blood of the murdered Person is nothing but the free Gift of Nature. This was all that appeared on my Shift, and it was the same on my Apron, for I wore the Apron under me next to my Shift. My Master going out of town desir'd me to lye in his Chamber, and that was the Occasion of my foul linen being found there. The Woman who wash'd the Sheets I lay in can testify that the same was upon them. ... That this was the Case is plain: for how is it possible that it could be the Blood of the murder'd Person? If it is supposed that I kill'd her [Ann Price] with my Cloaths on, my Apron indeed might be bloody, but how should the Blood come upon my Shift? If I did it in my Shift, how should my Apron be bloody, or the back of my Shift? And whether I did it dress'd or undress'd, why was not the Neck and Sleeves of my Shift bloody as well as the lower parts? (*Old-Bailey Session Papers* 26–27)

This speech is a lucid and logical refutation of the court's claims.[18] She overtly questions the court's reading, and her presentation of the physical evidence makes a compelling case for her innocence. However, her words present a narrative unspeakable in the context of a court of law. Defiantly mentioning the unmentionable "free gift of nature," Malcolm transgresses what was considered appropriate feminine behavior by representing that which should, by virtue of her sex, be unnatural to modest feminine discourse. The court deliberated fifteen minutes after hearing her defense (actually a rather long time for such deliberations at the time) and found her guilty.

Malcolm's speaking out is figured as extraordinary and as evidence of her guilt. Accounts of the trial dismiss Malcolm's defense and define her active role in her own defense as perverse: "She behav'd in a very extraordinary Manner ... often

---

[18]   Magrath notes that "although her explanation for the location of the blood suggests a rather unconventional ordering in the layers of her clothes ... it is possible that Malcolm ... wore aprons under her dresses ... to protect her outer garments from blood" (227).

times requesting the Court for the Witnesses to speak louder, and spoke upwards of a half and Hour in her Defense … in a trifling Manner" (*London Magazine* 95–96). As in the narratives of Hayes, Malcolm's refusal to confess to the murder charge is positioned as further evidence of her improperly gendered behavior. The *London Magazine* writer locates Malcolm's protestations as evidence, not of her innocence, but of her obvious guilt as they reveal her unsuitable insistence on self-representation. He comments that, after being sentenced, Malcolm "behaved in a most bold and impudent Manner; still persisting on her Innocence of being concerned in Murder." The ordinary describes her as a "most obdurate, impenitent sinner" who was "void of all virtue and the grace of God" (22).

Her persistence in rejecting the court's decision is portrayed as an indication of Malcolm's wickedness. Unlike Blandy, Malcolm was unable to present herself within a successful frame of femininity: she articulated her own defense within a rhetoric of logic rather than seductive victimization, and the sign of femininity, menstrual blood, upon which she drew for her defense, marked her both as hysterically feminine (menstruation was seen to enfeeble what little morality and capacity for reason women had) and as dangerously indelicate.

Malcolm is most famous today for being the subject of a portrait by Hogarth, who sketched Malcolm two days before her execution (Illustration 3.6).

Illustration 3.6.   Sarah Malcolm. (William Hogarth and John Trusler. *The Works of William Hogarth Containing One Hundred and Fifty-Eight Engravings, by Mr. Cooke, and Mr. Davenport, with Descriptions in Which Are Pointed Out Many Beauties That Have Hither to Escaped Notice, with a Comment on Their Moral Tendency.* London: Tegg.) This item is reproduced by permission of *The Huntington Library, San Marino, California.*

His sketch, upon which the painting was based, was published with the accounts of her trial.[19] The painting depicts Malcolm as a looming presence with a direct gaze, and she appears far older than her twenty-five years. Hogarth emphasizes Malcolm's bare muscular forearms, which rest heavily near her rosary beads on the table in her cell, and she is depicted in servant's dress with large shoulders and clawlike fingers. In the portrait, Malcolm's lack of conventional beauty and delicacy, her religious affiliation, and her servant status combine to depict her as triply criminal. Hogarth stated that he saw "by this woman's features, that she is capable of any wickedness." Malcolm's body—its overpresence, working-class strength, and unfemininity—was read as the text of her guilt. Her defense—that, in fact, her female body provided the text of her innocence—relied on evidence that was deemed inappropriate. She was seen as such a threat, such a monstrous anomaly, that "Professor Martin dissected this notorious murderess and afterwards presented her skeleton in a glass case to the Botanic Gardens at Cambridge where it still remains" (Hogarth and Cook 313).

While Sarah Malcolm received intense attention during her trial and shortly after her death, her fame did not touch that of Elizabeth Brownrigg. Like Catherine Hayes and Mary Blandy, Brownrigg's crime engendered hundreds of pages of exposition, repulsion, and fascination. Brownrigg's act of murder was an anomaly that resisted representational understanding; it proved nearly impossible for the biographers to craft narratives that could account for it. Eighteenth-century prosecutorial narratives and criminal biographies worked to make women's acts of murder understandable through narratives that delineate the ways in which the murderess's body failed properly to embody its sex. In Brownrigg's case, this discourse of sexual aberration reveals its weakness as it strains and fails to contain an inexplicable crime within a plot of transparent sexual codes.

Married to John Brownrigg, a painter and plasterer with a steady income, Elizabeth Brownrigg was a respected midwife whose 1767 torture–murder of a female apprentice in her charge was as shockingly violent as it was inexplicable (Illustration 3.7). The Old Bailey record opens with a description of the torture and murder:

> [T]hat the said Elizabeth, her the said Mary, willfully, and of malice aforethought, did make an assult, with divers large whips, canes, sticks, and staves, and did strike, beat, and whip, over the naked head, shoulders, back, and other parts of her naked body, in a cruel and inhuman manner, giving to her divers large wounds, swellings, and bruises; and with divers large hempen cords, and iron chains, round the neck of the said Mary, did bind and fasten ... under the stairs, leading into the cellar ... did fasten and imprison; by means of ... the said Mary, she did pine and languish till ... [she] did die. (102)

---

[19]   He offered the print for sale March 8, the same day newspapers described her execution. The painting was purchased by Walpole, who hung it at Strawberry Hill.

Illustration 3.7   Elizabeth Brownrigg. (George Daniel. *Merrie England in the Olden Time*. Vol. 2, pt. 2. London: R. Bentley, 1842; 194.) This item is reproduced by permission of *The Huntington Library, San Marino, California*.

Unsurprisingly, the horrific nature of the abuse combined with the stature of the murderer resulted in popular fascination with the case and it "roused the indignation of the populace more than any criminal occurrence in the whole course of our melancholy narratives" (*Newgate Calendar* 171). The discovery that Brownrigg had tortured all three of the girls apprenticed to her was considered so grotesque that the crowd at her execution "cried out, they hoped he [the ordinary] would pray for her damnation, for such a fiend ought not to be saved" (*Annual Register*

197). Brownrigg is not only beyond sympathy, but also beyond the expiation and Christian redemption that lies at the heart of the criminal biographical project.

Despite its particularity, Brownrigg's case reveals the ways in which similar terms were used to define any eighteenth-century woman who committed homicide. Brownrigg, like Hayes, was portrayed as an archetypal anti-mother, a horrifying Medea, murderous witch, and "inhuman tygress" (*Universal Magazine*). Her motivation, however, was elusive. She murdered someone weaker than herself, someone who was not only physically weaker, but who was also below her hierarchically in age and position, who depended on her for sustenance, and by whose death she received no increase in economic or individual sovereignty.[20] What gave Augustan writers particular pause was that, unlike Hayes and Blandy— whose narratives could be written backward from their crimes—Brownrigg's life did not fit into the narrative her crime demanded. She was a married mother (most reports claim sixteen births and three living children at the time of the trial), a respected and financially secure midwife whose life presented no opportunity to mark her as a woman predisposed to extreme outbreak.

As a result of the biographers' inability to fix Brownrigg within a recognizable plot of feminine appetite gone amok, many accounts of her crime were so erroneous that even the Newgate ordinary objected to their fictionality. Margaret Doody notes that Brownrigg was accused in the popular press of being a "bawd, a baby farmer, and a practitioner of wholesale infanticide for gain" ("The Law" 146). These stories were patently false: as a midwife "she is said to have acted with great skill and humanity. She was also a faithful wife, and a tender and affectionate parent" (*Annual Register* 190). She apparently was a devoted mother; she had, by all accounts, a happy marriage; she was liked by her community; she was a respected and much sought after midwife; and, because of her adept and caring medical work, she was appointed by the overseers of the poor of St. Dunstan's parish to care for women taken to labor in the workhouse. Faced with a woman so properly feminine in her maternal, marital, and charitable roles, the writer could only turn to notions of biblical sin for an explanation of her crimes, which can only be accounted for "by that depravity of human nature which philosophers have always disputed, but which true Christians will be ready to allow" (180). The devil as instigator, however, does not adequately address the complicated issues of domestic abuse that the case brought to light.

---

[20] Interestingly, another female torture–murder case of an apprentice took place in 1762, only five years before Brownrigg's offences. Sarah Metyard and her daughter Sarah Morgan Metyard were convicted and executed for starving, torturing, and murdering Ann Naylor, a thirteen-year-old apprentice. Case coverage seems mostly to focus on the fact that each of the convicted women laid the blame with the other and that they were forced to be incarcerated separately. I have found no reference to this case in any coverage of the Brownrigg crimes.

Brownrigg took in three parish apprentices, all young girls named Mary, whom she systematically starved and tortured.[21] One of the girls, Mary Jones, escaped and returned to the foundling hospital, where her wounds caused such alarm that the hospital solicitor wrote a letter to James Brownrigg threatening prosecution if he did not give reason for the child's injuries. When there was no response, the governors of the hospital decided it was imprudent to indict at common law, so they simply sent the girl away to safety. The other two girls remained and continued to be tortured until a neighbor apprentice boy, spying on the house at the behest of one of the girls' relatives, witnessed the abuse.

When the authorities were brought in, Mr. Brownrigg was caught and arrested while Elizabeth and her son fled. Despite medical care, Mary Clifford died soon after the arrest as a result of her wounds. Brownrigg and her son were soon caught and all three were charged with the crime of Willful Murder. Elizabeth confessed, passionately defended her son and husband as only accessories to the crimes, and was found guilty and hung, while the father and son were charged with misdemeanors that carried six months' imprisonment.

The husband and son, who were proven to be aware of, and in the son's case actively involved in, the girls' abuse, were let off with a lesser punishment than they would have received for stealing a loaf of bread. Such inequitable punishment points to the fact that it was Brownrigg's sex and position that engendered extraordinary public outrage, not simply the horror of the crime itself, a crime in which both father and son were unequivocally implicated. Evil was consolidated into the aberrant woman rather than implicating the familial and social units within which that woman existed.

Both Sarah Malcolm and Elizabeth Brownrigg were tried in this climate rife with tensions regarding shifting conceptions of domestic labor. Sarah Malcolm's case writ large the common fear of the employing classes that servants posed a threat; Brownrigg's case calls attention to the competing (and more likely) fear that the domestic is a legal subordinate whose fate rests on the caprice of the fairness of her employer. Both cases point to an eighteenth-century anxiety about the status of domestic servants. As Eve Lynch explains, "the vexed relationship between the public and private within the home [was] complicated for a servant who entered into a 'situation,' rather than a 'home,' a term that would carry a connotation of privacy and privilege too close to the family's status in the household."

These crimes once again highlight the domestic realm as battleground rather than safe haven and call attention to the inequities masked by marking the home

---

[21]   There is no record of sexual abuse, but it seems highly probable, given the sadistic nature of the crimes and the fact that the girls were kept naked for long stretches of time, that sexual abuse did occur and may have been instigated by all three of the Brownriggs. It is unclear whether or not James Brownrigg participated in the abuse, but he witnessed it and also refused to reply to the formal inquiry posed by the Foundling governors. As such he was legally an accessory to the crime. The son was witnessed actively participating in the abuse, and the apprentices testified to his involvement.

as separate from the realm of the civic and supposedly free from the pressure of market economy. While Hayes's and Blandy's crimes suggested the dangers posed by wife and daughter within the household, Malcolm's and Brownrigg's emerged from and shed light on the discomfort between the unclear boundaries between the "situation" and the "home." Throughout the century, servants were consistently linked with a perception of rising crime and declining morality, and pamphlets and treatises that warned of and bemoaned servant perfidy abounded. Defoe's comment is typical of the hyperbolic discourse regarding the perceived criminality of domestic servants: "Our sessions-papers are crowded with instances of servant-maids robbing their places, this can be only attributed to their devilish pride; for their whole inquiry nowadays is, how little they shall do, how much they shall have" (*Everybody's* 6).

Each murderess represented an opposite side of deep-seated cultural fear: Malcolm embodied employers' fears that they would be attacked in what should be the safety of their own beds; Brownrigg embodied servants' fear that employers might violate and even murder their domestic staff with impunity, that servants in fact had no "homes" but only "situations." Like a wife who kills her husband, to kill one's employer was a crime marked as extraordinarily dangerous and immoral—as petty treason rather than simple homicide. To kill one's servant, however, was not to commit a crime marked as extraordinary, even though—as in the case of spousal murder—the threat to one whose physical chastisement and subordination is legally assured is far greater than the reverse feared "rebellion." While no one would have argued that starvation and torture were appropriate methods of disciplining servants, such discipline, like that of wives by husbands, existed on a continuum in the eighteenth century—it was not the assault that was illegal per se but the extent of it. It is telling that, in an attempt to appeal to others of her class, Brownrigg defended her violence as necessitated by the girls' theft and lack of work ethic, trying to situate her behavior within a continuum of reasonable frustration and victimhood. Patty Seleski notes that while the press was concerned with presenting Brownrigg as the "ultimate 'bad mother'" to servants she was probably "less the bad mother … than the mistress from hell" (211, 212).

A 1767 comment in *The Annual Register* hints at the larger issues of social responsibility that surrounded Brownrigg's case; the writer insists upon the social context in which the crimes took place and the general culpability of the community in the violence. How, the writer asks, could such crimes remain uncommented upon? "Who could have believed," he writes, "that two wretches of the age of fifteen or sixteen years, could, in such a metropolis as London, and such a neighborhood as Fetter-Lane, continue to suffer as Mitchell and Clifford suffered for two years, without discovery or escape, especially as there was no other servant in the family but the apprentice-boy to go on errands" (197). The *Annual Register* calls attention to the community's role in Brownrigg's guilt and highlights the vulnerability of servants within the household or the abuse of the powerless by the powerful. [22]

Brownrigg's capacity for evil was contextualized exclusively according to her sex. She was painted as a sexually perverse woman—a madam or baby butcher—or she was defined as fatally un-feminine, not a woman at all.[23] Like Malcolm's body before her, Brownrigg's body was dissected and anatomized; however, in Brownrigg's case, the procedure was undertaken to reveal the physical signs that would prove she was not, in fact, biologically a woman (her skeleton is still in preservation today) (McAdoo 185). The objective of this anatomization was to prove Brownrigg was not physically female, that she had, despite her seemingly female body (including prodigious childbirthing), the physical attributes of a man. This desire to prove Brownrigg to be biologically male implies that for a man to commit such a terrible crime would be far more credible and less threatening than for a woman to have done so. If a woman's crime of violence could not be contextualized and contained within a narrative that read the criminal's life according to its revelation of unnatural sexual dispositions then that criminal body must be proved not to be female at all. Otherwise, what remains is the conclusion that all women's bodies present unreadable texts of possible fury that cannot be predicted or managed by lawful representation. For a male body to demonstrate this potential law-breaking fury was a fact both comprehensible and sometimes necessary in Augustan visions of masculine subjectivity; for a female body to do so was unimaginable and unspeakable.

Malcolm's and Brownrigg's crimes were read through the lens of their female bodies, rather than according to their individual, situational particularities. On trial was not only the individual woman who would live or die, but also the status of the female body itself as a category. The particularities of evidentiary issues were subsumed within a narrative of gender that relied on deep-seated attitudes about female nature. Malcolm's lack of conventional feminine attributes caused as well as proved her guilt, and the logic of her defense was levied as additional proof of her failure adequately to embody the feminine. Brownrigg was assumed to be either a monstrous specimen of her sex or a monstrous aberration from it. Specifics of context were erased as any woman charged with murder fell into a category of sexual deviance. The chain of circumstance necessary to support this claim relied on an irrefutable "fact": for a woman to commit an act of violence was either to violate her natural sex role or horrifically to embody it.

Eighteenth-century female criminal biographies position female subjectivity uncomfortably between the wishful idea that woman is inherently good and the fearful idea that she is inherently abhorrent. In these texts, the female criminal is defined in opposition to "true" womanhood, yet her configuration also reveals the underlying fear that violent criminality is, in fact, woman's true state. The biographies remain vested in the notion of femininity as a positive property, its

---

[22]   The trial took place amid a campaign to improve conditions for parish children.

[23]   The two approaches were about equal in number, according to surviving narratives.

presence recognizable by qualities such as passivity, propriety, thrift, and modesty. Simultaneously, they are invested in the notion of femininity as a negative property, recognizable by qualities such as assertiveness, immodesty, extravagance, and rapaciousness. In their framings of violent female criminals, these narratives move uncomfortably between these dual approaches. If the murderess is an "unwomanly" monster, the biography must delineate how one may read *all* female behavior so that one can recognize such a creature masquerading in one's community. If the explanation for female violence is that of unrestrained female nature, the biography must concern itself with the dangers of unregulated female nature. In either case, the texts, like conduct books, must concern themselves with the control of the behavior of all women, not simply those who have committed a crime.

Criminal biographies of violent women display the fear they work to repress: the possibility that any woman might explode into a murderous frenzy and that social codes cannot prevent this possibility. The schizophrenic imagining of criminally violent women relies on the erasure of particulars of context: the female criminal is defined categorically, not individually. She is imaginatively subsumed into a sex-defined type that refutes individuation even as it requires a discourse of improper individuation to support it. Within the discursive arena of the Augustan criminal biography, the female killer is at once she whose existence is impossible and she whose presence is inevitable.

Chapter 4
"The Confines of Virtue and the Frontiers of Vice": Daniel Defoe's *Roxana* and Henry Fielding's *Amelia*

And where are the Bounds between Duty and Crime? The Confines of Virtue reach
to the Frontiers of Vice, and where this ends that begins.

Daniel Defoe, *The Commentator*, No. 46 (June 10, 1720)

This chapter focuses on the portrayals of murderous women in two well-known eighteenth-century novels: Daniel Defoe's *Roxana, the Fortunate Mistress* (1724) and Henry Fielding's *Amelia* (1751). Defoe and Fielding are central players in critical discussions of the history of the novel; they are also essential to the newer scholarship of Augustan law and literature. The chapter draws from both legal and feminist approaches to eighteenth-century fiction to explore these novels' representations of the eighteenth-century female criminal subject. Positioning Defoe's and Fielding's novels in the context of my readings of nonfiction narratives of female crime and the fictional narratives of Behn and Manley provides new ways of thinking about these texts' imaginings of both gendered and criminal subjectivity. *Roxana* and *Amelia* demonstrate formal and plot links to *The History of the Nun, The Fair Jilt*, and *The Wife's Resentment*; however, in contrast to Behn's and Manley's novels, these texts provide explicitly didactic visions of social control that criminalize female agency and attempt to demonize female criminality. The novels, however, cannot fully sustain their regulatory missions. Like the criminal biographies of the previous chapter, these texts recursively reveal the basic paradoxes that underlie their limited visions of female criminality and, by extension, female nature. And yet *Roxana* and *Amelia* differ from the more static nonfiction prose narratives that inform them; as fiction, they share the complexity of voice and vision that Behn's and Manley's texts exhibit, a complexity that renders their murderesses tantalizingly available for readings that challenge the explicit moral agendas of their authors.

Representations of female homicide in these novels differ in important ways from those I discuss in Chapter 2. First, their plots do not center on the murderess or on murder. Roxana is a prostitute who is deeply implicated in, but does not commit, the murder of her daughter. Amy, Roxana's servant, is the novel's actual murderess, and yet it is the question of Roxana's guilt, not Amy's, that drives Defoe's narrative. In *Amelia*, the murderess, Miss Mathews, is a minor character that functions as a foil to the novel's eponymous heroine. With her fellow prisoner, Blear-Eyed Moll, Miss Mathews is presented less as a character in her own right than as a shorthand symbol of violently dystopic femininity.

Second, *Roxana* and *Amelia* include no explicit textual presentations of murder; they do not define their homicidal women through detailed expositions of violence. As we saw in the previous chapter, nonfiction narratives of the murderess include the gory details of her crime as "news" that shores up her monstrosity and irrational nature. Behn's and Manley's texts revel in the unrestrained textual license of their murderous women, engaging in gleefully detailed scenes of violent female agency, either through mordant humor or frenzied fantasy. In contrast, Defoe and Fielding offer restrained visions of female violence; their portrayals of female homicide are bled of graphic detail and occur entirely "off stage." The restraint of these portrayals does not result in the softening of the portrayal of the murderess's wicked nature but instead mutes her power in the text. In Defoe's and Fielding's novels, the murderess takes up little literal narrative space.

Third, *Roxana* and *Amelia* differ from the novels of Chapter 2 in that they share, at least in part, the criminal biographies' overt ideological project of preventing and restraining female criminality through a didactic plot. While these novels resemble earlier female-authored fictions in their critiques of men who fail at their patriarchal duties, they differ from them in their positing of marriage and its assumed correlatives—motherhood and domesticity—as the sole proper and desirable scope of female experience, however fraught.[1] To this end, each novel negatively contrasts female criminality with domestic, chaste, and maternal femininity: in Defoe's novel, an idealized female subject is implicit in what Roxana and Amy are not; in Fielding's novel, she is explicitly represented in Amelia herself.

Despite their conservative impulses, Defoe's and Fielding's novels, like Behn's and Manley's fictions, ultimately destabilize schematic notions of female violence. In fact, at the level of plot, Fielding's and Defoe's murderesses fare better than those of Behn or Manley: while Isabella and Violenta are praised and mourned, they are executed; in contrast, Amy and Miss Mathews live on, free of either juridical punishment or death. Neither *Roxana* nor *Amelia* excises its murderess, and each novel provides the material to critique the limits of its culturally orthodox visions of female violence. However, this destabilization is a function of the limits of the ideologies themselves rather than the overt project of the texts. In this way, these novels resemble the nonfiction narratives of the previous chapter and differ importantly from Behn's and Manley's fictions, fictions that explicitly position the murderess's crimes within a flawed legal and social system and advocate for the necessity and logical justice of increased female sovereignty. To read *Roxana* and *Amelia* in conversation with other eighteenth-century narratives of the murderess

---

[1]   In my use of the terms *domestic* and *domesticity*, I do not refer to a consolidated domestic but to a set of conventions of female positionality within a familial and patriarchal structure that predates the eighteenth century.

recalibrates the ongoing critical discussion about each text's configurations of both femininity and crime.

Roxana

"Whatever was done, Amy had done it."
—Daniel Defoe, *Roxana, or, the Fortunate Mistress* (1724)

To identify Amy as the murderess in *Roxana* and to consider her as a character worthy of explication in her own right reframes critical discussions of the text's presentations of female subjectivity. When we focus on Amy instead of Roxana as the text's violent criminal body, the novel reveals a set of concerns and assumptions we are otherwise unable to see. *Roxana*'s concern is the "proper" woman of a higher class who, when no longer properly contained by the plot of marital domesticity, joins forces with the lower-class female domestic in an alliance that produces violence and chaos.

Roxana is famous for its tension, at the level of plot and narration, between moral gestures and fetishistic delineation of the pleasures of its criminal antiheroine. Critic Madeleine Kahn persuasively argues that "to participate in *Roxana*, we must be willing to resist the anxious desire to fix Defoe reassuringly in one single narrative perspective" (69). I agree with Kahn and suggest that it is useful to consider this tension as evidence of the simultaneous structural and thematic influence of both feminocentric fictions and criminal and spiritual narratives. Not only does Defoe draw on these contesting narratives of female criminality, but also *Roxana*'s narration is multiply mediated, shifting between claimed autobiography and historical relation. The implied first-person discourse opens a space of reader identification with the criminal, implicitly untrustworthy, who is herself the source of the moral approbations that confound her (and our readings of her). Rather than a failed didactic text *or* an inelegant primer on female independence, *Roxana* exists simultaneously as a regulatory and revelatory vision of female violence and the imagined feminine self.

When we focus on Roxana herself as the novel's criminal woman, the text strikingly resembles the fictions of Chapter 2 in its incisive critiques of the perilous social positions of women, the negligence of men, and the ways in which female criminality may be caused or affected by situation rather than inexplicable alterity. While Defoe delineates Roxana's acts as increasingly wicked and impugns her motivations, the narrative imagines her as a character who *has* complex motivations rather than as simply a fiend in female form. As in *The History of the Nun* and *The Wife's Resentment*, Roxana's motivations for turning to prostitution are explained as logical, and the novel presents Roxana's sexual crimes and even her implication in Susan's murder within an identifiable frame of human reference rather than as evidence of inherent wickedness. Roxana's criminality is lamented and censured, but her initial fall into crime is not the result of a naturally "uncontrollable disposition" (*Newgate*, 1824, 170), but of unfortunate, and male-generated, circumstance. Despite its prefatory declaration to the contrary, the novel provides a paean to female independence and a radical critique of the limits of domestic femininity. *Roxana*'s focus on its heroine's sexual and monetary pleasure and its depiction of the logic that underlies her refusal of marriage and distaste for motherhood resembles the overt social critiques leveled in the novels of the "Fair Triumvirate."[2] Rather than positioning the home as dangerous because of uncontained female influence, Defoe dramatizes the ways in which the private sphere does not guarantee economic or affective security for women, and his fiction probes the dangers that lurk for women in the home. It is marriage that introduces Roxana to the deprivation that is the foundation for her entrance into crime and to the "masculine" world of capital exchange and accumulation, a world in which she proves eminently successful. Through Roxana's marriage with the brewer, Defoe scripts a plot often seen in early female-authored prose narratives: the account of an arranged marriage whose consequences to the woman prove disastrous. Her father marries her to a brewer who is the "foundation of [her] ruin" (7); when her husband leaves her impoverished, Roxana is left "all misery and distress"; she, her five children, and her servant are destitute. Like Behn and Manley, Defoe presents a plot driven not by providence, but by a woman's will to move outside of the plot of socially appropriate femininity when it does not reward her rightful action.

Roxana's desires for economic, sexual, and subjective liberty are presented as rational, and the novel luxuriates in the enumeration of their benefits. Yet the text finally defines the cost of such objectives and pleasures as too high. In contrast to Behn and Manley, Defoe uses elements of criminal biographies and spiritual autobiographies to elaborate the novel's concern with the state of the individual female criminal's soul and to argue that female salvation depends on woman's containment within the plot of chastity, marriage, and motherhood. Roxana's descent into prostitution and murder begins with the loss of her husband and home, and the novel's overlying message—one it cannot finally sustain—is that female crime occurs and women's souls are tragically "lost" when women are not properly contained within marriage. Roxana regularly bemoans her guilt and sin in passages that could come straight from a criminal biography; she cautions, for example, that "there can be no substantial Satisfaction in a Life of known Wickedness; Conscience will, and does, often break in upon them at particular times, let them do what they can to prevent it." If one takes Roxana, character and text, at face value in these moments of guilt, the novel may be read as a powerful moral exploration of the psychologically damning effects of shame and sin.

---

2   Interestingly, the novel's title was, according to Max Novak, "probably an allusion to *The Unfortunate Mistress* by Eliza Haywood" ("Defoe as an Innovator" 64). Novak points to an additional link between the novel and the "Fair Triumvirate" in his note that Roxana's views of marriage may have been modeled on Charles Gildon's version of Behn in *All the Histories and Novels Written by the Late Ingenious Mrs. Behn* 1700 (Novak *Realism* 164n31).

However, the novel's shifts between hyperbolic delineations of the gains Roxana receives by breaking free of domestic and maternal obligations and the horror that she has done so create a more disjunctive effect than such readings allow.[3] As Novak comments: "Money is power in Defoe's society, and Roxana, once reduced to a state of misery paralleling that of Job can choose how and where she wishes to live and in what state of opulence" (*Realism* 66). Roxana's descriptions of her sexual liaison with the prince point to the contradictions that fuel the narrative of her criminality. She comments that

> tho' Poverty and Want is an irresistible temptation to the Poor, Vanity and Great Things are irresistible to others. ... I was the Mistress of ten Thousand Pounds before the Prince did anything for me ... and [yet] I gave myself up to ... a Man ... [who] was the most tempting and obliging, that I ever met within my Life. (*Realism* 64-65)

Here Roxana acknowledges that she lacks the rationale of need to support her sexual pleasure. On the one hand, this passage is a typical formulation of the domino effect of women's departure from the moral path. Yet such a reading elides the presence of Roxana's undeniable exuberance. She does not berate herself overmuch for sleeping with the prince and relishes articulating her achievement of the "Great Things" of sexual and economic satisfaction. While the text is critical of the familiar figure of the libertine, Roxana is portrayed not as a one-dimensional character, but as a complex one that is never fully shut down or punished by the narrative.

The double-edged nature of the following account Roxana makes of her sin exemplifies the tension to which I point above: it provides evidence of Roxana's moral decline as it also validates her sexual and material power. The passage exemplifies the ways in which Roxana's pleasure in her body and her money is consistently bracketed with her discourses on the base status of each. Moments after admiring herself with the prince, bedecked in diamonds, she bemoans that she:

> knew what this Carcass of mine had been but a few Years before; how o'erwhelmed with Grief, drown'd in Tears, frightened with the Prospect of Beggary, and surrounded with Rags, and Fatherless Children ... and sat on the Ground, despairing of Help ... 'til my Children were snatch'd from me, to be kept by the Parish; I, that was after this, a Whore for Bread ... that I should be caress'd by a Prince, for the Honour of having the scandalous Use of my Prostituted Body, common before his Inferiours; and perhaps wou'd not have denied one of his Footmen but a little while if I cou'd have got my Bread by it. (74)

It is a critical commonplace that Defoe's narrative is replete with similar enumerations of the goods and pleasures that entice and engulf not only Roxana,

---

[3] See Novak, *Realism* 99–121, and Faller, *Crime* 200–44, for compelling readings to this effect.

but also the reader, no matter the counterpoint of restrained Whiggish commentary. Roxana replaces the scene of her seductive pleasure with that of her past want and misery, presenting the latter as a filter for the first in a move that justifies her status as a highly paid whore through her earlier need for "bread" (a term used since 1719 to refer to a means of subsistence as well as food). But the terms of exchange have changed: Roxana no longer trades for bread, but diamonds. She debases herself by insinuating that she could even be taken by the footman for bread, while she simultaneously exonerates herself with a distorted memory—misremembering that her children were "snatched from her" when in fact they were dispatched *by* her. Her memory of being dressed in rags, surrounded by needy children, and in tears is a useful counterpoint to her current position: lovely, loved, caressed, and bedecked in jewels.

The double-sided argument presented by the text suggests a criminal trial in which the attorneys for either side levy oppositional readings of the accused for the benefit of the judge/reader: the prosecution attacks Roxana's crimes, and the defense counters with her mitigating circumstances. However, were she at the bar, Roxana would necessarily be on trial for adultery or for prostitution, not for murder, or even conspiracy to commit murder, despite her moral implication in her daughter's homicide. *Roxana* is fundamentally unconcerned with either the soul or the story of its *actual* murderess. In contrast to Roxana's guilt—or to that of socially stable historical murderesses Elizabeth Brownrigg or Mary Blandy— Amy's guilt does not require extensive narrative inquiry to square it against the notions of natural femininity her crime belies. Rather, Amy's position as servant renders her capacity for homicide unsurprising; like the position of the Catholic laundress Sarah Malcolm, her class status both explicates and underlines her guilt.[4] Defoe's disinterest in Amy in any other than a relational sense is paralleled in the critical history of this novel, one in which critics overwhelmingly focus on Amy as a vehicle by which we can better understand Roxana herself.

Focusing on Amy as the murderess calls attention to different tensions in this famously attenuated text. *Roxana* may be read as offering a radical view of some women's sexuality and social limitations, despite or in addition to its contrary narrative impulses, but the novel does not meaningfully address the woman for whom the idealized domestic is never a possibility because she herself is a domestic. I will argue, however, that despite its surface narrative disinterest in Amy's story, it is through her story and what is elided from it that Defoe's narrative ultimately reveals the contradictions and fears that underlie its assumptions about women, class, and violence.

Critics of the novel have framed Amy as the monstrous source of Roxana's downfall, an exemplar of Roxana's monstrosity, or as an aspect or facet of Roxana's split self.[5] As my focus in this project is representation of the murderess herself,

---

4   See Chapter 3 for an extensive discussion of these cases.

5   See Braudy, "Daniel Defoe"; Castle, "'Amy'"; Durant; Faller, *Crime* 200–44; Gladfelder 131–50; Hammond; Hentzi; Kahn 57–102; Moglen 44–52; Novak, *Realism*

I do not approach the location of female criminal behavior onto the socially fraught body of the servant as primarily significant as a narrative enactment of familial or criminal psychosocial relations. Rather, considering, instead of simply naming, Amy as the murderous woman shifts the terms by which she, and the novel, have been read. I am concerned with the ways in which *Roxana* imagines the *particular* body of its murderess—Amy—and the terms by which it frames *her* crime.

From the novel's beginning, Amy's status as servant complicates our understanding of its engagement with notions of femininity and of criminality. For example, the erasure of paid domestic labor as even an option for the impoverished Roxana interestingly suggests that for a woman to transgress class boundaries is more unthinkable than for her to transgress moral and/or sexual ones. Despite their social differences, as women both Roxana and Amy have limited options as a result of Roxana's abandonment by her feckless husband. In some ways, Roxana's and Amy's options are similar: without a husband, Roxana turns to prostitution, and without employment, prostitution is also a potential plot for Amy. Defoe, in a 1725 tract, bluntly defines the options for female servants who lose their positions as prostitution or death: "If they are out of Place, they must Prostitute their bodies or starve" (*Everybody's* 5). In fact, Amy at least has the option of attempting to gain employment as a servant elsewhere, something the text does not even consider for Roxana, who considers and abandons the idea of work at the needle as not viable.

Perhaps the most compelling dramatization of the inequities of class position between Amy and her mistress is that of Amy's rape by the landlord, or, as Roxana terms it, "Amy's Disaster." In this critically contested scene, Roxana strips Amy, pushes her into bed with the landlord, and watches him rape her so that, as she explains, "my Maid should be a Whore too, and should not reproach me with it." Critics commonly read the jarring scene as evidence of Roxana's increasingly criminal nature and immoral or "unnatural" actions. Critics have also described the scene as Roxana's revenge—justified or otherwise—on Amy for pushing her mistress to sin by her use of "Rhetorick"—her encouragement of Roxana to have sex with the landlord and to accept his definition of a marriage. The scene reads differently when looked at specifically through the lens of class. First, Roxana's

---

99–120. Hammond, for example, argues that "the maid Amy, whose loyalty to her has been so powerful throughout her life, and with whom she has almost mystically bonded by the sharing of sexual partners, has become a loose cannon, pursuing her own monomaniacal mission to murder Susan" (228), and Faller refers to Amy as "Mr. Hyde." Castle argues for their status as doubled character, claiming that "Amy is the secret sharer in Roxana's life: she acts out her mistress's fantasies, she accepts the functions Roxana projects, both consciously and unconsciously, onto her … Amy and Roxana share a paradoxical relation of sameness and otherness" (84). Gladfelder contends that the text displaces its violence onto Amy in ways that implicate the upper-class heroine: "Defoe suggests through his shadowing of Roxana, the most damaging crimes emerge from the repressed inward violence of the respectable self" (144).

physical control over Amy's person and her sexual chastity dramatically enacts the class differences between them. To contend that Amy "deserves" her rape at Roxana's hands because of her "Rhetorick" erases this difference and requires a number of logical leaps that do not hold up to inspection: the reader must accept that a maid would have such power over her mistress; she must erase Roxana's self-will; and she must rely on Roxana's version of events, as it is Roxana who makes the self-interested claim that Amy is the "Viper, and Engine of the Devil" responsible for her sexual sins. Amy is necessarily more pragmatic than her bourgeois mistress and is in no position to "force" her mistress to do anything. As Novak argues, her "Rhetorick" of sex rather than starvation is one supported by natural law (*Realism* 102). For Amy, want trumps wantonness as something justly to be feared; as she tells her Roxana "if I will starve for your sake, I will be a Whore, or any thing, for your sake; why I would die for you, if I were put to it" (62). Rather than a declaration of demonic loyalty or moral equivocation, this statement may be read as a pragmatic and sobering comment on Amy's social and economic reliance on her mistress and her powerlessness to remedy their economic crisis.

In contrast to this reading, critic Helene Moglen views Amy not as a victim, but as an active participant in the scene. Moglen argues that:

> Amy participates in the landlord's game of seduction by playing pimp and acting as a voyeur. Roxana then reverses their roles, undressing her maid, thrusting her into the landlord's bed, and remaining to watch their coupling. Amy must not only be neutralized as Roxana's conscience, she must share her mistress's pleasures and desire. (48)

To read Amy's rape as shared "pleasures and desire," is to erase the violence and class inequity of the scene.[6] Amy's lost sexual innocence is caused by Roxana and is not self-generated; thus her "fall" into criminality should rightfully be more poignant and mitigating than that of her mistress. And yet, for Defoe, and for many critics, Amy's rape is of interest for what it tells us about her mistress, and Amy's loss of virtue is treated, by the narrator and critics, as of far less consequence than that of Roxana. Similarly, Amy's birthing and abandonment of a child by the landlord is not a narrative issue and is rarely mentioned by critics—her illegitimate lower-class offspring, like her virtue, is seen as important only as a foil to Roxana's upper-class plot.

According to a conventional plot articulated in criminal biographies, female violence must be relocated from the aristocratic and lovely body to the lower-class less "valuable" body. Defoe's portrayal of Amy reveals cultural anxieties about the roles both of servants and of women; like women, servants functioned as a catchall

---

⁶ In addition, as a student pointed out in our class discussion, to blame Amy or Roxana is effectually to erase the landlord's responsibility as the instigator of both the "Rhetorick" and the actual sexual violence.

for anxieties about shifting social arrangements and fears of criminality.[7] In this light, Amy exists as a cardboard cutout of female criminal violence, a stock figure from a criminal biography rather than—as one may argue for her mistress—one from the fiction of Behn or Manley. According to such a view, Amy's moral and sexual status as a woman (a debauched virgin, a mother) is less important because of her class status. Her poor moral status, as exemplified by her encouragement of Roxana to prostitute herself, is inherently located in her debased nature, a nature aligned with her class. Such a reading damns Amy as a lady *manquée*, evoking the familiar tropes of dangerous servant and social pretender.

Read thus, Amy is a character "utterly corrupted save for her intense loyalty to her mistress" (Faller, *Crime* 225). And yet it is precisely this exception to her monstrosity that Faller notes—Amy's servile loyalty—that is interesting and worthy of investigation for the ways in which it operates at multiple levels and refutes easy configurations of both her character and the novel's narrative of female homicide. Defoe's question—"Where are the Bounds between Duty and Crime?" (see the epigraph with which I frame this section)—takes on a particular resonance when we read "Duty" in the context of servitude. As her maidservant, Amy is subject to Roxana: her duty, in both narrative and plot, is to serve her mistress. Roxana notes that she "was always at my Elbow" (238), and indeed this is where she should have been according to contemporary delineations of the maidservant's role. Throughout the novel, Amy is described as an ideal servant: she is "diligent," a "clever manager," and "a resolute Girl" who adroitly mitigates Roxana's needs, desires, and contact with the outside world. While this role is open to useful psychological readings (see note 5 in the introduction to this volume), it is also an accurate description of the concrete expectations of an eighteenth-century servant.

On the one hand, Amy's guilt in the novel is mitigated because of her dutiful position. If Roxana, as mistress, is the instigator of her loyal servant's actions, then Amy is the selfless servant who is the tool of the authorized heroine. When looked at from this angle, Amy's dispatching of Roxana's children by the brewer, her defense of Roxana's decision to bed the landlord, and her continual service to Roxana throughout the novel—culminating in the murder of Susan—may be framed in the context of her role as obedient servant.

Amy's faithfulness to the beleaguered and impoverished Roxana initially evokes a romanticized devotion that signifies a servant's economic and moral value, a value figured in terms of the servant's unquestioning acceptance of her servile *identity* rather than position. Roxana comments that "to the Praise of this poor Girl, my Maid, that tho' I was not able to give her any Wages ... yet she would not leave me ... [she is as] faithful to me, as the Skin to my Back" (16, 25). The idealized vision of the loyal servant imagines the servant as part of an affective domestic alliance that serves her desire as well as that of her mistress, and it thus

---

[7]   As I will discuss later in this section, Amy is partially a threat because of the potential (if not probable) social mobility inherent in a class- versus a status-based system.

perniciously denies the economics that govern the mistress/servant relationship. In his tract *Everybody's Business Is Nobody's Business* Defoe bemoans the absence of an ideal of loyalty from servant to master and argues that loyalty should be legislated. He advocates new laws to ensure that servants "should be restrain'd from throwing themselves out of place" (*Everybody's* 25). Defoe's language suggests both violence and anxiety: servants must be forced to remain in their "places"—of employment and society—or they will violently abandon them. Such a configuration belies the trope Amy's free labor suggests as it points to the utter folly of the notion that a servant in a class- versus caste-based society would work for free.

Within the mercantile system of *Roxana*, Amy's selfless acceptance of her lot and her load thus simultaneously mitigates her guilt and calls into question her motives. For Amy's devotion to her mistress also embodies a horrible excess of duty, a duty that is itself a crime: as Roxana notes, Amy kills Susan as an act of fealty: "owing to her Excess of Care for my Safety" (317) and her "steddy Kindness to me" (317). In this light, Amy's figurative status as part of her mistress's body—"the Skin" to Roxana's "Back"—is a source of textual unease as well as a naturalized model of class loyalty. Contemporary critics, such as Terry Castle, have explored the suggestive and disturbing nature of Roxana's sexualized simile, linking it to the presence of a shadowy lesbian erotics or a psychic doubling. Whatever lens one brings to the image, its visceral nature emphasizes the closeness and the narrative longevity of Roxana's and Amy's attachment. (It is worth noting that the comment is related through the free direct discourse of Roxana's accounting *after* Amy's murder of Susan.) That Amy remains with Roxana without remuneration suggests that their bond is based on affect rather than economics. That she is unpaid for her labor removes the contractual economic link between the two women, hinting at an older model of fealty with which Defoe was uncomfortable.

Amy's extreme loyalty, her hyperbolic duty, however, also offers a space by which to critique a flawed system.[8] Notions of proper servitude, like those of proper femininity, required loyalty and the sublimation of the servant's self to the mistress's desire and then condemned the servant for following immoral orders. The paradoxical nature of this formulation recalls that of the married woman who has no legal identity unless she is charged with the murder of her husband. In the case of the servant, the condemnation assumes a right of and capacity for refusal that is predicated on her having that very self-will and ability to "rebel" for which she is castigated. This formulation suggests the disturbing logical extension of ideas of servitude: it implies that no moral core is possible if one must always act on or act out another person's desires. Ideas of femininity and of servitude (or slavery) based on inherent difference contend that the woman, servant, or slave

---

    8   Or a flawed heroine; Gladfelder persuasively contends that Roxana, rather than Defoe, is the one who displaces the guilt onto the servant body of Amy: "far from being confined to a distinct social class, Defoe suggests through his shadowing of Roxana, the most damaging crimes emerge from the repressed inward violence of the respectable self" (144).

is, by virtue of position or nature, fundamentally other than the authorized social subject and thus unworthy of equal legal and social rights and privileges. When the subservient "other" commits a legal crime these notions reveal their patent illogic: to hold someone legally responsible implies her status as an authorized subject, a status and responsibility that narratives of naturally debased social status or debased class position refute.

Defoe's hyperbolic rendition of Amy's selflessness recalls the ways in which Behn and Manley similarly constructed their murderous antiheroines in conventional terms so overdetermined they beg critical attention. In each case, the extremity of the depictions—ideal and horrific—that constitute the conventional type—woman or servant—calls attention to the absurdity of the terms of that type itself. And yet Behn and Manley create narrators who clearly align themselves with their murderous characters and the critiques their texts mount regarding conventions of femininity. In contrast, Defoe's portrayal of Amy, while open to counterreadings, tellingly suggests horror at a world gone topsy-turvy.

According to the logic of Defoe's novel, the relationship between Amy and Roxana is too close for comfort, and the blurred class lines between them create a powerful narrative disquiet. For while readers may balk at Roxana's existence as a "She-Merchant," and her resultant mercantile success, Amy's increased social and economic power poses an even more dangerous threat, as she is both female and lower class. Amy's class transgression comes up early when she "put on her best Clothes too, and came down dress'd like a Gentlewoman" (31). Amy's sartorial sin occurs at the dinner during which Roxana will finally agree to have sex with the landlord. Amy's dressing "up" is usefully glossed by Defoe's writings elsewhere on the dangers of misreading the bodies and thus the statuses of female servants, as these comments suggest the discursive arena in which the novel's imaginings of servants take place. Defoe calls for a return to sumptuary laws that would prohibit the misidentification of servants due to dress: "[T]he Apparel of our Women-Servants should be ... regulated, that we may know the Mistress from the Maid" (*Everybody's* 13, 17). He analogizes this problem of mistress misidentification to an illness whose "first Symptoms are only trifling ... but by Continuance and progression, their Periods terminate in the Destruction of the whole Humane Fabrick." It is the potential of the lower-class female body for social and sexual mobility that poses a danger both serious and common enough that it should be criminalized. By the middle of the novel, Amy embodies Defoe's dreaded and deadly hybrid: she is dressed "like a Gentlewoman" with three maids, a coachman, and a footman who, Roxana explains, were "particularly order'd to show her the same Respect as they wou'd to me, and to call her Madam Collins" (194). Here, the closeness between Roxana and Amy may be read, not as a pastoral of servant devotion, but as a connection between women that dangerously belies appropriate class divisions: both women "throw themselves out of place" (*Everybody's* 25).

It is a critical commonplace that Susan's murder at the novel's end is a strangely disjunctive plot device through which the narrative seems laboriously to attempt to restrain and rework the illicit pleasure the novel has so far granted its reader. If we look at Amy as a character in her own right, then the locus of female criminality shifts from the fallen heroine and her monstrous shadow self to the material partnership of two women of differing classes, each of whom is necessary for the committal of a murder. Amy eventually becomes a business woman, wealthy in her own right, and by the end of the novel she has successfully moved out of her servant status and become "partnered" with her bourgeois employer. In addition to wealth, Amy becomes Roxana's "companion" (105) and has "[a]uthority to manage everything in the Family" (197). Here we see the carnivalesque social order Defoe fears: "[I]n a little time our Servants will become our Partners; nay, probably, run away with the better Part of our Profits, and make Servants of us vice versa" (*Everybody's* 15). But rather than gaining her upward mobility through heterosexual romance, like Pamela, through which the servant *cum* lady is still subjugated through patriarchal marriage, Amy shifts her status through an illicit and ultimately deadly partnership with another woman. This narrative disquiet culminates in Amy's final act of "service": the murder of Roxana's eldest daughter and namesake, Susan.

The Susan plot is complex enough to merit a brief recapitulation: Susan is Roxana's eldest daughter by the brewer; she has been in service as a chambermaid and eventually, in a highly unlikely plot device, as a cook/maid of Roxana herself, until she is fired by Amy so that she does not discover her parentage. Roxana has retired from prostitution and married the Dutch merchant when Susan eventually tracks her down and threatens to expose her past through her insistence that Roxana claim her as her legitimate daughter by the brewer. Once Susan suspects Roxana of being her mother, she doggedly pursues her, a pursuit consistently deflected by Amy at Roxana's behest. When Amy suggests murdering Susan, Roxana castigates her in terms that explicitly equate the thought of murder with the act. She declares that "having resolv'd on it, is doing it, as to the Guilt of the Fact; you are a Murtherer already, as much as if you had done it already" (272). In this superficially moral declaration, Roxana effectively gives Amy room to commit the murder as she judges her guilty of it already, a conclusion Amy makes explicit in her retort that killing Susan in fact "can be no worse" than desiring it, and both Amy and Roxana desire her dead.

Ironically, it is Roxana's transformation back into a woman with a reputation to protect that puts her at risk, and it is the domestic—in both senses of the word—that proves her undoing. It is Roxana's decision to provide economic support to her long-abandoned children that provides Susan the key to her origins, and it is Roxana's marriage that makes Susan's exposure of her maternal status a threat. Roxana has practical reasons to avoid her daughter's claims: conventional notions of femininity would put her marriage at risk, and her lack of legal self-sovereignty puts her money at risk. As a married and respectable woman with a title—and no further ownership or control of her own fortune—Roxana has much to lose. Her fears that her daughter will make her simply another "German Princess" speak to a fear not only of being the object of public ruin but also of losing her entire income and being too old to remake a fortune through sex-work.

Critical discussion of the import of the murder tends to elide the complex relationship Defoe poses between Amy and Susan and to center on the mother–daughter relation between Susan and Roxana. It is crucial, however, to attend to the fact that, whatever Susan's origins, both Amy and Susan are servants, and each is or has been a servant of Roxana's. Both women also rely on Roxana for economic and social mobility out of the limitations of that shared role: Amy by the authority and wealth she has gained as Roxana's companion and manager, Susan by the money she has been given through Amy and by the increased income and the bourgeois status she would presumably gain if she were acknowledged as Roxana's legitimate daughter.

Defoe emphasizes the link between Amy and Susan with the fact that Susan first takes Amy for her mother. While Roxana and Susan share blood ties, their connection is marked as meaningful because of the *absence* of any intimate connection between them. For all her retroactive claims of maternal *jouissance* in Susan's presence, an erotics that suggests narcissism more than nurture, the novel systematically portrays Roxana's relation to maternity in terms more common to having a litter of kittens than our post-Romantic notions of motherhood. It is Amy, not Roxana, who develops a frequent and "intimate acquaintance" with Susan (206).

It would seem that Amy's betrayal of the "intimate acquaintance" she shares with Susan, another upwardly mobile female servant, should make the murdering of Susan more terrible and Amy herself more culpable, as she violently kills a woman with whom she has become close and who poses her no personal threat. And yet most critics, and the novel itself, position Susan's homicide as meaningful because of the ways in which it signifies Roxana's abdication of her maternal role and/or the nature of Amy's link to Roxana rather than to Susan. Reading Susan according to contemporary notions of abandonment or loss imbues her death with poignancy, as we see in Faller's moving descriptions of Susan and Roxana: "Roxana's daughter loves her (poor creature!) and means her no harm. All she really seems to want to do is to throw herself at her mother's feet" (*Crime* 235). "[H]ow could any mother retell this tale as Roxana does, with only an occasional, intermittent sense of what is properly at stake? … Her heart remains unpierced and iron-natured to the end" (*Crime* 68). While I share Faller's horror at the level of plot, issues of class complicate the dynamics of gender in the novel and render the murder and its context less clear-cut. Susan's status as a servant trumps her origins, and recognizing that her murder is one of a servant by a servant changes its resonance in the novel.

However wronged she may be in the family romance, Susan is presented in the text as an unappealing character. While she is Roxana's abandoned daughter by her first marriage, Susan's entire role in the novel is that of a servant, and an ambitious one at that. As Novak contends, "Susan is not to be regarded as an innocent, loving daughter seeking maternal affection, for Roxana has failed her both as a parent and as a member of the upper classes" (*Realism* 108). In the cosmology of *Roxana*, circumstantial reasons for ignominy do not erase its stain, and once a woman has "fallen"—whether into sexual sin, criminality, or servitude—she cannot regain her previous status. When Susan hears of the largesse that her brother has received (from Amy, acting as Roxana's agent) and thinks she has missed her chance of receiving her share, she bemoans: "I have lost it all, and all the Hopes of my being any-thing, but a poor Servant all my Days" (196). Susan's desire for upward mobility is never located in her "misplacement" from her upper-class origins, but is presented as the threatening (and logical) longing of any servant to escape her lowly status and climb the social ladder.

Roxana's response to Susan's reaction to her gift of money to move Susan out of servitude reveals that Roxana views her daughter as a servant, regardless of her economic status or her origins: "The Girl was overjoy'd with this News, you may be sure, and at first a little too much elevated with it, and dress'd herself very handsomely indeed" (198). Roxana herself is consistently "overjoy'd" at her economic successes and "handsome" appearance; her appreciation of her plate and her beauty takes up a great deal of narrative space in the novel. One may read Susan's vanity and greed as an example of inherited character, a reading enhanced by the fact that Susan is Roxana's given name. However, the novel positions the cause of such illicit female behavior as the woman's expulsion or departure from the class and domestic arenas that should properly contain her. Roxana's and Amy's criminal behavior stems from their circumstantial misplacement in the social schema, and Susan, too, is implicated in the novel's vision of the dangers of women "thrown out of place."

Since we view the novel through the lens of its antiheroine, while Roxana's distaste for her daughter points to her failure as a mother, it also affects our readerly judgment of Susan, and by extension Susan's murder. As well as an economically ambitious servant, Susan is described in terms more frequently used to describe a stalker than a love-sick child. Her daughter's existence affects Roxana like "being upon the Rack" (278). After learning that Susan plans to follow her on her travels, Roxana complains: "I was continually perplex'd with this Hussy"; she "haunted me like an Evil Spirit" (301). While Roxana waxes outraged at Amy's vocal willingness to murder Susan to protect Roxana's interests, she makes it clear that she, too, desires her difficult daughter's demise. The following passage, in which she recounts this desire after Susan has already been murdered, is indicative of Roxana's wickedness, but its strangely burlesque tone also works against our reading of Susan's death with any tragic solemnity.

> It is true, I wanted as much to be deliver'd from her, as ever a Sick-Man did from a Third-Day Ague; and had she dropp'd into the Grave by any fair Way, as I may call it; I mean had she died by any ordinary Distemper, I shou'd have shed but a very few Tears for her. (302)

Here, Roxana responds to the murder of her eldest child by clarifying it is the *means* of her death that is upsetting, not the fact of it. Susan's death by any "fair Way," a scale determined by Roxana, one assumes with great leeway, would have been a fine outcome. She describes her recently murdered daughter as an "ague," refers to her death in oddly crude and comic terms (she "dropp'd into the Grave"), and straightforwardly admits her desire to be "deliver'd" from her by death (rather than considering any other less drastic measure by which Susan could be dispatched as a threat). Roxana also recalls her murdered daughter's threat in terms of servitude: "I must for-ever after have been this Girl's Vassal" (280). For Roxana, murder is a better option than serving, particularly than serving a servant who has "thrown herself out of place."

In *Roxana*'s moral economy, Susan's death only matters in any *particular* sense when read through her association with Roxana's upper-class, if debased, body. Defoe includes nothing about the murder to frame our response to her death as specifically tragic in terms of Susan's victimization rather than Roxana's wickedness. The text does not generate nearly as much energy for the murder as it does for Roxana's enumeration of assets or lovers, and the effects of guilt Defoe assigns Roxana are ambiguous. Textually, the murder is strangely absent of detail. Susan's homicide is only obliquely referred to, never described. The displacement of any actual discussion of the murder works to mute rather than stress its import and power. We are never specifically told that Amy kills Susan, and we are told nothing about the details of Susan's death; rather this central event is hinted at and dismissed. Roxana recounts that she had a "fear the wicked Jade shou'd make [Susan] away which my very Soul abhorr'd the Thoughts of; which, however, *Amy* found Means to bring to pass afterwards; *as I may in time, relate more particularly*" (220). Her more particular relation is as follows: "*as I said, Amy* effected all afterwards, without my Knowledge, for which I gave her my hearty Curse ... But this Tragedy requires a longer Story than I have room for here: *I return to my Journey*" (350). While one can argue that this displacement demonstrates the horror of the scene, such a reading seems unlikely in a novel replete with the almost frenetic elaboration of concrete details. Rather, Susan's murder is described in terms very like those used to describe Roxana's illegitimate births and abandoned children. In both cases, we are told the act happened, appraised of its immorality and of Roxana's guilty conscience, but the terms of the telling are so oblique it is hard to keep track of what we are actually being told. There is simply no "room" in the narrative for the murder itself, an accounting of which would by necessity foreground and particularize the servants—murderess and victim—rather than the absent mistress.

Whatever Defoe's intent, the novel does not support a vision of Roxana's collapse or of the collapse of the narrative because of the loss of one more of her oft-abandoned or misplaced offspring. Even if we accept the existence of an early eighteenth-century maternal economy by which Roxana is deemed monstrous, the blood of her child is not literally on her hands, no matter how she may be implicated. Rather, we have a murder of a female servant by another female servant, a deed to be castigated, but one that is within the bounds of conventional eighteenth-century narrative expectation. Isabella and Violenta confound social and narrative expectation as they kill across class lines and across gender lines, murdering those in positions of unearned power; and through them, Behn and Manley crafted sly narrative commentaries on the absurdity of contemporaneous visions of women's nature and unequal status under the law. In *Roxana*, however, the murderess is of a class that erases expectations of positive conventions of femininity, and her victim is of a class and a gender that renders her death an unfortunate event, but not a threat to social signification.

What *is* a threat to social signification in this novel is not the "particular" act of murder or the "particular" body of the murderess but the "particular" affiliation of the maid and the mistress—the deadly and generative capacity of their collaboration and conspiracy as partners in crime. Like Behn and Manley, Defoe imagines his textual female homicide through a murderous cross-class female alliance. In *Roxana*, however, such a vision is a terrifying one. And yet, while the novel legislates against the dangers of its cross-class female bond, *Roxana* has, in its final effects, much in common with Manley's text in its articulations of the logic of such female criminal alliances. In both *The History of the Nun* and *The Wife's Resentment*, the murderesses rely upon their female servants for essential help in the murders of their spouses. In Behn's text, however, the alliance is based on abused fealty rather than active female partnership. Isabella's maid Maria is the unwitting protector of her mistress when she agrees to keep secret Isabella's late-night visit from her first husband, an agreement the maid makes because of her love of and loyalty to her idealized mistress: "all that her mistress said was gospel" (188). While duty may be misplaced here, it is not criminally so. In Manley's text, however, the slave Ianthe is an active participant in the actual plotting and murder of Violenta's errant husband; her role is never criticized, and she is paid for her help with money and freedom. In both *The Wife's Resentment* and *Roxana*, servants and mistresses forge illicit and ultimately deadly partnerships for their own gain. While Defoe is clearly discomfited by his female characters' self-motivated alliance, the novel ultimately fails to discipline either its murderess or her criminal accomplice, who exit the novel together and free of any domestic bonds. Amy and Roxana flourish for some years after Susan's murder, seemingly enjoying themselves and their wealth. Neither Amy nor Roxana is convicted or executed, nor do they die at the vengeful hand of providence. Rather, they end the novel together, free of husbands and legal consequences.

The novel's truncated ending demonstrates the success and the nature of the destructive cross-class link between the murderous maid and her scheming mistress. The concluding paragraph censoriously nods toward bad fortune but in terms so vague and syntactically oblique as to approach the patently bizarre. Roxana comments:

> I fell into a dreadful Course of Calamities, and Amy also; the very Reverse of our former Good Days; the Blast of Heaven seem'd to follow the Injury done the poor Girl by us both; and I was brought so low again, that my Repentance seem'd to be only the Consequence of my Misery, as my Misery was of my Crime. (330)

The "dreadful Course of Calamities" into which she and Amy fall is "the very Reverse of our former Good Days." As "good days" for Roxana and Amy imply wealthy days of prostitution and child-free existence, it is unclear of what their reverse would consist. The "Blast of Heaven" only *"seem'd"* to "follow the *Injury* done the poor Girl" (emphasis added). The "Blast," whatever it was, may have had nothing to do with Susan's death, a murder that Roxana has rescripted to an "injury"—neither syntactic move suggests Roxana's radical remorse or change. For Roxana repents, if indeed she does, only as a consequence of *misery*, not guilt. And Roxana has levied such protestations of guilt throughout the narrative, guilt that should, in the textual economy of the criminal biography, result in the cessation of sin.[9] But, as Faller notes, Roxana's expressions of guilt and repentance are consistently followed by more sinning, a cycle that suggests at the level of form that Roxana and Amy will continue, as they have throughout the novel, to circulate as active sinners.

Roxana claims she requires an "account" from Amy of her innocence of the murder, and yet she accepts Amy back without any accounting at all. Roxana explains, when describing her inability to manage her estate without her partner, that Amy "kept my Accounts" (366), not the reverse. The novel cannot finally "account" for Amy nor hold her "accountable"—in either sense of the word. There is no "accounting" for these two criminal women who move together outside of the heroine's plot of marriage and death. Rather than a psychic doubling or prismatic vision of "woman," the relationship between Amy and Roxana suggests an intimate cross-class bond between women that trumps the marital and the maternal. Defoe's novel vision of the link between the servant murderess and her prostitute mistress replicates destructive and rote notions of female criminality as it simultaneously enlivens and is enlivened by the collaborative female criminal agency it attempts to repress.

Amelia

> "You hear the resentment of the most injured of women. You have heard, you say, of the murder, but do you know the cause?"
>
> —Henry Fielding, *Amelia*

As I state in the introduction to this chapter, Henry Fielding's novel and paean to wifely virtue, *Amelia*, shares crucial elements with *Roxana* in its representations of the murderess. Like Amy, the murderous Miss Mathews is a secondary character that exists as a foil to the novel's eponymous protagonist; and as in *Roxana*, the violence takes place "off stage." Fielding, however, mocks female violence and thus erases the import and the power of the murderess as a threat to individual and social bodies. In contrast to Amy's crime, which, while invisible, is essential

---

9   See Faller's and Kahn's previously cited chapters on *Roxana*.

to *Roxana*'s plot, Miss Mathews's homicidal rage is, at first glance, peripheral to the novel's design; we hear of the murder as part of what will become the far more central crime in the novel: the "criminal conversation" (149) between Miss Mathews and the virtuous Amelia's husband, William Booth—a long exchange in which she and Booth tell one another their stories and which precedes their adulterous affair.[10]

Fielding's novel—like Defoe's and like nonfiction accounts of the murderess—articulates a moral goal that rests upon traditional ideological formulations of female nature that imagine female violence as inexcusable and that criminalize female agency.[11] *Amelia's* bifurcated vision of femininity evokes both criminal biographies and conduct literature; the novel opposes idealized passive femininity and demonized active femininity to dramatize the import of stable marriage and family as the source of civic harmony. As critics such as Jill Campbell and John Zomchick have argued, *Amelia* suggests that affective female morality is the sole remedy for a debauched public sphere; the novel explicitly positions the redemptive power of the lady as the cure for the toxicity of England's "Diseases in the Political Body" (Fielding, *An Enquiry* 75), diseases that include a dysfunctional and deadly legal system. In this vein, as Zomchick explains, Fielding posits female criminals—particularly Miss Mathews—in clear opposition to the domestic ideal, Amelia, whose role is to ameliorate masculinity and nation. The novel contrasts the restrained figure of the female exemplar, the beleaguered wife Amelia, with the excessive figures of the novel's female criminals—particularly Miss Mathews and the monstrous prisoner, Blear-Eyed Moll.

---

[10]   The term "criminal conversation" (crim. con.) also refers to a tort law regarding adultery. The first cases of crim. con. dated from the 1690s; Lawrence Stone defines crim. con. as "a writ of trespass, the theory being that, by using the body of the wife, the seducer had damaged the property of her husband, for which he could sue for damages, like any other tort" (*Broken Lives* 23). These actions were highly popular in the 1750s, when Fielding published *Amelia*. Crim. con. actions were solely concerned with female adultery; just as a woman could not use male adultery as grounds for divorce, so too, crim. con. was a legal avenue open only to men. In these cases, it is once again femininity, here explicitly female sexuality, that is on trial: the plaintiff and defendant did not debate the fact of the adultery, but the passivity or activity of the wife's sexual nature. What is disputed is whether or not the wife instigated the action (in which case the husband rarely collected) or whether she was the innocent, passive partner and the unsuspecting victim of the defendant's seduction, in which case the husband could collect substantive damages (Binhammer 7).

[11]   However, the novel differs sharply from criminal biographies in its articulation of the need for legal reform; for example, Fielding opens the novel with a series of scenes of miscarriages of justice that mount a radical critique of the class, national, and sex biases at play in England's legal system. The novel opens with a flat rejection of the law as an always-successful arbiter of morality. The "trading justice" called "Thrasher" operates with a cynicism and venality Fielding strongly indicts and symbolizes judicial corruption; by the end of the second chapter he has erroneously committed the novel's hero, Booth, to Newgate.

Like *Roxana*, however, *Amelia* reveals the paradoxes at work in such frangible conventional formulations of female nature. Ultimately *Amelia*, like *Roxana*, presents a complex vision of female criminal violence that challenges the novel's overt regulatory agenda. Fielding's plot, like Defoe's, belies the novel's thematic moral thrust. Rather than dying of shame, being executed, or even living under a cloud (as in *Roxana*), *Amelia's* female criminals exit the novel alive and happy: Miss Mathews is wealthy and married in the colonies, and the prisoner Blear-eyed Moll continues to reign "merrily" in Newgate.[12]

In addition, while Fielding does not explicitly take on the limitations of women as juridical subjects and their exclusion from civic power, as do Behn and Manley, he provides evidence for the ways in which patriarchy and economics entwine to motivate female criminality as well as to engender women's wrongful convictions. For example, early in the novel, Fielding introduces a female servant who is falsely accused of being a whore and is wrongly found guilty and sentenced to prison for a month—she cannot prove her innocence as she cannot afford to send for her neighbors as witnesses (17). In this instance, Fielding reveals the ways in which poverty and sex combine wrongly to define a woman as criminal.

Finally, despite its conservative impulses, Fielding's novel crafts a moral argument that explicitly resembles those of his predecessors whose texts acknowledge and do not demonize female sexual desire. Looking closely at Miss Mathews and her narrative allows us to see the ways in which Fielding's novel reveals a concern with the material consequences of women's lack of knowledge of desire and of the socioeconomic context in which that desire is produced and understood. More specifically, *Amelia*, like the novels of Behn, Manley, and Haywood, demonstrates the dangers to women of being uncritical consumers of the text(s) of seduction.

Amelia's representation of the murderess and of the murder itself seems, however, far more conventional and delimiting than any of the previous texts, fictional or nonfiction, that I have so far discussed. In *Amelia*, Fielding satirizes female violence and thus drains the female act of homicide of its radical potentiality. While the criminal biographies demonize the murderess, she is a figure whose agency and power threatens social signification as well as individual bodies. In *Amelia*, in contrast, the violent woman's sword poses no real danger to masculine or civic bodies, but is instead a nuisance. Miss Mtthews's attack on her treacherous seducer reads not as a terrifying spectacle but as a burlesque—a ridiculous and ultimately impotent act. Fielding's description of the crime highlights her ineffectiveness and the futility of a feminine attack on masculine power. Miss Mathews declares: "I plunged a drawn penknife, which I had prepared in my pocket for the purpose, into his accursed heart" (51). As

---

[12]   Fielding argued that providing detailed narratives of the executions of prisoners was ill advised as they would create sympathy for the criminal, and, as Gladfelder notes, "his solution was for writers to carry out a judicial 'Murder behind the Scenes'" (15); however, *Amelia's* female criminals are punished neither on nor off stage.

Margaret Doody comments, "Miss Mathews's use of alliteration is a sign for the reader not to take her too seriously" ("The Law" 128). Moreover, her power, such as it is, is revealed to be illusory, as we soon discover (as does she) that Miss Mathews in fact only gave her victim a surface wound, and that he has fully recovered. Her crime is premeditated, which is evidence of her wickedness and monstrosity, and yet the caricature of the murderess is rendered absurd rather than terrifying. Female homicide has become miniaturized here; the impotence of the protophallic weapon— the penknife—sharply contrasts with the fatal and dismembering sword of Manley's Violenta and suggests the futility of women wielding either pen or knife.

The female criminals that populate the Newgate of *Amelia* are notable not for their violence but for their excessive and criminalized sexuality. While she fails miserably at stabbing a man to death, according to the topoi of the novel Miss Mathews can destroy a man—and by extension a nation—through seduction. She has an "air of most bewitching softness" (34), a seductive power connected to the black arts. As a female rake, she is licentious, vain, hypocritical, and a home-wrecker; she is aligned with the "very pretty" prostitutes whose "innocent countenance[s]" mask their "idle and disorderly" natures and thus lure hapless men into diseases of the body and spirit (25). In contrast to these superficially lovely female criminals, Fielding presents the prisoner Blear-Eyed Moll as a travesty of femininity, a gargantuan figure of abject and limitless female carnality. Blear-Eyed Moll is female nature and appetite gone amok:

> Her eye (for she had but one) ... constantly looked toward her blind-side ...
> Nose she had none; for Venus, envious perhaps at her former charms, had carried
> off the gristly part; and some earthly damsel, perhaps from the same envy, had
> leveled the bone with the rest of her face. (21)

Moll is the violent consequence of unrestrained sexuality; once beautiful enough to engender envy in Venus herself, she has been disfigured by female desire, her own and that of other women. Her nose is ravaged by syphilis and has been beaten by a sexual competitor. Her mouth is a cavernous *vagina dentata*, and her breasts no longer nurture, but have merged with her engulfing, nonproductive genitalia:

> About half a dozen ebony teeth fortified that long and large canal, which nature
> had cut from ear to ear ... Her body was well adapted to her face; she measured
> full as much round the middle as from head to foot; for, besides the extreme
> breadth of her back, her vast breasts had long since forsaken their native home,
> and had settled themselves a little below the girdle. (21)

Moll's body takes up too much space; she exceeds the boundaries of restrained femininity, and her desire suggests that of the hungry witch of fairy tales. Moll is the first female criminal with whom Booth interacts in the novel, and her desire for him and for his belongings further positions her as a castrating witch. Moll is "taken in fact with a very pretty young fellow" (21), and promptly "accosts" and "uncases" him (20), stripping him of his coat and his symbolic masculinity. Whether lovely or ludicrous, the novel's female criminals are presented as horrible for the violence of their illicit sexual desire rather than for their illicit legal crimes.

The novel's critique of and horror at its female criminals is writ clear not only through plot and characterization but through chapter titles and narrative asides that instruct us how to read the female criminals we encounter. Fielding clearly frames Miss Mathews as a *femme fatale* according to familiar classical and contemporaneous conventions. If readers are in doubt about how to approach the beautiful murderess, we are clearly instructed by the titular warning that comprises the title of the chapter in which we encounter her: "Containing the extraordinary behavior of Miss Mathews on her meeting with Booth, and some endeavors to prove by reason and authority, that it is possible for a woman to appear what she really is not" (bk. 1, ch. 6). Miss Mathews, while lovely and well born, will be revealed as lascivious and base. In case we have not learned our lesson from the chapter's title, the narrator explicitly informs us that we may not read Miss Mathews at face value: her "genteel" appearance belies her nature: the "vent of sorrow or shame" she reveals to Booth is rescripted "if the reader pleases, as rage" (34) and, at the chapter's end, Miss Mathews is indicted by age old notions of the viraginous woman. She:

> expressed sentiments becoming the lips of a Dalia, Jezebel, Media, Semiramis, Parysatis, Tanaquil, Livilla, Messalina, Agrippina, Brunichilde, Elfrida, Lady Macbeth, Joan of Naples, Christina of Sweden, Katherine Hays [sic], Sarah Malcolm, Con. Philips, or any other heroine of the tender sex, which history sacred or profane, false or true, hath recorded. (35–36)

Fielding explicitly places Miss Mathews within an infamous schema of female monstrosity that simultaneously incorporates mythic and contemporary examples of female deviance.[13]

And yet, despite its authoritative muster, the very presence of such overt instruction calls attention to Miss Mathews's and the novel's availability for multiple interpretations. The terms of the injunctions also emphasize this interpretive instability. Carefully looking at the narratival framing of the novel's murderess reveals its representations of female desire and agency to be more complex than they first appear. The great chain of horrible women is, for example, a more porous passage than it appears. To deem these women "heroines of the tender sex," ("The Law" 35) as Margaret Doody points out, "[E]ndeavors to make us dismiss as unpleasant and absurd the idea of any kind of 'Heroine.' The strong woman who is her nation's defender seems but another type of murderess,

---

[13] Feminist critics have done excellent work on this oddly hysterical and richly evocative passage, a passage in which, as Doody points out, Fielding defines a "heroine" as an active and criminal female subject. See, for example, chapters on *Amelia* in both Campbell and Castle (*Masquerade*).

and both are assimilated to the sexually voracious woman, the insatiable whore" ("The Law" 129). Doody's reading points to the ways in which this condemnation implicates Amelia herself as the novel's heroine, and thus vexes the very notion of the ameliorating power of the lady, what Jill Campbell calls the novel's "proleptic cultural dream" of the redemptive power of the angel in the house.[14] Moreover, while Fielding's strange assimilation of exemplars of female fortitude and female infamy works as Doody explains—to lower the virtuous to the level of virago—it also suggests the opposite. The virago is not defined as a monstrous other but is a "heroine" of the "tender sex," a group that includes Amelia and Miss Mathews. Both have been, like Medea before them, wronged by perfidious men. However unintended such a reading surely is, the rhetorical gestures of the passage create an ambiguous effect that troubles the text's formulaic oppositions.

The narrator's instruction that we beware of misreading Miss Mathews calls attention to the fact that character and moral are open to interpretation, rather than fixed and emphasizes that "if the reader pleases," she may read Miss Mathews's story, or indeed the story of any "tender heroine" with sympathy rather than scorn. The instruction is surely intended to circumvent such sympathy with the criminal woman. However, the textual acknowledgment of the *potential* of such sympathy differentiates Fielding's novel from the realm of didactic simplicity of the criminal biography in which such a possibility would remain repressed. As she is imprisoned for an attempted murder of which she is guilty, Miss Mathews's character should not need such authorial gloss. Booth, Amelia's husband, is a hapless misreader of character, but Fielding's chapter heading is addressed to the reader of the novel, a reader whose vision and accuracy of interpretation clearly exceeds that of Booth, and thus suggests that we, too, are at risk of being seduced, as Booth soon will be, by the sympathy and beauty of the novel's convicted murderess.

While much critical attention has rightfully been paid to the ways in which *Amelia* is concerned with the interpretive skills of men, I argue that the novel also explicitly addresses the danger that being an uncritical reader poses to women.[15]

---

[14] Campbell argues convincingly that "there are a number of ways in which the character Amelia may slip the moorings of her safely 'feminine' identity, as constructed for masculine ends, and raise at least the possibility of real female moral power" (241). Conway builds on Campbell's argument and uses the portrait of Amelia as the center of her persuasive argument that Amelia gains a large measure of authority through her location in the material world (135–49).

[15] In the world of *Amelia*, for a woman to seem to be one thing while she actually is another endangers not only the individual man, in this case Booth (and by extension the reader), but also the nation. If men misread femininity, if women seem to be that which they are not, then the ameliorative potentiality of feminine virtue in which the text is invested is revealed to be as fallible as the legal system the novel so savagely denounces. If that is the case, we cannot be assured that either Miss Mathews or Amelia is in fact necessarily what the narrator would have them appear. As Castle points out, if women can pretend to virtue, then Amelia herself, the novel's moral center, is destabilized. Castle argues that Amelia is in fact revealed as a dissembler (through Amelia's nonplussed reaction to Atkinson's

Amelia, like the amatory fictions that precede it, reveals the ways in which the rhetoric of seduction imperils women who are naive readers. "If the reader pleases," she may see, "[b]y reason and authority," that Miss Mathews is herself victimized by virtue of being an unskilled reader rather than simply being the occasion or object of others' misreading.

Miss Mathews's seduction at the hands of a faithless lover reads like an amatory cautionary tale in its critique of the mechanisms of heterosexual romance in mid-eighteenth-century England. While the description of the *act* of her crime itself is bled of power, it is Miss Mathews's narration of her crime and her motive that most weakens Fielding's creation of a fiendish female criminal. Its content, language, and rhetorical strategies could come from a fiction of any of the "Fair Triumvirate," and the narration opens a space of identification, explanation, and critique that belies the narrator's conclusions or the novelist's stated intent. Miss Mathews resembles a sympathetic Haywoodian heroine more than she does the monster Fielding claims her to be. The content of the tale serves as a cautionary fiction to women about the untrustworthiness of men. Miss Mathews asks: "You have heard, you say, of the murder, but do you know the cause?" Her narrative details that "cause," providing a motive that is emotionally if not legally defensible: her lover cruelly mocked and left her after having wooed and won her without legal marriage.[16]

As in all of the novels I have discussed, female criminality begins when male protectors fail to protect their female charges; in Miss Mathews's case, a daughter should be able to trust a man her father makes "a part of our family" (9). Like Mary Blandy, Miss Mathews falls for the gallant officer Hebbers, who has been invited into the family circle by her father, a character whose lack of sense is designated by his status as "a hearty well-wisher to the present government" (8). Miss Mathews is "inflamed" by Hebbers's beauty, gentility, and protestations of love, and assumes him trustworthy because of her father's approval of him and his seductive rhetoric. His claim that it is poverty rather than inclination that has made him cold to her convinces her of the "disinterested" nature of his passion for her. He dupes her; she is ruined, and, like Violenta, she attempts to kill him.

While her "sword" fails, her "words" do not, and Miss Mathews crafts a narrative that articulates and defends her own honor.[17] Criminal biographies of violent women repress particular material motives for female violence; they define female homicide as caused by the murderess's essential lack of "natural" feminine

---

declarations of love and her hiding of her knowledge of Booth's affair with Miss Mathews). Gladfelder extends Castle's argument and convincingly reads Amelia as an actively desiring sexual being rather than an asexual domestic one.

[16]   Until 1753, a year after *Amelia*'s publication, English courts recognized a promise of marriage (male to female) as legally binding; the erasure of this protection represents a social shift in notions of seduction and the sexual contract.

[17]   That Miss Mathews has turned to the "sword" to defend her honor resonates in a novel preoccupied with dueling and shifting notions of masculine honor.

submission and locate that lack in the murderess's failure to embody proper feminine traits. The murderess's legal sentencing—her execution—is presented as synonymous with justice and as the only appropriate conclusion to the narrative of her crime. In contrast, Miss Mathews has a recognizable and logical motive for her crime, and she clearly differentiates legal punishment from justice. As the narrator of Behn's *The History of the Nun* argues that abused male fiat is responsible for "an abundance of mischiefs and miseries" (154), so Miss Mathews locates female crime in masculine wrongdoing rather than abased female nature: "From the damned inconsistency of your sex to ours proceeds half the miseries of mankind" (84).

Fielding's text parallels those of Behn, Manley, and Haywood in its revision of the common story of seduction; rather than ending the tale of a ruined maiden with simple ruin—shame, expulsion to a convent, or death—it ends with female vengeance. Like Violenta, Miss Mathews refutes the standard arc of the seduction tale: she fights back and defends her violent revenge with logic and passion. She declares:

> Is the killing a villain to be called murder? Perhaps the law calls it so.—Let it call it what it will, or punish me as it pleases.—Punish me!—no, no—that is not in the power of man—not of that monster man, Mr. Booth. I am undone, am revenged, and have now no more business for life; let them take it from me when they will. (34)

Critics have argued that the passage positions Miss Mathews as monstrous for her lack of remorse; however, the facts of the history and her logical rationale for the crime work against such a reading. "Man" is the monster here—both the villainous seducer and the masculine realm of the law that refuses to punish him for his "undoing" of her. Fielding calls attention to the gaps between the letter of the law and its spirit through her questioning of the very term "murder" as the word to describe the defense of her honor. And while Miss Mathews calls into question the efficacy of the legal system, in line with the novel's larger critique of justice versus law, she also heroically accepts the terms of that law, however specious. Like Violenta, she claims her guilt as she turns herself over to a legal system that has itself failed her as, ruined, she "has no more business for life."

Miss Mathews dangerously misreads the text of heterosexual exchange as a romance while Hebbers, more accurately, sees it as a bill of trade.[18] Miss Mathews cannot recognize Hebbers's claims as false because they so ideally fit a romantic script she has uncritically consumed. During her narrative she omits the details of seduction, commenting that "I am come to a part of my narrative in which it is impossible to be particular, without being tedious; for as to the commerce between lovers, it is, I believe, much the same in all cases; and there is, perhaps,

---

[18]   Eliza Haywood presents a similar situation in *The City Jilt, or, the Alderman turn'd Beau* (see Saxton, "Telling Tale" 115–42).

scarce a single phrase that hath not been repeated ten millions of times" (43). This comment echoes a narrative aside in Haywood's *The City Jilt* in which the female narrator states: "Nothing happening between them but what is common to persons in the Circumstances they were, I shall pass over in Silence the Days of their Courtship" (67). Each of these comments calls attention to the familiarity of the script of romance, both literary and lived. By marking these moments as stock, Miss Mathews, like Haywood's narrator, asserts that they and their hyperbolic vicissitudes are common. She subtly warns female readers of the rote and well-scripted nature of the language of courtship, unworthy even of textual inclusion, as well as the truly common nature of the failed romance she relates.

Miss Mathews's tale reveals the dangers for women of being uneducated in the ways in which marriage works within a system of economic exchange rather than affection. Miss Mathews's narrative suggests that she was complicit in her own ruin, not because she is inherently a "bad" woman or because she had premarital sex per se, but because of her lack of interpretive knowledge and her thus uncritical acceptance of feminine roles. It is this status as uncritical consumer rather than critical reader that results in her inappropriate devotion to her lover and her lack of awareness of her value in a system of male exchange. For example, when Hebbers falsely declares his "abhorrence at the thoughts of marrying for interest," she innocently agrees that "*none but fools and villains did so*" (42). By the time we encounter Miss Mathews, she has shifted from being an uncritical consumer of romance fictions to a worldly-wise narrator who includes her own authorial cautions to the female reader; her comment that "a woman who hath given her consent to marry, can hardly be said to be safe until she is married" (43), is not for Booth's edification, but for that of the female reader.

Miss Mathews has learned self-consciously to inhabit and act out the feminine roles she previously inhabited as natural; and when she is conscious of the roles, she may use them to her own advantage. During her narration to Booth and while she is listening to his narration, Miss Mathews gains authority over her own representation, becoming a subject who manipulates male desire rather than an object who is governed by it.[19] She is no longer actually soft and innocent, a state that gained her nothing but ruin; instead she has the "most extraordinary power of displaying softness" (35).[20] To enact softness rather than to embody it grants

---

[19]   As I have mentioned, critics have tended to accept Fielding's framing of Miss Mathews's manipulation of Booth and her sexual desire for him as evidence of her monstrosity—a monstrosity either that positions her in opposition to Amelia or that she and Amelia share. In contrast, Haggerty offers a welcome empathy for Miss Mathews; he reads her narrative as a confession through which she is "exposing herself to Booth as a way of liberating herself from the confines of her own guilt" and that the confession is "an attempt to establish a relation, albeit sexual, with someone who stands outside her private desolation" (389, 390).

[20]   "Softness" evokes an appropriate constellation of terms for Miss Mathews, its simultaneous associations with ease, gentleness, and pusillanimity.

Miss Mathews the power of the active subject; as the active subject, she recognizes her status as an object of desire in a system of sexual exchange. This recognition allows her to manipulate her status as desired object in order to serve her own desires. Her manipulation of male desire is eminently successful: through it she gains the attention and sexual performance of Booth—her long-ago lost first love —money to support her in prison, freedom from prison, and finally marriage and wealth in the colonies. For Miss Mathews, lost maidenhood does not result in lost maiden, but in satisfied health and wealth for a woman who has learned to manipulate gendered expectations to serve her own ends. Miss Mathews has nothing left to lose; she has learned from her earlier experience of real softness to display softness while no longer being so vulnerable and thus to look after her own self-interest.

Fielding presents the violent history of seduction and betrayal Miss Mathew narrates to Booth in contrast to Booth's narration of his courtship of Amelia. Rather than being oppositional, however, these dual seduction narratives are conspicuously similar in content and form and work together to educate the female reader to the dangers of uncritical acceptance of the apparatuses of heterosexual romance. The narratives are strikingly parallel at the level of content: like Hebbers, Booth is an impoverished military man. Like Hebbers, Booth attempts to trick Amelia and pleads his poverty and ultimate interest in her welfare as the excuse for his feigning. In contrast to Miss Mathews's father's approval of Hebbers, which is a mitigating factor in her ruin, Amelia's mother explicitly forbids the union between Amelia and Booth because of his poverty. Just as Miss Mathews responds to Hebbers's romantic declarations, Amelia eagerly accepts and responds to Booth's; Booth explains: "We were upon the footing of lovers; and Amelia threw off her reserve more and more, till at length I found all that return of my affection which the tenderest lover can require" (65). Finally, driven by her erotic passion, Amelia, like Miss Mathews, runs away with the unsuitable man who has promised to marry her, "Performing the part of a Heroine all the way" (84).[21] The hackneyed description of their elopement emphasizes the tropic nature of the seduction fiction: on a dark night, by a moonlit garden wall, "a female voice, in a whisper cried out, 'Mr. Booth'" (76). The conventional nature of the scene is further stressed when Booth responds to his lover in actually scripted lines; he answers "in a line of Congreve's, which burst from my lips spontaneously ... '*Who calls the wretched thing that was Alphonso?*'" Amelia, knowing her part, cries out, "O it is indeed my Alphonso" (76). These lines not only point to the scripted nature of heterosexual romance, but also are darkly ironic when we consider their source, William Congreve's tragedy *The Mourning Bride*. The title comments on the eventual marital stress that awaits the now breathless Amelia, and the play's famous quote, with which Fielding's audience would have been familiar, extends

---

[21]   Miss Mathews points to her jealousy of other women and Hebbers's manipulation of that jealousy as a source of her downfall (and presumably as evidence of her status as a "bad" woman). Interestingly, Booth's seduction of Amelia turns on his false seduction of Miss Osborne, a woman Amelia refers to as "her known enemy" (63).

the irony to gloss Miss Mathews's tale: "Heaven has no rage like love to hatred turned, nor hell a fury like a woman scorned" (3.8).

Amelia, like Miss Mathews, is a sexually desiring woman whose desire and lack of education about the nature of heterosexual romance lead her uncritically to accept Booth's seduction. Booth's protestations of love and his desire for marriage are of course true, but the rhetoric of seduction and mutual desire is identical in each narrative. While critics may posit Amelia's wifely virtue as entirely oppositional to Miss Mathews's criminal carnality, their roles in their respective primal seduction narratives are parallel. Amelia's escape from being "undone" is, according to the logic of these histories, pure chance. As Hugh Gladfelder adroitly notes, Amelia and Booth's relationship, and thus the entire novel, occurs because of her bold youthful disobedience of her family, a disobedience engendered by her desire for Booth (195). While Booth does marry Amelia and thus she does not lose her imperiled reputation, the entire novel is concerned with the ways in which Amelia is at risk because of his poverty and bad behavior. For all of Amelia's protestations that love in a cottage would be a delight, the novel firmly demonstrates the ways in which money is necessary for marital harmony and familial survival. Amelia and Booth prosper at the end only because of Amelia's maternal legacy. The novel is openly dedicated to the exploration of the effects of male foolishness, deceit, and bad behavior on its virtuous heroine: Booth is a bad judge of character, a liar, a spendthrift, an adulterer, an intellectual lightweight, and a mediocre Christian whose recuperation happens in the novel's famously unbelievable ending, in which Amelia's money and his conversion save the marriage.

Booth's behavior, past and present, links the two women and the two stories, providing an indictment of male behavior that mitigates the novel's sentencing of Miss Mathews. The narrator rescripts Booth's adultery as acting in a "manner inconsistent with the strict rules of virtue and chastity" (148) and provides a quasilegal plea to the reader in Booth's defense:

> [F]ortune seemed to have used her utmost endeavors to ensnare poor Booth's constancy. Let the reader set before his eyes a fine young woman, in a manner a first love, conferring obligations, and using every art to soften, to allure, to win, and to enflame; let him consider the time and place; let him remember that Mr. Booth was a young fellow, in the highest vigour of life; and lastly, let him add one single circumstance, that the parties were alone together; and then if he will not acquit the defendant, he must be convicted; for I have nothing more to say in his defence. (148)

On the one hand, this defense recalls the narratival tone of *Tom Jones*, with its impatience for moral prudery and its avuncular affection for male high jinks and the women who engender them. Read in this light, the passage does not seriously damn either Miss Mathews or Booth, but rather chides their youthful antics. On the other hand, the narrator soon reminds us of the effect the affair may have on Amelia, a sobering counterpoint that is later weakened by our realization that

Amelia knows all along about the affair and that her knowledge has certainly had no visible effect on her character throughout the novel. The passage is also notable for its direct contradiction of one of the novel's central moral themes: the debunking of those who blame their ill status or actions on fortune. The novel opens with the injunction that "the public voice hath in all ages done much injustice to Fortune, and hath convicted her of many facts in which she had not the least concern" and argues that, in fact, it is following the "blind guidance of a predominant passion" that is responsible for most individual and social ills. If we read the narrator's defense of Booth according to the novel's framing moral precepts then indeed Booth "must be convicted" and Miss Mathews, while "guilty," is not the primary criminal in the "conversation."

Even if we ignore the sexist sirenlike notions that underlie the narrator's defense of Booth, Booth is defined as markedly more implicated in their "criminal conversation" than the narrator admits. Miss Mathews's narrative reveals that Booth used the rhetoric of seduction with her years ago while he was engaged to Amelia; this flirtation implicates him in their adulterous affair as it also provides us with evidence of her past love for and once proper behavior with him. The narrator informs us that "[i]n real fact, Mr. Booth had been her first love, and had made those impressions on her young heart, which the learned in this branch of philosophy affirm, and perhaps truly, are never to be eradicated" (146). Booth was Miss Mathews's first love, and yet she notes that she hid her affection for him in those days since his affections were "more happily disposed of to a much better woman than myself" (39). Miss Mathews appropriately refused her attraction for Booth in the past, while Booth's behavior hints that he is more culpable and less moral than the text claims (and perhaps than she).

Booth's tendency to seduction, and thus his link with Hebbers and with male perfidy in general, is first marked by his observations on the lovely beauty of a nameless young female prisoner, his immediate remark that Miss Mathews "was so remarkably handsome" upon noticing her in the prison, and the narrator's multiple comments about Booth's "many handsome acknowledgements of her favour" (33), acknowledgments that occur before she has begun to flirt with him and that continue, undetailed, throughout their exchange. Issues of blame in Miss Mathews and Booth's "criminal conversation" are also interestingly complicated when we consider the ways in which "blame" infers authority. Whatever responsibility the text assigns for their sexual congress, Miss Mathews functions in the novel as the author of her narrative. As she tells her story to Booth, she is the multivalent author of her own seduction tale: she scripts herself as the wronged heroine as she simultaneously scripts the present seduction between herself and Booth. As narrator, she skillfully positions herself, to Booth and the reader, as the ruined maid—a figure whose lost innocence engenders both sympathy and concomitant desire.

Her narrative borrows from amatory writers not only at the level of plot, but also at the level of form. Miss Mathews's narrative employs the strategies of immediacy, direct testimony, emotional appeal, and lavish language familiar from earlier fiction: she begins her story, "[W]hen you know of what hath happened since our last meeting, your concern will be raised. ... O, sir, you are a stranger to the cause of my sorrows. ... Tell me do you know my wretched story?" (34, 35; first ellipses added). Her first-person narrative functions at the level of the somatic as well as the didactic; she makes her argument through an appeal to the emotions as well as to the intellect. In her role as author, she controls her own representation for her own ends. For example, in the following description of Hebbers's ploys, she cannily evokes sexual innocence, active desire, and her current debauched status. At the same time, she makes a convincing analysis of women's endangerment as a result of their innocent consumption of the text of romance:

> In moments when he fell into the warmest raptures, and exprest the greatest uneasiness at the delay of his joys, he seldom mentioned the word marriage. ... Indeed women cannot be cautioned too much against such lovers ... a woman who hath given her consent to marry, can hardly be considered to be safe till she is married. (43)

Her narrative of his perfidy is designed to produce the tear and sigh of sympathetic outrage, the reasoned cautionary message to women, as well as the frisson of sexual pleasure, a response that will become literalized in Booth's erotic response to her tale.

When she has finished her story, Miss Mathews then becomes the editor of his. She has refused to narrate the particular "commerce between lovers," claiming it to be stock and "tedious." However, Miss Mathews insists that Booth include the details of his romance of Amelia, details that he tells her he will omit, not for her reasons—their stock nature—but out of propriety. Her insistence on his inclusion of these details points to the ways in which she recognizes their erotic effectiveness. Here, Booth's articulation of the conventional details of romance, of his seduction of Amelia, works to seduce him. He complies and recounts his courtship and early marriage with Amelia in pointedly sexual terms:

> I caught her in my arms with raptures not to be exprest in words, called her my heroine, sure none ever better deserved that name after which we remained for some time speechless, and lock'd in each other's embraces. (98)

She has already told us she finds such details rote. She is interested in them now as editor of his text so that, for her own benefit, she can manipulate the mechanisms/tropes of seduction once used against her. After being duped, ruined, and imprisoned, Miss Mathews has learned how accurately to read the text of heterosexual romance and the male author of that text with "reason and authority." The novel reveals the ways in which she has, like one of the heroines of the "Fair Triumvirate," learned to "appear what she really is not" (bk. 1, ch. 6) in order to manipulate the narratives that have previously ensnared her.

Miss Mathews not only exceeds formulaic conventions of female criminality but also critiques them, and she does so through the narration of her own history in terms that strikingly parallel feminocentric seduction fictions. Fielding's portrayal of the murderess Miss Mathews uses tropic notions of female criminality and libertinism, yet it formally and thematically evokes the tropes used by Behn, Manley, and Haywood to critique such limited visions. Miss Mathews's behavior *is* "extraordinary," and her narrative reveals Fielding's ultimately failed attempt to portray her as "that which she is not": a monstrous she-devil. Rather, Miss Mathews is a complex character whose motive and behavior engender the sympathy the novel attempts to preclude.

Amelia's fantasy of femininity is haunted by its larger-than-life murderous women, whom the text can finally neither accept nor expel. Fielding, as a magistrate, was faced with an actual murderess—one who insisted on telling her own story rather than remaining within the confines of juridical discourse; he responded by creating a counternarrative to her text. The fictional dictates Fielding the novelist attempted in *Amelia* are formulated by Fielding the magistrate in the powerful arena of judicial opinion in his legal treatise on the case of Mary Blandy. Miss Mathews's case parallels the story of seduction and abandonment recounted by Mary Blandy in her trial for her 1751 parricide—a crime she committed the year *Amelia* was published. Both Blandy and Miss Mathews claim that they were deceived by men who promised to marry them but who married others and left them ruined. In the next chapter, I will argue that through the narrative fiction of the law, the lawless body of the woman, who has escaped Fielding's fictional authority, can be sentenced, contained, and eliminated.

Chapter 5
"The Prisoner at the Bar":
Mary Blandy and Henry Fielding

If only she [Mary Blandy] had been the creature of some great novelist's fancy, imagine her made visible to us through the exquisite medium of Mr. Henry James' incomparable art—the subtle individual threads all cunningly combined, the pattern wondrously wrought, the colours delicately and exactly shaded, until the rich texture of the finished tapestry, the figure of the woman she lived stood perfectly revealed.
—*The Trial of Mary Blandy*, ed. William Roughhead, Edinburgh (1914)

This chapter brings us full circle back to Mary Blandy, hung on April 6, 1752, for poisoning her father. Rather than focus on what popular discourse about her crime reveals about the constructions of women and violence, as I did in Chapter 3, this chapter examines two texts from the juridical arena whose formal techniques demonstrate contesting conceptions of narrative authority: Mary Blandy's defense of her innocence in her autobiographical apologia, *Miss Mary Blandy's Own Account of the Affair Between Her and Mr. Cranstoun* (1752), and Henry Fielding's exposition of Blandy's guilt in his theological-jurisprudential account, *Examples of the Interposition of Providence in the Detection and Punishment of Murder* (1752).

The debate between Blandy's and Fielding's versions of her truth does not simply center on the guilt or innocence of Blandy herself; it encapsulates a battle for narrative primacy in both the literary and legal arenas. As critic Alexander Welsh explains, Blandy's and Fielding's nonfiction texts exemplify mid-century changes in fictional practice, specifically the trend toward the privileging of realism and objectivity over romance and subjectivity. While neither is a novel, these narratives use what we now see as rhetorical strategies associated with fiction, strategies already explicitly aligned with the novel by mid-century. Convicted murderess Blandy attempts to support her plea for clemency through the narrative strategies associated with feminocentric amatory fiction.[1] The nature and context

---

[1]   Building on Welsh's arguments about Blandy's case and his larger arguments about circumstantial narrative, Sage Heinzelman notes Blandy's associations with "sentimental novels of late seventeenth- and early eighteenth-century women writers"; however, Heinzelman's comments on amatory fiction reveal our different understandings of such fictions. She states: "[T]his is not to say that Mary might not also have had access to novels in which female vulnerability was explored and in which the failure of the law to provide

of her narrative is transparently personal; Blandy wrote the account in prison after her sentencing in an attempt to gain a pardon. She turned to a narrative form that offered her a platform from which to construct herself as a victim rather than a virago. The seduction tale allows Blandy to take the familiar position of the gull of the sinister seducer; like the amatory heroines of Chapter 2, she represents herself as weak, but not wicked; ashamed, but not amoral. Her narrative explicitly and implicitly posits the personal and the emotional as essential to an understanding of crime and to the telling of a story. Blandy insists on complexity and fallibility and, as such, does not offer an easy social panacea to the problem of the parricide.

In contrast, novelist-magistrate Fielding attempts to define and contain Blandy through rhetorical strategies we now associate with realism, strategies that recall his fictional treatment of female criminals in *Amelia*. Written in his capacity as a magistrate, the *Interposition* explicitly and implicitly rebukes the personal and posits legal and religious authority as the means by which to understand crime and as the vantage point from which to tell a story. His narrative refuses complexity and fallibility and attempts to solve the problem of the parricide by invoking unwavering legal, moral, and textual authority. Ultimately, however, Fielding's *Interposition* offers a plea rather than a ruling; and the text finally may be read as a wishful fantasy that imagines the natural state of fathers and daughters as incapable of violence rather than the authoritative textual mandate Fielding intended.

Miss Mary Blandy's Own Account is thematically and formally organized according to conventions of amatory seductive fictions, those texts, often erotic and hyperbolic, that portray a heroine in distress and endangered by a male seducer. She positions herself in the familiar role of the innocent and abused heroine, victimized by a scheming seducer who took advantage of her naiveté, a circumstance possible because of the loving but irresponsible actions of her rightful protector, in this case, her father.

Formally, the narrative relies on first-person testimony, elaborate verbiage, and emotional appeal to an explicitly female audience. While Fielding simply asserts his views as fact without attendant claims to veracity, Blandy, like earlier fiction writers, insists outright on the truth of her text. As a female author, her status is already suspect; that she is a literal criminal further weakens her claims to veracity. In addition, the very insistence she offers may diminish the success of her attempt to argue with those narratives that present their conclusions within a frame of assumed fact.

Blandy's account is immediate and extravagant in its appeal to sympathy. She opens her narrative with an impassioned exhortation, "*Oh! Christian Reader*" (11), and continues with a direct and emotional plea to an explicitly female audience:

> My Misfortunes have been, and are such, as never Woman felt before—— Oh!
> let the Tears of the Wretched move human minds to Pity, and give Ear to my

---

women with protection came under attack" (336); I argue that women's amatory fictions do not run counter to but exemplify these characteristics.

Case, here wrote with greatest truth. It is impossible, indeed, in my unhappy Circumstances to recollect half of my Misfortunes, so as to place them in a proper Light—Let some generous Breast do that for the Miserable—and God will reward Goodness towards an unhappy, deceived, ruined Woman! Think what Power Man has over our Sex, when we truly love!——and what Woman, let her have what Sense she will, can stand the Arguments and Persuasions Men will make use of? (11)

Here, Blandy directly petitions the sympathy of female readers, explicitly linking her position with that of all women who are undone by the "power and persuasions of men." She refers to the power of Cranstoun, whom she accuses of leading her to poison her father without her knowledge, but her statement also offers comment on the power and persuasion of the masculine legal representations of life and circumstance, representations to which she can offer no remonstrance in kind.[2] For, while Blandy may have "sense"—her relatively high level of education is levied against her in court—for her to attempt to evoke the control of masculine political, legal, or religious authority would be unspeakable.

She adopts this air of beleaguered innocence throughout, admitting she was errant and foolish, but laying the blame for the murder on her perfidious lover. Blandy goes on at length regarding the ways in which Cranstoun did her wrong, and she intersperses her narration with exclamations of her filial love and heartache. She includes sections of letters between her and Cranstoun, letters that testify to her seduction and ruin-to-be and create a sense of intimacy in her account that contrasts with the more distant reportorial tone of Fielding's text. She claims her innocence of the poisonous nature of the love potion and explains that the letter to Cranstoun in which she worries about discovery (a major piece of evidence in the trial) only referred to the possibility that her father's discovery of the love potion might set him against Cranstoun.

In a move common to seduction fiction, Blandy subtly inserts a political aim within a narrative of extravagant desire. She includes a petition for pardon into the dramatic account of her ruin at her lover's hands:

When I fatally obeyed Mr. Cranstoun's orders, and was innocently the instrument of Death, as they say, to the best of Fathers; brought Disgrace to my family, and shameful Death to myself, unless my hard Case, here truly represented, recommends me to Royal pity, Clemency, and Compassion. (12)

Having failed to be excused by the court of law in which her case was tried, Blandy turns her case to the public and seems to hope that her version of the crime will induce an outpouring of support that might earn her a royal pardon. Rather than

---

[2]   Keep in mind also that there were no women in any legal positions in eighteenth-century England, so the only time a woman would appear in court would be as a defendant or witness.

overtly attacking the male authorities—the judges and lawyers—by whose dictate she has been convicted, Blandy astutely positions herself as a victim in need of the bountiful protection of masculine authority. Her hope for a pardon was not a vain one. As J. M. Beattie notes, at the conclusion of the assize sessions the judges virtually always reprieved some of those they had condemned to death at court, a reprieve being in Blackstone's words, "the withdrawal of the sentence for an interval of time" (Beattie 430).[3] Beattie explains that, when dealing with convicted murderers, judges issued reprieves mainly for those they thought had been wrongfully convicted on the evidence, as a way of overcoming juries who ignored their advice and direction. Blandy attempts to appeal to the judges, who could overturn the decision, as well as to a popular audience. While the trial reports show the lawyers for the crown approached her as, at best, a misguided, irrational hysteric and as, at worst, a subhuman, she praises the judges' and lawyers' treatment of her. Blandy is shrewd in her ladylike appeal to what she positions as the innate chivalry of the judges versus the base and unruly demeanors of the jury.[4]

Blandy counters the image of herself as formulaic she-devil by positioning herself as the image's flip side: the beleaguered heroine, the woman who presents a stoic vision of Christian fortitude despite the cruel treatment she has received at the inferior, and implicitly lower-class, hands of the jury. She appeals to the public by dramatizing her status as frail and proper woman, one inherently unfit to be in such base and public conditions and thus implicitly incapable of committing the crimes of which she is accused. Blandy's presentation of herself as a damsel in distress explicitly counters the arguments put forth in court that her lack of visible emotion proved her unnaturalness and lack of remorse. Instead, she poignantly presents herself as a martyr who has borne her trial with resolve and grace:

> The Untruths which have been told of me, the Messengers sent after me to see if I was safe, the putting me in Irons, (tho so weak and ill, that my own Body was too much to carry about), the Baseness and Wickedness of printing the

---

[3]   In 1728, judges were advised not to "appoint an unusual distant time for the Execution" when they left a convict to be hanged, to discourage the prisoner from appealing for a pardon (Beattie 432). That Blandy had six weeks within which to order her affairs before her execution allowed for her to write and circulate her own version of her innocence. It is unclear why she was given this much time; the Murder Act of 1752 fixed the time between conviction and execution at three days in order to prevent campaigns for pardon (434); it is speculation, but interesting, to consider whether Blandy's 1752 case and attempts to garner public sympathy might have influenced this decision.

[4]   Her positioning of the jury as uncouth and unchivalric would have resonated with contemporary tensions regarding the sense that juries were composed of "lower" sorts of men, and that those who were best able to serve on juries were able to avoid the duty: "The better informed and more opulent persons, to whom this duty of attendance belongs, escape through private avenues ... the weight, therefore, of this important concern, falls upon the lower class, who are utterly unable to sustain it. ..." (Hutton 22–23).

> Depositions to hurt me with the Jury; under all this I bore up, from knowing my Innocence. … Enemies call Innocence and Christian Courage, hardened Guilt. (13)

Blandy attempts to save herself by rescripting her plot from that of female criminal monstrosity to one of female victimization. Like Amelia, Blandy essentially dissolves within the base confines of the prison. She counters the image of an actively sexual and violent criminal female body with that of an ineffectual and vaporous no-body that presents no threat to social signification.

Like the narrator in Behn's *History of the Nun*, Blandy authorizes the position of the beleaguered heroine as one of fundamental innocence as her misdeeds are caused by originary male sin. Blandy accepts the tropes of female frailty and folly in exchange for freeing herself of the charge of premeditated guilt for which she is to be hung. She pleads, in a statement that could come straight from any fiction of the "Fair Triumvirate," or, for that matter, from Miss Mathews: "Let me be punished for my follies, but not lose my Life. Sure it is too hard to die for ignorance and too good an Opinion of a Villain?" (13). She appeals to her reader's personal affective response, a response grounded in emotional as well as logical sense. She insists upon the inevitable contextual and subjective nature of law and of morality.[5]

Blandy concludes her narrative with an appeal to God that emphasizes her narrative's roots in the sentimental and affective. Blandy presents God as a sympathetic entity who will reward the generous beneficence of the kind and loving soul who will help to save her unhappy life. She invokes God as suggestive model for her emotion-based appeal, associating herself with passive victim and posing the reader as the empowered subject. Blandy's God is linked to His subject in a chain of sympathy, not circumstance. Rather than appealing to religion as abstract law, she employs religion as a cajoling entreaty to her reader, and she locates religious duty in the defense rather than prosecution. She asks her readers to:

> Remember what blessings will attend you for defending the Orphan, the Injured and the Deceived … in memory of her parents who pray for her rescue from their places in Heaven—Drop pen,—my Spirits harassed out with Sorrow, fail.—God Almighty preserve you and yours from such Misfortunes.—Amen. Whoever thou art whose eyes drink in this sad and moving tale,—indulge one Tear: Remember the Infallibility of sublunary Things, and judge no man happy till he dies. (13)

Blandy's narrative insists on immediacy and embodiment, focusing on connection versus separation and the individual versus the abstract. Here, the murder victim—her father—is not the prosecuting witness in a heavenly trial, but the worried parent, and Blandy is figured, not as the monstrous sinner, but as the particular

---

5   See Faller ("Tales" 197) for an interesting argument regarding the ways in which Blandy's narrative constructs the man-of-feeling as its reader.

and loved child of the deceased. She calls our attention to the body she represents as frail and marked by sorrow: she is unable even to hold the pen with which she writes. Blandy makes her discourse immediate and specific, presenting herself as a spectacle of female sorrow and imperiled flesh. She seeks a sensational response (the tear) from her reader and, rather than pontificating truth, asks that her reader remember that truth itself is always contextual and that our "sublunary" capacity to judge is limited by our human frailty. The reader and author, the judge and the criminal, are linked as individuals who cannot possibly "judge" from outside of that subjective state.

That she articulated her own defense as a woman marked Blandy as guilty, as did the fact that she had been brought into the arena of law at all. Since she was already convicted, her attempts to change the terms of her representation were construed by many as evidence of the depths of her capacity for deliberate misrepresentation and treasonous turpitude.[6] The act of writing further implicated Blandy in a criminal conversation: her eagerness to narrativize her own experience served to condemn her as improperly feminine and thus shored up the originary terms of guilt upon which the prosecution formulated their chain of circumstance. Moreover, she offered her own narrative as that which should supplant the prosecutors' narrative, one defined as divinely ordered—a narrative that, as Fielding claimed, was proof of providence as "circumstances that tally with one another are above human contrivance." Her proposal of an alternative and oppositional narrative was itself blasphemous as she attempted, through her own account, to contest the supra-authority of God, state, and man with that of individual, female desire.

As a convicted murderess who had been involved in an illicit and illegal love affair, Blandy turned to the sole available narrative form that offered her the chance to shape her motivations and change the terms of her sentence. But while her narrative was deemed too romantic and hyperbolic, in fact it was— like the fictions of Behn, Manley, and Haywood—too authoritative and too realistic. Blandy structured her tale along the lines of those feminocentric fictions that alarmingly reveal women's crimes and desires to be viable, motivated, and specific. She appealed to notions of chivalry and female passivity, notions belied by her very writing of the text.

While Blandy's narrative garnered much disapproval and did not result in a pardon, it did, as I discuss in Chapter 3, create a bastion of popular support. Blandy manipulated fictions of gender in order to produce herself as a feminine victim of avaricious masculine seduction and failed male protection, and this manipulation worked to no small extent. However, her presentation of her case in a fictional mode overtly coded as feminine, while opening the space for popular sympathy, simultaneously marked her text and her case as a romance: an escapist, fantastical,

---

[6]   As Doody notes, having failed to convince the judge and the jury, Blandy ought either to have confessed her guilt, like the traditional subject of the criminal biography, or to have kept quiet ("The Law").

transgressive fiction that held great popular appeal, but had no authoritative claim for veracity or primacy. While her account gained popular sympathy, it carried little weight against the legal, theological, and seemingly objective authority wielded by the court or by Fielding's text.

In contrast to the insistence on the contextual and the personal appeal of Blandy's text, Fielding's text combines miracles with manacles to infuse juridical and textual authority with divine prerogative. He evokes God as originary proof for his argument, associating himself as author with that divine prerogative to which the reader must submit. Fielding's treatise concludes with a spate of rhetorical questions that fairly tremble with impersonal righteousness, evoking a patriarchal vision of a vengeful God and a furious murdered father:

> What are the terrors of earthly judgment, compared to this tremendous Tribunal? … where is the fortitude which can look an offended Almighty in the face? … who can bear the dreadful thought of being confronted with the spirit of one we have murdered, in the presence of all the Host of Heaven, and to have justice demanded against our guilty soul, before that awful judgment-seat, where there is infinite justice, as well as infinite power? (67)

These rhetorical questions function emotively as givens rather than as an argument open to debate. God, the human father, the judge at the bench, and the (male) writer coalesce into one "tremendous tribunal" that is the source of "infinite justice as well as infinite power."[7]

Fielding's formal structure works according to a principle of removed authority. In *Strong Representations: Narrative and Circumstantial Evidence in England*, Alexander Welsh demonstrates that, in the eighteenth century, this notion of removed authority becomes associated with the authority granted to literary realism and circumstantial evidence in court. As Susan Sage Heinzelman notes, Fielding claims authorship only for the introduction and conclusion of the narrative, "as if the intervening tales, 'collected from various authors, ancient and modern' have fallen into a natural and logical order of their own accord" (325). The tales appear to be either directives from God or simple historical truth not mediated by authorship, resembling facts in a legal case that, with careful management, present an incontrovertible truth that hides the artifice of its telling. Each is simply titled "Example I," and so on, and is presented as a set of listed facts that add up to a clear conclusion. The *Interposition* does not elaborately claim its truth status, but presents its cases as though they are simply facts. Fielding asserts that "there is …

---

[7] Fielding, in both his fiction (particularly *Tom Jones* and *Amelia*) and in other legal commentary (such as his writings on prostitutes, and his 1753 *Proposal for Making Effectual Provisions for the Poor*) is not uniformly as harsh regarding the poor and the criminal as he is in this text or in the 1751 *An Enquiry into the Causes of the Late Increase of Robbers*. As *Amelia*'s critique of the justice system demonstrates, he had little patience for laws and social systems that criminalized poverty.

no truth whatever, which can be supported by so many authorities from history, as this of the divine vengeance against Murder" (11).

In fact, Fielding's text quite delightfully embodies the absolute presence of human contrivance in narratives, particularly those narratives predicated on persuasion. Fielding's "evidence"—his text's plot—is explicitly presented as the reportage of examples of the hand of God, a titular claim that presumes his examples to be rooted in what we might call truthful representations. But, in fact, the narrative presents factual and fictional stories as equal forms of evidentiary truth, intermingling examples from the Bible, myth, hearsay, and the contemporary press. This presentation of factual and fictional narratives as interchangeable recalls *Amelia*'s inclusion of the stories of Medea, Lady MacBeth, Catherine Hayes, and Sarah Malcolm as equivalent records of history (35–36). Fielding's field day with "truth" and "fiction" occurs not only in his inclusion of both as equal, but also in his fictionalization of facts. Fielding not only uses tales that are explicitly fictional, but also takes great liberties with actual cases; for example, in his discussion of Catherine Hayes, he erroneously claims she was struck down with guilt by the sight of her dead husband's coat and that, after this interposition of divine providence, she passively and willingly accepted her punishment of death by burning.

Rather than an objective and unembellished authority, the text amply displays its own fictionality. Fielding's full title itself demonstrates the artifice of his purportedly factual narrative: *Examples of the Interposition of Providence in the Detection and Punishment of Murder. Containing above thirty Cases, in which this dreadful Crime has been brought to Light in the most extraordinary and miraculous manner; collected from various authors, ancient and modern. With an Introduction and conclusion. Both written by Henry Fielding, Esq*. His title reveals the formal and thematic inventiveness and conjuring character of the tales— murder is revealed through "*the most extraordinary and miraculous Manner*"—as it simultaneously insists on their providential source and logic.

In this collection of "examples," with the air of history such a title lends, Fielding's reportorial and authoritative tone is at odds with the wildly unlikely scenes he narrates. He presents outrageous generalizations as clear facts. For example, "the most authentic histories, as well as the traditions of all ages and countries" support the assertion that ghosts of those murdered haunt the murderers. The examples themselves read like excerpts from tabloid articles on wild children, freak births, or shocking scandals. The Bible, Greek history, and current news all translate into comparable lurid and unlikely tales of blood and vengeance. The limbs of the long dead bleed when the murderer returns to the room where they have been hung, and God (literally) writes the story of murders in ink visible only to a clergyman. The Bible, Plutarch, "a gentleman whose great-grand-father was an Irish judge ... before whom the thing happen'd [*sic*]" (63), *Wanly's Wonders of the little World*, and *Beard's Theatre of Wonders* are equivalent sources. The rollicking audacity and largesse of the text make it, like *Tom Jones*, great fun to read; yet it is a piece of juridical-theological propaganda that consistently claims its own authoritative power, not as crafted text, but as natural fact.

The contradictions of Fielding's text are not available simply to the chary contemporary critic. Fielding himself calls attention to the unbelievability of his narrative in an admonishment to his readers that recalls the defensive positions of novelists to accusations of falsity or immorality. He warns readers that to be skeptical of his arguments speaks more of "an obstinate and stubborn infidelity, than of a sound and sober reason" (9). Such a preemptive strike is well founded, as his actual discussion of Blandy's case is as paradoxical and convoluted an exposition of the "nature" of female criminals as he offers in *Amelia*.

He opens his discussion of Blandy's case by stating confidently that "[i]n Miss Mary Blandy is seen, the strong infatuation which often attends those who commit Murder, and which seldom fails of leading them to justice" (67). Here, in a move familiar from criminal biographies, Blandy is immediately categorized as a type, one who is predestined to face juridical punishment. Yet Blandy was widely recognized to be a generally well-behaved woman, and Fielding must go to some lengths to make her fit into the character type of murderess-to-be. Fielding states that it was, in fact, uncharacteristic for her to have "uttered speeches very unbecoming in a daughter," and then uses an impressively specious claim to reverse the positive import of the statement. He claims that, since she was a generally "good girl," that she could act out at all indicated the depth of her depravity. To counter the claim that Blandy was too smart to have purposively killed her father in a manner so obvious that it practically assured her arrest, Fielding argues that since she was known to "have had an exceeding good understanding, and great quickness of parts and invention," what else "but infatuation could make her go on in that horrid fact of poisoning her father, in so public and barefac'd a manner?" (67). But "infatuation" is what Blandy herself claimed in her apologia, in which she maintains that her infatuation for Cranstoun led her to follow his advice and administer the "love potion" to her father. Fielding accepts her infatuation, but refuses to accept that its consequence could be the foolish behavior of innocence versus ill intent.

Fielding's reading of Blandy as intentional murderess refutes her claim of innocence; his reading also positions her as inherently far more powerful than she appears in her own self-representation. Fielding presents Blandy, like Miss Mathews, as a smart and motivated female criminal whose violence is intentional. But while Fielding elaborates the details of the villainy that engenders Miss Mathews's attack on a perfidious seducer, he cannot articulate a motive for parricide other than natural evil. As Blandy's prosecutor, the Hon. Mr. Bathurst claims parricide is "a crime so shocking in its own Nature ... as will ... make our Children's Children, when they read the horrid tale of this Day, blush to think that such an inhuman Creature ever had an Existence." Like the prosecutor before him, Fielding cannot venture to ascribe to Blandy even the vexed motivation he ascribes to Miss Mathews. He not only makes Blandy a villainess, but also renders her outside of human representation, an "inhuman" anti-exemplar for the ages. For a daughter to kill her father strikes too hard at social structures to be explained by anything other than accident—what Fielding refutes and Blandy claims—or inherent evil.

From the time of her arrest, everyone knew *how* Blandy killed her father; what they did not know is why, and it is this lingering question, this desired revelation—not just of motive, but of the truth that explains an act considered beyond explanation—that requires fiction. I return to the epigraph with which I open this chapter, in which William Roughhead, the editor of Blandy's case for the *Notable Trials* series in 1914, wishes Blandy to have been the subject of "a great novelist's fancy." Roughhead assumes that the figure of the lived woman could only be perfectly revealed through the medium of novelistic fiction, that "cunning" cohesion is required to reveal the pattern behind the parricide. But the "wondrously wrought" image would rely on the novelist's own organizing fictions, the plots available to him to "reveal" the murderess. Fictional versions of crime create the illusion that we understand and thus can somehow master the criminal. Like Fielding's treatise, their authority comes from their promise of the revelation of providence as it simultaneously relies upon their transformation of providence into plot.[8]

Fielding's explanation of the value of his text asserts the power of plot to affect providence rather than the power of providence to affect plot. His exposition of the didactic value of the *Interposition* makes the authoritative power of fiction explicit and positions fiction, not as the genus for crime, but as its antidote. He explains that the *Interposition* is

> very proper to be given to all the inferior Kind of People; and particularly to the Youth of both sexes, whose natural Love of Stories will lead them to read with Attention what cannot fail of Infusing in to their tender Minds an early Dread and Abhorrence of staining their Hands with the Blood of their Fellow-creatures. (Qtd. in Godden 158)

Like those writers who locate the cause of criminality in fiction, Fielding assumes that stories have a direct affect on the behavior of readers of a certain status; it is the "inferior" readers—the young, women, the lower classes—who remain at risk of criminality. These reading audiences are presumed to be affected not by reason but by the "Dread" that fiction may induce in their "tender Minds."

The *Interposition* makes a telling case for the ways in which novels may "master" crime itself. Fiction is imagined here not as the instrument through which to reveal the murderess, but as the means to prevent her existence. The inefficacy of laws may be, by implication, ameliorated not through the body of the domestic heroine, as in *Amelia*, but through fiction itself. It is finally not God, or the judicial system, but the "natural love of Stories" that "cannot fail" to prevent murder.

* * *

---

[8]   I am indebted to Lennard Davis for the enviable phrasing of the idea that novelists "put themselves in the blasphemous position of equating plot with providence" (134).

I end this chapter with a brief musing on Fielding's defense of *Amelia* (from which the chapter's title is taken), a defense that speaks to the interrelated status of competitive modes of eighteenth-century narration. Through this small example, I call attention to the ways in which these narrative modes are levied by various writers in particular rhetorical situations and demonstrate the short-sightedness of the tempting critical equation of narrative strategies with essential authorial selves.

In response to stinging criticism of *Amelia*, Fielding published, in *The Covent Garden Journal* in January 1752, a mock-trial in which *Amelia* is the criminal woman, the "Prisoner at the Bar" who has been indicted before the "*Court of Censorial Enquiry.*" Fielding's description of *Amelia* (text and character) strikingly parallels Blandy's description of herself in her apologia. In contrast to the prosecutorial stance he takes in the *Interposition*, here Fielding casts himself as the prime witness for the defense: the father of the beleaguered accused heroine. He writes:

> I declare I am the Father of this poor Girl, the Prisoner at the Bar ... I go further and avow, that of all my Offspring, she is my favorite Child. If her Conduct be fairly examined, she will be found to deviate very little from the strictest Observation of those Rules. I do not think my Child is entirely free from Faults. I know nothing human that is so; but surely she doth not deserve the Rancour with which she hath been treated by the Public. (65–66)

Fielding explicitly parallels Blandy's defense of herself in his characterization of *Amelia* as the wrongly accused daughter. In place of the victimized father and murderous daughter of the *Interposition*, he presents the scenario of the worried father, and the at-risk daughter of Blandy's apologia: Blandy invokes her father who "pray[s] for her rescue," and Fielding is the distraught father who pleads for his "poor Girl." His plea for tolerance and degree in the sentencing of his "Offspring" echoes Blandy's plea that she "be punished for my follies, but not lose my Life." As narrator, Fielding appeals to a sympathetic, rather than simple, audience with personal testimonial rather than magisterial authority. He configures his female criminal, not as a monster to be condemned through a chain of circumstance, but as a victim of circumstance, whose story is subjective and whose faults, while present, do not render her outside of sympathetic identification.

I do not see this shift as an indictment of Fielding's shifting stances, but rather as an example of the ways in which all eighteenth-century writers in this study adopt rhetorical strategies and authorial positions according to the particular nature of a text and its context. Rather than mark shifts of sentiment and style in eighteenth-century writers as anomalies, or oversimplify theoretical and material divisions between writers, it is useful to see the ways in which eighteenth-century writers make their subjects "visible to us" through a "rich tapestry" of art. Blandy's and Fielding's dueling narratives of her case explicitly have a material stake—that of Blandy's life; in contrast, most casualties of the battle for narrative primacy that this chapter traces are less overtly violent, the victims the reputations of authors and their works. And yet, as Fielding reveals above and Manley dramatizes in *The Wife's Resentment*, losses of reputation have material effects, and the binary nature of verdicts—innocent or guilty, realistic or romantic, serious or melodramatic, rational or emotional—means that they often elide essential nuances.

Epilogue

This epilogue briefly considers three novels of the 1790s whose visions of female criminals allow me to gesture toward continuities as well as shifts in English fictional visions of female crime at the cusp of the nineteenth century: Elizabeth Inchbald's *Nature and Art* (1796), Mary Wollstonecraft's *Maria, or the Wrongs of Woman* (1798), and Mary Robinson's *The Natural Daughter* (1799). Each novel takes the criminal woman as its subject and builds on, as well as diverges from, representations of female criminality familiar from the fictions and criminal narratives of the past century. These novels engage with and critique the vexed history of eighteenth-century narratives of criminal female violence in ways that reflect their shared fictional inheritance.

By the 1790s, the novel itself was no longer a new or marginal form but a recognizably dominant mode of cultural expression. Inchbald, Wollstonecraft, and Robinson use themes and formal devices from amatory and criminal narratives, as well as more newly emergent "moral realism," to dispute regulatory and positivist visions of female nature.[1] Their late-eighteenth-century narratives frame female criminality within a contemporaneous and specific legal historical moment while using narrative elements of older romantic and criminal forms to shore up their radical political critiques. Inchbald, Wollstonecraft, and Robinson cloak their visions of violent female rage within a newly viable discourse of radical reform.

Nature and Art, Maria, and The Natural Daughter all overtly challenge orthodox patriarchal formulations of women and crime. However, they also amplify the literary trend, initiated by Defoe and Fielding, to displace female violence. Rather than murderesses, the female criminals in these novels are nonviolent victims of unjust masculine prerogative. The displacement or erasure of female violence and the focus on female victimization that occur in these novels of the 1790s are prescient given the actual state of late-eighteenth-century English women. These writers focus on the criminalization of female agency and the violent circumstances that uphold patriarchal rule and offer politically astute calls for vitally needed social and legal reforms. The muting of female violence does not, in other words, align with the regulatory impulse we see in Defoe's and Fielding's texts.

Like earlier fiction by women, *Nature and Art, Maria,* and *The Natural Daughter* use the female criminal character to reveal the ways in which female

---

[1] The sophisticated effects of each novel's use of formal montage have often been misread, and each writer has been critically castigated for her perceived aesthetic unevenness or lack of stylistic felicity. Recent criticism is beginning to provide more complex readings.

agency is rendered criminal by oppressive and sexist social and juridical systems. All three novels explicitly critique sexist and sexualized configurations of female criminality and pointedly locate female crime in social circumstance rather than in female nature. *Nature and Art*, *Maria*, and *The Natural Daughter* reveal the horror at the heart of women's position in patriarchal society, particularly in relation to the institution of marriage: Inchbald demonstrates the fatal status of women seduced without the legal protection of marriage, while Wollstonecraft and Robinson dramatize the imprisoned status of women legally trapped within marriage.

In *Nature and Art*, Inchbald critiques the multiple levels of oppression that lead to female crime through her tragic character Hannah Primrose, who is seduced, impregnated, and then abandoned by the villainous William Norwynne. After working as a prostitute to support herself, she eventually falls in with a band of robbers and adopts a protosocialist Robin Hood–like ethic toward crime:

> [T]aught by the conversation of the dissolute poor, with whom she now associated, or by her own observation on the worldly reward of elevated villainy, she began to suspect "that dishonesty was only held a sin, to secure the property of the rich; and that, to take from those who did not want, by the art of stealing, was less guilt than to take from those who did want by the power of law. (113)

While the novel overtly claims Hannah's logic as false, its plot nevertheless supports her radical claims regarding the entitlement of the disenfranchised— women and the poor of both sexes—that the passage ventures to make. At the level of plot, *Nature and Art* indicts the socially powerful, wealthy, and morally sanctioned man who is responsible for the woman's sexual ruin and subsequent fall into poverty, criminality, and death.

Inchbald plays directly with the criminal narrative, whose regulatory form and content her novel contests. Hannah is eventually arrested for forgery, and her case is tried by her former seducer, Norwynne, now the assize judge, whose failure to recognize her explicitly emphasizes his callow nature.[2] Having figuratively taken her life by taking her honor, he now sentences her to death by hanging. After Hannah's execution, Inchbald ironically includes a criminal narrative of Hannah's execution and gallows' repentance, a narrative we know to be false and one that conceals the culpability of the novel's true criminal—Judge Norwynne:

> The last dying words, speech, and confessions; birth, parentage, and education; life, character, and behavior, of Hannah Primrose, who was executed this morning between the hours of ten and twelve having been led astray by the arts and flattery of a seducing man. (118)

---

[2]   The alignment of his guilt with class privilege and the power of the law recalls the fiction of both Manley and Richardson.

Inchbald frames her pitch-perfect version of an ordinary's account within a novel that exposes the official patriarchal narrative to be a lie, and thus calls into question the lawful records of both church and state that collaborate in the wrongful death of the criminal woman.

Maria strikingly resembles *Nature and Art* in the broad scope of its social critique and its commingling of prose modes. Wollstonecraft's unfinished novel of a woman incarcerated for madness by her abusive husband dramatizes the criminalization of female self-governance caused by English marriage laws. Maria declaims the legal state of sexist oppression that criminalizes mother love and female labor:

> But a wife being as much a man's property as his horse, or his ass, she has nothing she can call her own. ... The tender mother cannot *lawfully* snatch from the grips of the gambling spendthrift, or beastly drunkard, unmindful of his offspring, the fortune which falls to her by chance, or (so flagrant is the injustice) what she earns by her own exertions. (91, 92)

The criminal conversation trial in which her husband sues her lover for damages may or may not provide Maria restitution of her fortune or liberty; but the trial itself, like the novel, offers Maria a space of testimonial that may affect public, if not judicial, opinion.

Like Inchbald, Wollstonecraft moves between didactic moralism and what may seem to be hyperbolic calamities to reveal the horror that is women's oppression.[3] Her novel most resembles Inchbald's in the embedded plot of Maria's prison guard, Jemima. Jemima's suffering begins with her "natural" birth and includes beatings, rape, prostitution, thievery, and abortion. Her story, as critic Hugh Gladfelder notes, is "a distillation of the whole tradition of ordinaries' accounts and halfpenny criminal lives" (214). In contrast to this tradition, however, Wollstonecraft locates Jemima's guilt as socially constructed and her crimes as the result of sexist and classist social and legal structures that institutionalize female oppression.

The violent plot lines of criminal biographies and amatory fictions provide the embodied underpinnings to the notions of radical political protest that inform these late-eighteenth-century fictions of female possibility.[4] As I have argued, while the criminal narratives fulfilled an overtly regulatory project that feminocentric texts purposefully trouble, both criminal narratives and early fiction tell similarly violent tales. Some critics argue that the language of sentimentalism reinforces the social institutions that these radical political novels attack. In contrast, I see the novels' use of exaggeration and extremity—plot and prose familiar from amatory

---

[3]   Inchbald and Wollstonecraft are often pitted against one another by feminist critics; my argument focuses on the similar rhetorical devices they use in crafting polemical fictions that rely upon the strategies of romantic and criminal forms to make their rational arguments.

[4]   I borrow the term "fictions of female possibility" from my mother, Ruth Saxton.

and criminal narratives—as a useful rhetorical strategy. This strategy grounds the novels' political rhetoric in the somatic—reminding the reader, at the levels of both content and form, of the real violence that lurks behind seemingly abstract social facades. The presence of what we may variously deem romantic, amatory, or gothic elements in these novels of reform does not stem from the inevitable, but likely unintended, revelations of the fissures in sexist ideologies—as in more regulatory fictions—but from the acknowledged horror of the violence done *to* not *by* women.

These novels locate criminal violence in the bodies of the legitimate husbands and judges whose power over female bodies renders women victims rather than perpetrators of violent crime. As in earlier fictions, women are criminalized victims who are seduced and abandoned, separated from or forced to abort their children, forced into sexual or criminal labor, and then wrongly accused and sentenced. But no murderesses appear in these novels; female criminality is either nonviolent or the violence is an attack on the self, either directly or indirectly.[5] Female crime takes the form of forgery, theft, adultery, and prostitution.

Robinson's *The Natural Daughter* castigates aristocratic male privilege as it traces the history of Martha Morley, who is thrown out of her home by her hypocritical sadistic husband for staying true to her honorable principles. Like Wollstonecraft, Robinson renders explicit masculine abuse and the resultant criminalization of female agency. In the following passage, she imagines male seduction as murder and equates female homicide with self-defense:

> If a man is stopped on the highway, he may shoot the depredator: and he will receive the thanks of society. If a WOMAN were to act upon the same principle, respecting the more atrocious robber who has deprived her of all that rendered life desirable, she would be punished as a *murderer*. (74)

The passage continues with a long discourse on the frequency and violent effects of males breaking marital oaths. Robinson's biting critique of the inequality and illogic of gendered laws and the exclusion of seduction from enforceable ill-doings explicitly recalls Behn's lengthy pronouncement in *The History of the Nun* on the breaking of romantic vows. But while Behn specifically damns the male justice system and religious institutions for their support of male sexual prerogative and its resultant criminalization of women, Robinson widens her net to accuse "British females" for their complicit status in upholding male privilege. Like Wollstonecraft, Robinson is concerned with the ways in which British women participate in their own oppression and consequent criminalization. The murderess is relegated to an "if/then" clause that erases her action even as it challenges the terms of that erasure as unjust.

---

[5]   Infanticide does appear in the novels of this era; as I discussed earlier, infanticide was legally differentiated from homicide and, as is still true, it does not legally or popularly signify the externalized violence of female homicide.

In *The Natural Daughter*, Robinson neatly displaces female homicide onto providential plot. The role of murderess falls to the author, rather than a character, and the violence exists not as a bloody footprint we trail to male guilt, but as a wishful authorial enactment of petty treason free even of the taint of imagined homicide. Women were no longer legally burned at the stake for killing their husbands in England in the 1790s, but husband-murder still remained a locus for social anxiety and archetypal notions of female venality. In *The Natural Daughter*, the consummately evil husband—Mr. Morley—symbol of all that is wrong with coverture and male governance, is not killed by his abused wife, but rather dies a convenient death at the hands of the female author on the last pages of the novel. As Mr. Morley is poised to throw a baby off a cliff, its deserted mother exclaims "[M]y infant! Oh, Morley, Morley, thou inhuman *father*!" (294). His subsequent death by a fall over the cliff, a fall caused by the shock of his newly discovered paternity, is rhapsodically rendered:

> Mr. Morley heard the fiat of his destiny! ... They had witnessed the just vengeance of insulted Heaven! They had seen the libertine who, under the mask of sanctity, had violated all the laws of honour and religion, who had assumed through life the name of a philanthropist ... perish! (294)

Robinson's tone recalls the similarly ecstatic and triumphant tenor of the murder scene in *The Wife's Resentment*. In contrast to the more vexed textual presence of the murderess, however, this displacement allows the female writer, reader, and character guilt-free celebration at the death of the despised husband. Here, fiction does not prevent murder, as Fielding claims in the *Interposition*, but enacts it.[6] Plot works as providence. The words of the female author are responsible for the villain's death: the language of Robinson's plot and of Martha's declaration (Martha has become a writer to support herself[7]) kill Morley, but no female character lifts a hand against him.

By the 1790s, murderesses seem to be relegated by novelists to that romantic realm associated with the extra-real, with the scandalous and outré fictions that were not seen to offer a platform for serious political or moral inquiry. It is in the

---

[6] While elements of bloody crime narratives and of amatory fictions remained at play for the next century, novels praised for their moral fortitude and realism continued to mute violent female agency by displacing it to plot (as in Casaubon's fall or Rochester's maiming) or to peripheral characters such as Hortense, in Charles Dickens's *Bleak House*, whose status as French maid evokes the criminal biography in its national and class shorthand, but who has no real character in the novel.

[7] Robinson uses Martha Morley's experience as a writer as a means to comment upon what she posits as the sexist and anti-intellectual nature of the fiction market; Martha receives only ten pounds for her "first born" (208) and when she is wrongly incarcerated in a private madhouse and she discovers that the novel has gone through six editions, her frustration affirms her insanity to the doctors.

gothic novel that the murderess continues to appear as a larger-than-life force. Novels such as Matthew Lewis's *Ambrosio, or, The Monk* and Charlotte Dacre's *Zofloya* recall the fiction of a century earlier in their hyperbolic fetishizing of unrestrained female agency. Gothic novels resemble amatory fiction in that the themes of political oppression, criminal violence, miscegenation, incarceration, and prohibited sexuality are not framed within a sociospecific or local legal context, but instead are cloaked in the guise of the fantastic, the exotic, and the exaggerated. From the end of the eighteenth century, the murderess takes center stage only in the press and in subgeneric fictions. In addition to media accounts of actual murderesses, the gothic novel, the sensation novel, and the penny dreadful become the space of imagined violent female agency. These fictions' association with the somatic, the feminine, and the fantastic links them in a chain of critically debased popular fictions that begins with the female-authored fictions of the Restoration and first half of the eighteenth century.

The story of the murderess remains a compelling one: "[A] female Offender [still] excites our curiosity more than a male" (Charles Johnson 327), and the underlying terms of her representations remain constant even as the idioms and forms through which she is articulated necessarily shift according to era, location, and genre. Fictional visions of murderesses continue to fascinate, and homicidal women are the frequent protagonists of popular novels, comics, plays, television shows, and films. Actual murderesses remain rare, and true-crime accounts of their cases continue to excite curiosity and to proliferate within the popular and mainstream press. The murderess is still perceived as an anomaly whose violent crime violates not only legal, social, and moral sanctions, but also naturalized notions of gender, as the following example makes clear. The case of murderess Elizabeth Brownrigg embodies the arcane and outlandish nature of eighteenth-century visions of the murderess: Brownrigg's body remains in the British Museum since her 1767 execution, awaiting the scientific developments that her peers thought would surely prove this mother of sixteen children to be male and thus explain her otherwise inexplicable violence. Aileen Wuornos, an impoverished, abused, and mentally ill twentieth-century prostitute, was executed in Florida in 2002 for the murder of seven men; like Brownrigg's body, her brain has been saved for scientific study in the hopes that it will someday explain her crimes according to a biological anomaly. I repeat the quote from Margaret Atwood's *Alias Grace* with which I opened this book: "'Murderess, murderess,' he whispers to himself. 'It has an allure, a scent almost. Hothouse gardenias. Lurid but also furtive.'"

Select Bibliography

Aercke, Kristiaan P. "Theatrical Background in English Novels of the Seventeenth Century." *Journal of Narrative Technique* 18.2 (1988): 120–36.

Allestree, Richard. *The Ladies Calling: In Two Parts*. Oxford: Printed at the Theatre, 1673.

Amory, Hugh. *Law and the Structure of Fielding's Novels*. New York: Columbia UP, 1964.

The Annual Register, or a View of the History, Politicks, and Literature, for the year 1767. London: Printed for J. Dodsley in Pall-mall, 1768.

Armstrong, Nancy. *Desire and Domestic Fiction: A Political History of the Novel*. New York: Oxford UP, 1987.

Astell, Mary. *Some Reflections upon Marriage*. London, 1700.

Atwood, Margaret. *Alias Grace*. New York: Nan A. Talese, 1996.

Backscheider, Paula R. *Daniel Defoe: His Life*. Baltimore: Johns Hopkins UP, 1989.

—. *Moll Flanders: The Making of a Criminal Mind*. Boston, MA: Twayne, 1990.

—. and John Richetti. *Popular Fiction by Women, 1660–1730: An Anthology*. Oxford: Clarendon, 1996.

Bakhtin, M. M. *The Dialogic Imagination: Four Essays*. Ed. Michael Holquist. Trans. Caryl Emerson and Michael Holquist. Austin: U of Texas P, 1981.

Ballaster, Ros. "'Pretenses of State': Aphra Behn and the Female Plot." Hutner 187–211.

—. *Seductive Forms: Women's Amatory Fiction from 1684–1740*. Oxford: Clarendon, 1992.

Barbauld, Anna Laetitia. "On the Origin and Progress of Novel-Writing." *The British Novelists, with an Essay, and Prefaces, Biographical and Critical*. Vol. 1. London, 1820.

Beasley, Jerry C. "Politics and Moral Idealism: The Achievement of Some Early Women Novelists." Schofield and Macheski 216–36.

Beattie, J. M. *Crime and the Courts in England, 1660–1800*. Princeton: Princeton UP, 1986.

—. "The Criminality of Women in Eighteenth-Century England." *Journal of Social History* 8.4 (1975): 80–116.

Behn, Aphra. *The Fair Jilt, or The History of Prince Tarquin and Miranda. Oroonoko, The Rover and Other Works*. Ed. Janet Todd. London: Penguin, 1992.

—. *The History of the Nun, or, The Fair Vow-Breaker. Popular Fiction by Women, 1660–1730, an Anthology*. Ed. Paula R. Backscheider and John J. Richetti. Oxford: Clarendon, 1996.

—, and Charles Gildon. "The History of the Life and Memoirs of Mrs Behn By One of the Fair Sex." *All the Histories and Novels of the Late Ingenious Mrs Behn.* 5th ed. London, 1705.

—, and Charles Gildon. "Memoirs of the Life of Mrs Behn Written by a Gentlewoman of her Acquaintance." *All the Histories and Novels Written by the Late Ingenious Mrs. Behn Entire in One Volume: Together with the History of the Life and Memoirs of Mrs. Behn Never Before Printed.* 3rd ed. London: Printed for Samuel Briscoe, 1698.

Bell, Ian A. *Defoe's Fiction.* London: Croom Helm, 1985.

—. *Literature and Crime in Augustan England.* London: Routledge, 1991.

Bender, John. "Eighteenth-Century Studies." *Redrawing the Boundaries: The Transformation of English and American Literary Studies.* Ed. Stephen Greenblatt and Giles Gunn. New York: MLA of America, 1992. 79–99.

—. *Imagining the Penitentiary: Fiction and the Architecture of Mind in Eighteenth-Century England.* Chicago: U of Chicago P, 1987.

Benedict, Barbara M. "Recent Studies in the Restoration and Eighteenth Century." *Studies in English Literature, 1500–1900* 42.3 (2002): 619–74.

Bingham, Victor. *The Noose Around the Wrong Neck.* Henley-on-Thames: Bingham Press, in press.

Binhammer, Katherine. "The Sex Panic of the 1790s." *Journal of the History of Sexuality.* 6.3 (January 1996): 409–34.

Blackstone, Sir William. *Commentaries on the Law in England.* 4 vols. Oxford: Clarendon, 1766–69.

Blandy, Mary. *Miss Mary Blandy's Own Account of the Affair Between Her and Mr. Cranstoun: from the Commencement of the Acquaintance, in the year 1746, to the Death of her Father in August 1751, With all the circumstances leading to that unhappy Event.* London, 1752. London: Printed for A. Millar, 1752.

Bonamy, Dobree. *English Literature in the Early Eighteenth Century, 1700–1740.* Oxford: Oxford UP, 1959.

Bowers, Toni. *The Politics of Motherhood: British Writing and Culture, 1680–1760.* New York: Cambridge UP, 2005.

—. "Sex, Lies, and Invisibility: Amatory Fiction from the Restoration to Mid-Century." *The Columbia History of the British Novel.* Ed. John Richetti. New York: Columbia UP, 2005. 50–72.

Braudy, Leo. "Daniel Defoe and the Anxieties of Autobiography." *Genre* 6 (1973): 76–67.

—. *Narrative Form in History and Fiction: Hume, Fielding, and Gibbon.* Princeton: Princeton UP, 1970.

Brewer, David. "'Haywood': Secret History and the Politics of Attribution." Saxton and Bocchicchio 283–99.

British Journal. London (May 14, 1727).

Brown, Laura. *Ends of Empire: Women and Ideology in Early Eighteenth-Century English Literature.* Ithaca: Cornell UP, 1993.

Burford, E. J., and Sandra Shulman. *Of Bridles and Burnings: The Punishment of Women*. New York: St. Martin's, 1992.

Butler, Samuel. *Prose Observations*. Ed. Hugh de Quehen. Oxford: Clarendon, 1979.

Cameron, William J. *New Light on Aphra Behn: An Investigation into the Facts and Fictions Surrounding her Journey to Surinam in 1663, and her Activities as a Spy in Flanders in 1666*. Auckland: U of Auckland, 1961.

Campbell, Jill. *Natural Masques: Gender and Identity in Fielding's Plays and Novels*. Stanford: Stanford UP, 1995.

Castle, Terry. "'Amy Who Knew My Disease': A Psychosexual Pattern in Defoe's *Roxana*." *ELH* 46.1 (1979): 81–96.

—. *Masquerade and Civilization: The Carnivalesque in Eighteenth-Century English Culture and Fiction*. Stanford: Stanford UP, 1986.

"Catherine Hayes, a Murderess." *Lives of the Most Remarkable Criminals Who have Been Condemned and Executed for Murder, Highway Robberies, Housebreaking, Street Robberies, Coining, or Other Offences; From the Year 1720 to the Year 1735*. London: Reeves, 1874.

Chandler, F. W. *The Literature of Roguery: in Two Volumes*. 2 vols. London, 1907.

Chudleigh, Lady Mary. "To the Ladies." *Poems on Several Occasions*. London, 1703.

Congreve, William. *The Mourning Bride. The Complete Plays of William Congreve*. Ed. Herbert John Davis. Chicago: U of Chicago P, 1967.

Conway, Alison. *Private Interests: Women, Portraiture, and the Visual Culture of the English Novel, 1709–1791*. Toronto: U of Toronto P, 2001.

Craciun, Adriana. Introduction. *Zofloya*. By Charlotte Dacre. Ontario, Canada: Broadview, 1997. 9–32.

Craft-Fairchild, Catherine. *Masquerade and Gender: Disguise and Female Identity in Eighteenth-Century Fiction by Women*. University Park: Pennsylvania State UP, 1993.

Dacre, Charlotte. *Zofloya, or the Moor: A Romance of the Fifteenth Century*. Ontario, Canada: Broadview, 1997.

Daniel, George. *Merrie England in the Olden Time*. Vol. 2, pt. 2. London: R. Bentley, 1842.

Davis, Lennard. *Factual Fictions: The Origins of the English Novel*. New York: Columbia UP, 1983.

Defoe, Daniel. *The Commentator*, No. 46 (June 10, 1720).

—. *Conjugal Lewdness: or, Matrimonial Whoredom: A Treatise Concerning the Use and Abuse of the Marriage Bed*. 1727. Ed. Maximillian E. Novak. Gainsville: Scholars' Facsimiles & Reprints, 1967.

—. *An Effectual Scheme for the Immediate Preventing of Robberies, and Suppressing all other Disorders of the Night*. London: Printed for J. Wilford, 1731.

—. *An Essay Upon Projects*. London: Printed by R. R. and T. Cockerill, at the corner of Warwick-Lane, near Pater-noster-Row, 1697.

—. *Everybody's Business Is Nobody's Business*. Kessinger Publishing's Rare Reprints. Web. 6 June 2008.

—. *A Hymn to the Funeral Sermon*. London, 1703.

—. *A Plan of the English Commerce, Being a Complete Prospect of the Trade of this Nation, as well the Home Trade as the Foreign*. Oxford: Blackwell, 1928.

—. *Roxana, The Fortunate Mistress, or a History of the Life and Vast Variety of Fortunes of Mademoiselle de Beleau, afterwards called the Countess de Wintelsheim in Germany Being the Person known by the name of the Lady Roxana in the time of Charles II*. Ed. Jane Jack. London: Oxford UP, 1964.

—. *Street-Robberies, consider'd: the Reason of their being so Frequent*. 1728. Stockton, NJ: Carolingian, 1973.

—. *A Trip Through London: Containing Observations on Men and Things*. London: Printed, and sold, by J. Roberts, J. Shuckburgh, and J. Jackson, 1728.

—. *A Trip Through the Town*, 4th ed., London, 1735.

—. *The True-Born Englishman: A Satyr*. London, 1701.

—, and Jack Sheppard. *The History of the Remarkable Life of John Sheppard, Containing a Particular Account of his Many Robberies and Escapes ... .* London: Applebee: 1724.

Dickens, Charles, George Harry Ford, and Sylvère Monod. *Bleak House: An Authoritative and Annotated Text, Illustrations, a Note on the Text, Genesis and Composition, Backgrounds, Criticism*. New York: Norton, 1977.

Dijkstra, Bram. *Defoe and Economics: The Fortunes of Roxana in the History of Interpretation*. New York: St. Martin's, 1987.

Dolan, Frances. *Dangerous Familiars: Representations of Domestic Crime in England, 1550–1700*. Ithaca: Cornell UP, 1994.

Donoghue, Denis. "The Values of Moll Flanders." *Sewanee Review* 71 (1963): 287–303.

Doody, Margaret. "The Law, the Page, and the Body of Woman: Murder and Murderesses in the Age of Johnson." *The Age of Johnson* 1 (1987): 127–60.

—. *The True Story of the Novel*. New Brunswick: Rutgers UP, 1996.

Doran, Dr. *"Their Majesties' Servants": Annals of the English stage, from Betterton to Edmund Keane*. New York: Widdleton, 1865.

Duncombe, John. *The Feminiad. A Poem*. 1754.

Durant, David. "Roxana's Fictions." *Studies in the Novel* 13.3 (Fall 1981): 225–36.

Dryden, John. "To the Pious Memory of the Accomplisht Young Lady Mrs. Anne Killigrew." London: Printed for Samuel Lowndes, 1686.

Eliot, George. *Middlemarch*. Berlin: A. Asher; Philadelphia: J. B. Lippincott, 1872.

Elton, G. R. "Crime and the historian." *Crime in England: 1550–1800*. Ed. J. Cockburn. Princeton: Princeton UP, 1977.

Faller, Lincoln. *Crime and Defoe*. Cambridge: Cambridge UP, 1993.

—. "Tales of a Poisoning Female Parricide and a Prostitute Treated 'in a Manner Too Shocking to Mention': Two Criminal Cases and 'the *Clarissa* Effect.'" *Eighteenth-Century Novel* (2006): 147–97.

—. *Turned to Account: The Forms and Functions of Criminal Biography in Late Seventeenth- and Early Eighteenth-Century England*. Cambridge: Cambridge UP, 1987.

Ferguson, Moira. *First Feminists: British Women Writers, 1578–1799.* Bloomington: Indiana UP, 1985.

Fielding, Henry. *Amelia.* Ed. David Blewett. Harmondsworth, UK: Penguin, 1987.

—. *A Charge Delivered to the Grand Jury, at the Sessions of the Peace Held for the City and Liberty of Westminster, &c. on Thursday the 29th of June, 1749.* Dublin: Printed by George Faulkner, 1749.

—. *Covent Garden Journal.* London, January 25, 1752.

—. *An Enquiry into the Causes of the Late Increase in Robbers &c. 1751.* Ed. Malvin R. Zirker. Oxford: Oxford UP, 1988.

—. *Examples of the Interposition of Providence in the Detection and Punishment of Murder. Containing above thirty Cases, in which this dreadful Crime has been brought to Light in the most extraordinary and miraculous manner; collected from various authors, ancient and modern. With an Introduction and conclusion. Both written by Henry Fielding, Esq.* London, 1752.

—. *The History of Tom Jones the Foundling in his Married State.* Dublin: Printed by S. Powell, for G. and A. Ewing, 1749.

—. *A Proposal for Making an Effectual Provision for the Poor.* London, 1753.

—. *A True State of the Case of Bosavern Penlez.* London, 1749.

Flynn, Carol Houlihan. *The Body in Swift and Defoe.* Cambridge: Cambridge UP, 1990.

Foucault, Michel. *I, Pierre Rivière, Having Slaughtered my Mother, my Sister, and my Brother ... : A Case of Parricide in the 19th Century.* Ed. Blandine Kriegel. New York: Pantheon Books, 1975.

Gallagher, Catherine. *Nobody's Story: The Vanishing Acts of Women Writers in the Marketplace, 1670–1820.* Berkeley: U of California P, 1994.

Gardiner, Judith Kegan. "Aphra Behn: Sexuality and Self-Respect." *Women's Studies* 7.1–2 (1980): 67–78.

Gatrell, V. A. C. *The Hanging Tree: Execution and the English People, 1770–1868.* n.p., n.d.

Gay, John. *The Present State of Wit.* London, 1711.

A General and Impartial Account of the Life of Mary Blandy, Particularly From the Time of her Commitment to Oxford-Castle, to her Execution at Oxford, Monday, April 6, 1752, for poisoning her Father. With Her own Account of the Affair between her and Mr. Cranstoun, from their first Acquaintance, in 1746: In a Narrative of the Crime for which she suffered. London: Printed and Sold by W. Jackson in the High-Street Oxford and the Booksellers there; and sold in London by R. Walker in the Old Bailey and by all the Booksellers and Pamphlet sellers, 1752.

Gentleman's Magazine. London, 1750. 532–33.

Gilbert, Sandra, and Susan Gubar. *The Madwoman in the Attic: The Woman Writer and the Nineteenth-Century Literary Imagination.* London and New Haven: Yale UP, 1979.

Gildon, Charles. *An Epistle to Daniel Defoe.* 1719. Rpt. London: Dent, 1928.

—, trans. *Phaeton: or, The Fatal Divorce. A Tragedy as it is acted at the Theatre Royal, in imitation of the ancients. With some reflections on a book call'd, A short view of the immorality and profaneness of the English stage. By Euripides*. London: Printed for Abel Roper, at Black-boy over against St. Dunstans Church in Fleetstreet, 1698.

Gladfelder, Hugh. *Criminality and Narrative in Eighteenth-Century England*. Baltimore: Johns Hopkins UP, 2001.

Godden, G. M. *Henry Fielding: A Memoir*. Whitefish, MT: Kessinger Publishing, 2004.

Goreau, Angeline. *Reconstructing Aphra: A Social Biography of Aphra Behn*. Oxford: Oxford UP, 1980.

Gould, Robert and Thomas Brown. *Love Given O're: or, a Satyr against the Pride, Lust, and Inconstancy, &c. of Woman*. London, 1682.

Granger, James. *A Biographical History of England*. Vol. 28. London, 1769.

Griffiths, Arthur. *The Chronicles of Newgate*. London: Chapman, 1884.

Guthrie, James. *The Ordinary of Newgate: His Account of the Behaviour, Confession, Demands, of the Malefactors, Who Were Executed at Tyburn, ... in the Mayoralty of Rt. Hon. Daniel Lambert, Esq*. London: Printed and sold by John Applebee, 1741.

Haggerty, George. "Fielding's Novel of Atonement: Confessional Form in *Amelia*." *Eighteenth-Century Fiction*. 8.3 (1996): 389, 390.

Hall, Edith. "*Medea* on the Eighteenth-Century Stage." *Medea in Performance: 1500–2000*. Ed. Edith Hall and Oliver Taplin. Oxford: European Humanities Research Centre of U of Oxford/LEGENDA, 2001.

Hammond, Brean S. *Professional Imaginative Writing in England, 1670–1740: Hackney for Bread*. Oxford: Clarendon, 1997.

Hart, Lynda. *Fatal Women: Lesbian Sexuality and the Mark of Aggression*. Princeton: Princeton UP, 1994.

Hartman, Mary. *Mary Hartman's Victorian Murderesses: A True Story of Thirteen French and English Women Accused of Unspeakable Crimes*. New York: Schocken, 1976.

Haywood, Eliza. *The City Jilt, or the Alderman turn'd Beau. Eliza Haywood: Three Novellas. Early English Women Writers, 1660–1800*. Ed. Earla A. Wilputte. East Lansing, MI: Colleagues, 1995.

—. *Memoirs of the Baron de Brosse, Who Was Broke on the Wheel in the Reign of Louis XIV*. 2nd ed. London: Browne, 1725.

—. *Reflections on the Various Effects of Love. According to the Contrary Dispositions of the Persons on Whom it Operates*. London, 1726.

Heinzelman, Susan Sage. "Guilty in Law, Implausible in Fiction: Jurisprudential and Literary Narratives in the Case of Mary Blandy, Parricide." *Representing Woman: Law, Literature and Feminism*. Ed. Susan Sage Heinzelman and Zipporah Batshaw Wiseman. Durham, NC: Duke UP, 1994.

Hentzi, Gary. "Holes in the Heart: Moll Flanders, Roxana, and 'Agreeable Crime'." *Boundary 2: An International Journal of Literature and Culture* 18.1 (Spring 1991): 174–200.

Hill, Bridget. *Eighteenth-Century Women: An Anthology*. London: Allen, 1984.

Hitchcock, Tom, and Robert Shoemaker. *Tales from the Hanging Court*. London: Hodder Arnold, 2006.

Hoffer, Peter C. and N. E. H. Hull. *Murdering Mothers: Infanticide in England and New England 1558–1803*. New York: New York UP, 1981.

Hogarth, William and Thomas Cook. *Hogarth Restored: The Whole Works of the Celebrated William Hogarth, as Originally Published: With a Supplement, Consisting of Such of his Prints as Were Not Published in a Collected Form*. London: Printed for John Stockdale ... and G. Robinson, 1808.

—, Thomas Cook, and John Trusler. *The Works of William Hogarth Containing One Hundred and Fifty-Eight Engravings, by Mr. Cooke, and Mr. Davenport, with Descriptions in Which Are Pointed Out Many Beauties That Have Hither to Escaped Notice, with a Comment on Their Moral Tendency*. London: Tegg, 1800s.

—, Thomas Cook, and Samuel Davenport. *The Works of William Hogarth: Consisting of One Hundred and Forty-Four Engravings Copied from the Large Originals, and Including Many of the Author's Minor Pieces*. London: Lewis, 1800.

Holmes, Geoffery. *British Politics in the Age of Anne*. London: Macmillan, 1967.

Humphreys, A. R. *The Augustan World: Society, Thought, and Letters in Eighteenth-Century England*. New York: Harper and Row, 1954.

Hunter, J. Paul. *Before Novels: The Cultural Contexts of Eighteenth-Century English Fiction*. New York: Norton, 1990.

Hutner, Heidi, ed. *Rereading Aphra Behn: History, Theory and Criticism*. Charlottesville: UP of Virginia, 1993.

Hutton, William. *A Dissertation on juries; with a description of the hundred court: as an appendix to the Court of Requests*. Birmingham: printed by Pearson and Rollason; and sold by R. Baldwin, London, 1789.

Inchbald, Elizabeth. *Nature and Art*. Ed. Shawn Maurer. Peterborough, ON, Canada: Broadview, 2005.

Johnson, Charles. *Lives of Most Remarkable Female Robbers*. London: Ann Lemoine, 1801.

—, and Alexander Smith. *A General History of the Lives and Adventures of the Most Famous Highwaymen, Murderers, Street-robbers &c. To Which is Added, a Genuine Account of the Voyages and Plunders of the Most Notorious Pyrates. ... By Capt. Charles Johnson*. London: Printed for and sold by J. Janeway, 1734.

Johnson, Samuel. *London: a Poem, in Imitation of the Third Satire of Juvenal*. London: Printed for R. Doddesley, 1738.

Jones, Ann. *Women Who Kill*. New York: Holt, Rinehart and Winston, 1980.

Jones, Benjamin M. *Henry Fielding, Novelist and Magistrate*. London: Allen & Unwin, 1933.

Jones, Jennifer. *Medea's Daughters: Forming and Performing the Woman Who Kills*. Columbus: Ohio State UP, 2003.

Jones, Vivien, ed. *Women in the Eighteenth Century: Constructions of Femininity*. New York and London: Routledge, 1990.

Kahn, Madeleine. *Narrative Transvestism: Rhetoric and Gender in the Eighteenth-Century English Novel*. Ithaca: Cornell UP, 1991.

Kappeler, Victor, Mark Blumberg, and Gary W. Potter. *The Mythology of Crime and Criminal Justice*. Prospect Heights, IL: Waveland, 1993.

Klein, Lawrence. "Gender and the Public/Private Distinction in the Eighteenth Century: Some Questions about Evidence and Analytic Procedure." *Eighteenth-Century Studies* 29.1 (Fall 1995): 97–109.

Knapp, Andrew, William Baldwin, and Henry Savage. *The Newgate Calendar: Comprising Interesting Memoirs of the Most Notorious Characters Who Have Been Convicted of Outrages on the Laws of England: with Speeches, Confessions, and Last Exclamations of Sufferers*. London: J. Robbins and Co., 1824; Hartford, CT: Mitchell, 1926.

Langbauer, Laurie. *Women and Romance: The Consolations of Gender in the English Novel*. Ithaca: Cornell UP, 1990.

Lewis, Matthew Gregory. *Ambrosio, or, The Monk: A Romance*. 4th ed., with considerable additions and alterations. London: Printed for J. Bell, 1798.

Lewis, W. S., ed. *The Yale Edition of Horace Walpole's Correspondence*. Vol. 20. London, 1937–83. 48 vols.

Lillo, George. *The London Merchant, or, The history of George Barnwell*. London: Printed for J. Gray ... and sold by J. Roberts, 1731.

Linebaugh, Peter. *The London Hanged: Crime and Civil Society in the Eighteenth Century*. Cambridge: Cambridge UP, 1992.

Lockhart, John Gibson. *Memoirs of the Life of Sir Walter Scott*. Vol. 3. Boston and New York: Houghton, 1902.

The London Magazine, or, Gentleman's Monthly Intelligencer, London (n.d.): 7 and 95–96.

Lorrain, Paul. *The Ordinary's Account*. June 6, 1709. London.

—. *Remarks On the Author of the Hymn to the Pillory. With an Answer to the Hymn to the Funeral Sermon*. London, 1703.

Lynch, Eve. "Domestic Empires The Victorian Servant and the British Literary Imagination." Diss. U of California Davis, 1996.

MacCarthy, B. G. *Women Writers: Their Contribution to the English Novel, 1621–1744*. Cork: Cork UP, 1944.

Magrath, Jane. "(Mis)Reading the Bloody Body: The case of Sarah Malcolm." *Women's Writing* 11.2 (2004): 223–36.

Maitland, F. W., and F. C. Montague. *A Sketch of English Legal History. American Commercial Legislation Before 1789*. By Albert Anthony Giesecke. Philadelphia: U of Philadelphia P, 1910.

Mandeville, Bernard. *The Fable of the Bees or, Private Vices Publick Benefits*. London: Printed for J. Roberts, 1714.

Manley, Delarivier. *The Adventures of Rivella*. London: Printed for John Morphew and J. Woodward, 1714.

—. *Secret Memoirs and Manners of Several Persons of Quality, of both Sexes. From the New Atlantis, an Island in the Mediterranean*. London, 1709.

—. *The Wife's Resentment. The Meridian Anthology of Early Women Writers: British Literary Women from Aphra Behn to Maria Edgeworth, 1660–1900*. Ed. Katherine M. Rogers and William McCarthy. New York: New American Library, 1987.

Maurer, Shawn Lisa. "'As Sacred as Friendship, as Pleasurable as Love': Father-Son Relations in the Tatler and The Spectator." *History, Gender and Eighteenth-Century Literature*. Ed. Beth Fowkes Tobin. Athens, GA: U of Georgia P, 1994, 14–38.

McAdoo, William. *The Procession to Tyburn: Crime and Punishment in the Eighteenth Century*. New York: Boni, 1927.

McBurney, William. "Mrs. Penelope Aubin and the Early Eighteenth-Century Novel." *Huntington Library Quarterly* 20 (1947): 245–67.

McDonagh, Josephine, ed. *Child Murder and British Culture, 1720–1900*. Cambridge: Cambridge UP, 2003.

McKeon, Michael. "Historicizing Patriarchy: The Emergence of Gender Difference in England 1660–1760." *Eighteenth-Century Studies* 28.3 (Spring 1995) 295–322.

—. *The Origins of the English Novel, 1600–1740*. Baltimore and London: Johns Hopkins UP, 1987.

—. The Secret History of Domesticity: *Public, Private, and the Division of Knowledge*. Baltimore: Johns Hopkins UP, 2005.

McLynn, Frank. *Crime and Punishment in Eighteenth-Century England*. New York: Routledge, 1989.

Messenger, Ann. *His and Hers: Essays in Restoration and Eighteenth-Century Literature*. Lexington: UP of Kentucky, 1986.

Misson, Henri. *M. Misson's memoirs and observations in his travels over England. With some account of Scotland and Ireland. Dispos'd in alphabetical order. Written originally in French*. London: Printed for D. Browne, et al., 1719.

Mist's Weekly Journal. London: Printed by N. Mist, 1722–27.

Moglen, Helene. *The Trauma of Gender: A Feminist Theory of the English Novel*. Berkeley: U of California P, 2001.

Montagu, Basil. *Hanging Not Punishment Enough*. London: Longman, Hurst, Rees, Orme, and Brown, Paternoster-row, 1701, reprinted 1813.

Morgan, Joan. *The Hanging Wood: Being the Story of Mary Blandy of Henley-on-Thames*. London: Macdonald, 1950.

Morris, Virginia B. *Double Jeopardy: Women Who Kill in Victorian Fiction*. Lexington: UP of Kentucky, 1990.

Nalson, John. *An Impartial Collection of the Great Affairs of State*. London: Printed for S. Mearne, 1682–83.

A Narrative of the Barbarous and Unheard of Murder of Mr. John Hayes, By Catherine His Wife, Thomas Billings, and Thomas Wood, on the First of March at Night. Published in London, 1726, "With the Approbation of the Relations and Friends of the Said Mr. John Hayes." Knapp, Baldwin, and Savage. Newgate Calendar. Vol. 3.

The Newgate Calendar: Comprising Interesting Memoirs of the Most Notorious Characters Who Have Been Convicted of Outrages on the Laws of England: with Speeches, Confessions, and Last Exclamations of Sufferers. Hartford, CT: Mitchell, 1926.

Novak, Maximillian E. "Defoe as an Innovator of Fictional Form." *The Cambridge Companion to the Eighteenth-Century Novel*. New York: Cambridge UP, 1998.

—. *Defoe and the Nature of Man*. London: Oxford UP, 1996.

—. Realism, Myth, and History in Defoe's Fiction. Lincoln: U of Nebraska P, 1983.

Nussbaum, Felicity. *The Brink of All We Hate: English Satires on Women 1660–1750*. Lexington: UP of Kentucky, 1984.

Okin, Susan Molle. "Women and the Making of the Sentimental Family." *Philosophy and Public Affairs* 11.1 (Winter 1982): 65–88.

The Old-Bailey Sessions Papers. The Old Bailey Proceedings Online. www.oldbaileyonline.org.

Painter, William. *The Palace of Pleasure Beautified, Adorned and Well Furnished, with Pleasaunt Histories and Excellent Nouelles, Selected out of Diuers Good and Commendable Authors. By William Painter Clarke of the Ordinaunce and Armari*. Imprinted at London, by [John Kingston and] Henry Denham, for Richard Tottell and William Iones, 1566.

Pateman, Carole. *The Sexual Contract*. Stanford: Stanford UP, 1988.

Pearson, Jacqueline. "The History of *The History of the Nun*." Hutner 234–52.

Perry, Ruth. *The Celebrated Mary Astell: An Early English Feminist*. Chicago: U of Chicago P, 1986.

—. *Women, Letters, and the Novel*. New York: AMS, 1980.

Pollak, Ellen. *The Poetics of the Sexual Myth: Gender and Ideology in the Verse of Swift and Pope*. Chicago: U of Chicago P, 1985.

Pope, Alexander. *The Dunciad*. Ed. James Sutherland. Vol. 5. *The Twickenham Edition of the Poems of Alexander Pope*. Ed. John Butt. 3rd ed. rev. 6 vols. London: n.p., 1963.

Rawlings, Philip. *Drunks, Whores, and Idle Apprentices: Criminal Biographies of the Eighteenth Century*. London: Routledge, 1992.

Rawson, Claude. *Henry Fielding and the Augustan Ideal Under Stress: "Nature's Dance of Death" and Other Stories*. London: Routledge, 1972.

Reeve, Clara. *The Progress of Romance and the History of Charoba, Queen of Aegypt*. Facsimile Text Society Ser. 1: Literature and Language, 4. New York, 1930.

A Refutation of the Narrative of the Trial of Mary Edmundson. London, 1759.

Richetti, John. "An Emerging New Canon of the British Eighteenth-Century Novel: Feminist Criticism, the Means of Cultural Production, and the Question of Value." *A Companion to the Eighteenth-Century English Novel and Culture*.

Ed. Paula R. Backscheider and Catherine Ingrassia. Malden, MA: Blackwell, 2005. 365–82.

—. "The Family, Sex, and Marriage in Defoe's Moll Flanders and Roxana." *Studies in the Literary Imagination* 15 (1982): 19–35.

—. *Popular Fiction Before Richardson, 1700–1739*. Oxford: Clarendon, 1969.

Robinson, Mary. *The Natural Daughter: With Portraits of the Leadenhead Family: A Novel*. London: Printed for T. N. Longman and O. Rees, 1799.

Rogers, Katharine. *Feminism in Eighteenth-Century England*. Urbana: U of Illinois P, 1982.

Rosen, George. "A Slaughter of the Innocents: Aspects of Child Health in the Eighteenth-Century City." *Studies in Eighteenth-Century Culture* 5 (1976): 293–316.

Roughhead, William, ed. *The Trial of Mary Blandy*. Edinburgh and London: Hodge, 1914. 55.

Salvaggio, Ruth. "Aphra Behn's Love." Hutner. 253–70.

Savage, Richard. *An Author to Be Lett. being a Proposal Humbly Address'd to the Consideration of the Knights, Esquires, Gentlemen, and other Worshipful and Weighty Members of the Solid and Ancient Association of the Bathos. By Their Associate and Well-Wisher Iscariot Hackney*. London: Printed for L. Gilliver, 1732.

Savile, George, Marquis of Halifax. *The Lady's New Year's Gift: or, Advice to a Daughter*. 1688. V. Jones 17–23.

Saxton, Kirsten T. "Telling Tale: Eliza Haywood and the Crimes of Seduction in The City Jilt, or, the Alderman turn'd Beau." Saxton and Bocchicchio 115–42.

—, and Rebecca P. Bocchicchio, eds. *The Passionate Fictions of Eliza Haywood: Essays on Her Life and Work*. Lexington: UP of Kentucky, 2000.

Scheuermann, Mona. *Her Bread to Earn: Women, Money and Society from Defoe to Austen*. Lexington: UP of Kentucky, 1993.

Schofield, Mary Anne. "Descending Angels: Salubrious Sluts and Petty Prostitutes in Haywood's Fiction." Schofield and Macheski 186–200.

—. *Eliza Haywood*. Boston: Twayne, 1985.

—, and Cecilia Macheski, eds. *Fetter'd or Free? British Women Novelists, 1670–1815*. Athens, OH: Ohio UP, 1986.

Secord, Arthur W., ed. *Defoe's Review*. 22 vols. New York: Columbia UP, 1938.

Seleski, Patty. "A Mistress, a Mother, and a Murderess Too: Elizabeth Brownrigg and the Social Construction of an Eighteenth-Century Mistress." *Lewd and Notorious: Female Transgression in the Eighteenth Century*. Ed. Katharine Kittredge. Ann Arbor: U of Michigan P, 2003. 210–34.

Sharpe, J. A. *Crime and the Law in English Satirical Prints, 1600–1832*. Cambridge: Chadwyck-Healey, 1986.

Showalter, Elaine. *A Literature of Their Own: British Women Novelists from Brontë to Lessing*. Princeton: Princeton UP, 1977.

"A Song, on the Murder of Mr. Hays, by his Wife To the Tune of Chevy-Chase." *A New Miscellany*. 1730. 34–36. Hitchcock and Shoemaker 53.

Speck, W. A. *Stability and Strife: England 1714–1760*. Cambridge, MA: Harvard, 1977.

Spencer, Jane. *The Rise of the Woman Novelist: From Aphra Behn to Jane Austen*. Oxford: Blackwell, 1986.

Spender, Dale. *Mothers of the Novel: One Hundred Good Women Writers Before Jane Austen*. London: Pandora, 1986.

Stallybrass, Peter, and Allen White. *The Politics and Poetics of Transgression*. London: Methuen, 1986.

Starr, G. A. *Defoe and Casuistry*. Princeton: Princeton UP, 1971.

—. *Defoe and Spiritual Autobiography*. Princeton: Princeton UP, 1965.

Staves, Susan. *Married Women's Separate Property in England, 1660–1833*. *Players' Scepters: Fictions of Authority in the Restoration*. Lincoln: U of Nebraska P, 1979.

Stone, Lawrence. *Broken Lives: Separation and Divorce in England, 1660–1857*. Oxford: Oxford UP, 1993.

—. *The Family, Sex and Marriage in England, 1500–1800*. New York: Harper, 1977.

Swift, Jonathan. *A Letter from a Member of the House of Commons in Ireland to a Member of the House of Commons in England, Concerning the Sacramental Test*. London: Printed for John Morphew, 1709.

—. *A Tale of a Tub, to Which is Added the Battle of the Books and the Mechanical Operation of the Spirit*. 1709. Ed. A. C. Guthkelch and D. Nichol Smith. 2nd ed. Oxford: Clarendon, 1958.

Thackeray, William M. *Catherine: A Story*. Kessinger Publishing's Rare Reprints. Web. 6 June 2008.

Thomas, D. A. *Principles of Sentencing. The Sentencing Policy of the Court of Appeal Criminal Division*. London: Heinemann, 1970.

Thompson, E. P. *Whigs and Hunters: The Origin of the Black Act*. New York: Pantheon, 1975.

Thompson, James. *Models of Value: Eighteenth-Century Political Economy and the Novel*. Durham, NC: Duke UP, 1996.

Thorn, Jennifer. *Writing British Infanticide: Child-Murder, Gender, and Print, 1722–1859*. Newark, DE: U of Delaware P, 2003.

Todd, Janet. *The Sign of Angellica: Women, Writing, and Fiction 1660–1800*. London: Virago, 1989.

The Tryal of Mary Blandy, spinster, for the Murder of her Father, Francis Blandy, Gent.: at the Assizes held at Oxford for the County of Oxford, on Saturday the 29th of February, 1752.. Published by Permission of the Judges. London: Printed for John and James Rivington, 1752.

Trumbach, Randolph. *The Rise of the Egalitarian Family*. New York: Academic, 1978.

Universal Magazine 41 (1767).

Warner, William B. *Licensing Entertainment: The Elevation of Novel Reading in Britain, 1684–1750*. Berkeley: U of California P, 1998.

—. "Licensing Pleasure: Literary History and the Novel in Early Modern Britain." *The Columbia History of the British Novel*. Ed. John Richetti. New York: Columbia UP, 1994.

A Warning Piece Against the Crime of Murder. [London]: Printed for William Owen, [1752].

Watt, Ian. *The Rise of the Novel*. London: Chatto and Windus, 1974.

Welsh, Alexander. *Strong Representations: Narrative and Circumstantial Evidence in England*. Baltimore: Johns Hopkins UP, 1992.

West, Benjamin. *Miscellaneous Poems, Translations, and Imitations*. Northampton, England: Printed for the Author by Thomas Dicey and sold by T. Evans, 1780.

Whicher, George Frisbie. *The Life and Romances of Mrs. Eliza Haywood*. New York: Columbia UP, 1915.

Wiegman, Robyn. "Economies of the Body: Gendered Sites in Robinson Crusoe and Roxana." *Criticism* 31.1 (1989): 33–51.

Wilson, Colin, and Damon Wilson. *Written in Blood: A History of Forensic Detection*. London: Robinson, 2003.

Wolff, Cynthia Griffin. "Fielding's Amelia: Private Virtue and Public Good." *Texas Studies in Literature and Language* 10 (1968): 37–55.

Wollstonecraft, Mary. *Maria, or the Wrongs of Woman*. New York: Norton, 1975.

Wood, Thomas. *An Institute of the Laws of England, or, The Laws of England in Their Natural Order, According to Common Use Published for the Direction of Young Beginners, or Students*. In the Savoy: Printed by E. and R. Nutt and R. Gosling, (assigns of E. Sayer esq;) for Richard Sare, 1720.

Woodcock, George. *The Incomparable Aphra*. London and New York: AMS, 1948.

Woolf, Virginia. *A Room of One's Own*. New York: Harcourt, 1957.

Wyndham, Horace. *The Mayfair Calendar: Some Society Causes Célèbres*. New York: Doran, 1926.

Zomchick, John P. *Family and the Law in Eighteenth-Century Fiction*. Cambridge: Cambridge UP, 1993.

—. "'A Penetration Which Nothing Can Deceive': Gender and Juridical Discourse in Some Eighteenth-Century Narratives." *Studies in English Literature, 1500–1900* 29.3 (Summer 1989): 535–561.

Index

(References to illustrations are in **bold**)

Adler, Lydia 61–2
Agamemnon 13, 14, 59
Alexander, Thomas and James 75, 76
amatory fiction 2, 3, 31, 69, 107, 112–13,
   115, 129
   gothic novels, resemblance 132
   in *Miss Mary Blandy's Own Account*
     116
Annual Register 82
Arbuckle, James 26
Atwood, Margaret, *Alias Grace* 1, 132

Backscheider, Paula 27
Beattie, J. M. 15, 118
Behn, Aphra 2, 27, 69
   The Fair Jilt 5, 31, 32, 40–46
     female desire 40, 41
     female rake 44
     femininity, devil/angel dyad 44
     textual fantasy 41, 42, 43
   History of the Nun 5, 31, 32, 32–40,
     46, 48, 85, 87, 108, 119, 130
     bigamy 32, 38, 44
     chastity 35
     criminal biographies, critique 39
     dedication, to Hortense Mancini 35
     female agency, denial 36, 40
     female desire, unnatural
       suppression 36–7
     female sexuality 36
     gender politics, critique 33–4
     inconstancy, male/female 34
     male sin, and female sin 40
     murders 38–9
     narrator/subject, alignment 33
     needlework, symbolism 38
     patriarchy 36
     plot 32

     realism 39
     vow-breaking 34–5, 130
     witchcraft trope 38
Billings, Thomas 58, 59, 60, 61, 72, 74
Bingham, Victor, *The Noose Around the
   Wrong Neck* 71
Blackstone, William 118
Blandy, Mary 3, 5, 55, 57, 62–71
   *A General and Impartial Account of
    the Life of Mary Blandy* 64, 67
   Cranstoun, affair with 68, 69, 72, 117
   as damsel in distress 69, 118–19
   execution **67**, 70
   Hayes case, similarities/differences
    71–4
   images **65**, **66**
   Miss Mary Blandy's Own Account 6,
    69, 115–21
     amatory fiction conventions 116
     criminal conversation 120
     female reader audience 116–17
     frailty, appeal to 120
     narrative use 120
     political aim 117–18
     popular sympathy 120–21
   murder, of father 68, 114, 115, 116
   poem about 71
   see also Fielding, *Examples*
Bobbitt, Lorena 5
bread, meaning 90
The British Journal 59
Brownrigg, Elizabeth 5, 6, 55, 74, 78–81
   body
     in British Museum 132
     dissection 83
   character 80
   femininity 80
   images **79**

torture accusations 78, 79, 81
Brownrigg, James 81

Campbell, Jill 102, 106
Cassandra 13
Castle, Terry 94
Charles II, King of England 35
Chudleigh, Lady Mary, "To the Ladies" 55
class
    and gender 74
    Nature and Art 128
    Roxana 91–2, 95–6, 98, 100
    and Sarah Malcolm 75
Clytemnestra 59
    eighteenth-century portrayal 13, 14, 17
conduct literature 20, 36
    The Lady's Calling 14
Congreve, William, *The Mourning Bride* 110
The Covent Garden Journal 125
crime panics, eighteenth-century 5, 20–23
criminal biographies 20, 23–4, 39
    didacticism 6, 61
    fictional conventions 24, 56–7, 61
    function 78
    narrative closure 61
    sales 56
    social functions 57
    types 56
    see also Blandy, Mary; Hayes, Catherine
Criminal Cases Review Commission 71
criminal conversation
    Amelia 102fn10
    Miss Blandy's Own Account 120
criminality
    anxiety 20
        and mobility 22
    and novels 24, 28, 124
    of servants 26, 82
    see also female criminality

Dacre, Charlotte, *Zofloya* 7, 132
Davis, Lennard 25
Defoe, Daniel 2, 3
    The Commentator 85
    *Everybody's Business Is Nobody's
        Business*, servants' loyalty 94
    History of...John Sheppard 23
    History of the Pirates 12

Roxana 6, 49, 85, 87–101
    Amelia, comparison 101–2
    class 91–2, 95–6, 98, 100
    criminality, context 87–8, 89
    female independence 88
    female violence 87, 92
    home, dangers in 88
    narratives, multiple 87
    servant loyalty 94, 100
Doody, Margaret 19, 70, 80, 104, 105–6
Duncomb, Lydia 74
Duncombe, John, *The Feminiad* 27–8

Edmondson, Mary 17
Elton, G. R. 15
English society, as sick body 21
Euripides, *Medea* 13

Faller, Lincoln 56, 57, 101
female body, perception 75
female criminality 6, 14, 20
    domestic 18
    eighteenth-century conceptions 75
    in the novel 1, 127
    roots 107–8
    see also female violence
female possibility
    fictions 129
    and murderesses 1
female violence 2, 74, 86
    Amelia 101, 102, 103
    cause, eighteenth-century view 11–12
    displacement 7, 92, 127
    present-day fears 8, 132
    Roxana 87, 92
    The Wife's Resentment 46–7, 49–52, 53
Fielding, Henry 2, 3
    Amelia 6, 85, 101–14
        character, reader's interpretation 106
        criminal conversation 102fn10
        criticism, Fielding's defense 125
        female agency 102
        female criminality, critique 114
        female desire 103, 104–5
        female monstrosity 104–5
        female violence 101, 102, 103
        fortune, debunking 111, 112
        legal reform, call for 102fn11

Roxana, comparison 101–2
A Charge Delivered to the Grand Jury 20
An Enquiry into the Causes of the Late Increase of Robbers 21
Examples of the Interposition of Providence 6, 7, 115, 116, 121–2, 131
  authorship, distanced 121–2
  didacticism 124
  fictionality 122–3
  inaccuracies 123
  rhetoric 121
  truth/fiction equivalence 122
History of the Pirates 12
Joseph Andrews 28
Tom Jones 28, 111
Freud, Sigmund 18

gender, and class 74
Gildon, Charles, *Phaeton* 13
Gladfelder, Hugh 111, 129
Glover, Richard 13
Gould, Robert, and Thomas Brown, *Love Given O're* 31
Guthrie, James, *Ordinary's Account* 61

Hanging Not Punishment Enough 22
Harrison, Elizabeth 74
Hayes, Catherine 5, 55, 57, 69
  as archetype of female evil 60
  ballad about 60–61
  biographies
    "Catherine Hayes, a Murderess" 58, 59, 61, 62
    A Narrative of the...Murder of Mr John Hayes 58–60, 61
  Blandy case, similarities/differences 71–4
  committing murder **64**, 65
  execution 62, **63**
  incest accusation 59–60
  in Thackeray's *Catherine* 74
  as victim 71
  violence against, by spouse 62
Hayes, John 58
  murder **64**
Haywood, Eliza 27, 69
  The City Jilt 109
  Love in Excess 29
Heinzelman, Susan Sage 121

Hill, Bridget 14
Hogarth, William, Sarah Malcolm sketch **77**, 78

Inchbald, Elizabeth, *Nature and Art* 6, 127, 128–9
  class 128
infanticide 11fn1, 130fn5

Johnson, Charles 13
  General History...Most Famous Highwaymen 1
  Lives of the Most Remarkable Female Robbers 19
Johnson, Samuel, *London* 22
Judith
  Biblical portrayal 12–13
  eighteenth-century portrayal 13, 14

Kahn, Madeleine 87

The Lady's Calling 14
Lewis, Matthew
  Ambrosio 132
  The Monk 132
Lillo, George, *The London Merchant* 31
London
  anonymity of 22
  population increase 22fn24
London Magazine 77
Lorrain, Paul 23
Lynch, Eve 81

McLynn, Frank 59
Malcolm, Sarah 5, 6, 55, 74–8, 81, 90
  body, dissection 78
  and class 75
  execution 75
  female body, perception 75
  Hogarth sketch **77**, 78
  menstrual blood defense 75, 76, 77
Mancini, Hortense, Duchess of Mazarin 35
Manley, Delarivier 2, 27, 69
  The New Atlantis 47
  The Wife's Resentment 5, 31, 46–54, 85, 87, 126, 131
    bigamy 49
    didacticism 53

execution 52–3
female honor 47, 48, 50, 51
female violence 46–7, 49–52, 53
femininity, stereotypes 50
letters, didactic use 48
male aristocratic excess 48–9
murder 52, 53
marriage, gender inequity 73
Medea 18, 52, 106
    eighteenth-century portrayal 13, 14
Mist's Weekly Journal 17, 62
Moglen, Helene 92
Morgan, Joan, *The Hanging Wood* 71
Mosaic Code, Old Testament 9
murder
    death as punishment 9–10
    narratives 10
    nature of 9, 71
murderesses
    domestic homicide by 16, 17–18, 19
    fear of 17
    and female possibility 1
    and feminine mythologies 11
    fictional narratives 4, 14, 20, 31–54,
        127–32
    and gender betrayal 11
    and gendered pathologies 11
    in gothic novel 132
    literary sources 2
    non-fictional narratives 4, 5, 14, 20,
        55–84
    present-day concerns 7–8, 132
    rarity 19
    threat to
        masculine authority 13, 19
        social order 11
    transgressive sexuality 12
    use of term 1fn1
    see also Blandy, Mary; Brownrigg,
        Elizabeth

Nairn, Katherine 15
Nebuchadnezzar 12
New York Times 71
Newgate Ordinaries 2, 23, 80
Novak, Max 89, 92, 97
novella 24
novel(s)

and criminality 24, 28, 124
criteria for 2, 3
as didactic tool 28
early 24, 25
female criminality in 1, 127
gothic 7, 132
histories of 3
legal narratives, influence of 24
moral health, threat to 25–6
progenitors 3
sensation 7, 132
women writers 27–8

Old Testament, Mosaic Code 9
The Old-Bailey Session Papers 75
Ordinaries, accounts of hangings 56, 61
    see also Newgate Ordinaries
Orestes 13

penny dreadfuls 7, 132
petty treason
    by men 16
    by women, 16, 61fn5
    death by burning 16
    definition 16
Philips, Katherine 27
Pope, Alexander, on women 36
Price, Ann 75
public/private space, women 18, 20

Rawlings, Philip 56
realist fiction 3, 6, 115
Reeve, Clara, *The Progress of Romance* 23
Richardson, Samuel 3
    Clarissa 28, 29
    Pamela 28, 47, 48
Robinson, Mary, *The Natural Daughter* 7,
        127, 131
    aristocratic male privilege 130
Roughhead, William 124
    The Trial of Mary Blandy 115

Salvaggio, Ruth 43
Savile, George, *The Lady's New Year's
        Gift* 73
Seleski, Patty 82
servants
    criminality 26, 82

loyalty
    Defoe on 94
    in *Roxana* 94, 100

Thackeray, William, *Catherine* 74
Thomas, D. A., *Principles of Sentencing* 8
Thomson, James, *Agamemnon* 14
Tollbooth Prison 15
Tracy, Mary 75, 76

Universal Magazine 80

Walpole, Horace 56
Watt, Ian, criteria for novel 2, 3
Welsh, Alexander 71, 115
    Strong Representations 121
wife-beating 72
Wilson, Colin, and D. Wilson, *Written in Blood* 74
Winchilsea, Countess of 27
Wollstonecraft, Mary, *Maria* 7, 127, 129
women

death by burning 16
eighteenth-century, legal nonstatus 14–15
homicidal instincts 16fn12
lack of
    reason 12
    self-control 12
novelists 27–8
nurturing nature 10
Pope on 36
pregnancy, lenient sentencing 15
proper role 18
public/private space 18, 20
virgin/whore dyad 12, 75
Wood, Thomas 58, 60, 61, 72, 74
Wuornos, Aileen 132
Wyndham, Horace, *The Mayfair Calendar* 71

Yates, Mary 13

Zomchick, John 102